TABLE OF CONTENTS

Back To School 5
A collection of preparation ideas, getting-to-know-you activities, teacher tips, and reproducibles designed for the first days of school.

Bulletin Boards 21
Seasonal, holiday, and anytime displays that feature student involvement; necessary patterns included.

Classroom Management 47
Tips and reproducibles to help you organize students and materials.

Motivating Students 67
Ideas for motivating students and building self-esteem.

Parent Communication 77
Teacher-tested tips for a successful Open House and keeping the lines of communication open.

Arts And Crafts 93
Projects for holidays and seasons, with recipes and patterns included.

Centers 113
Simple, easy-to-manage learning centers that serve as reinforcement and free-time activities.

Games 123
Ideas for classroom-review games, rainy-day recess games, and outdoor fun.

Five-Minute Fillers 129
Quick and fun activities to reinforce a variety of subject areas and skills.

Substitute Teacher Tips 135
Ideas to help prepare for a substitute teacher.

Language Arts 141
A collection of activities to use to reinforce the basic components of your language arts program.
- Grammar 142
   Includes parts of speech, capitalization, and punctuation.
- Sentence Skills 146
   Activities for using the correct punctuation, writing complete sentences, and determining subjects and predicates.
- Word Skills 150
   Vocabulary-building activities to reinforce spelling homophones, synonyms, antonyms, prefixes, suffixes, contractions, and abbreviations.
- Reading 156
   Skill reinforcers for sequencing, fact and opinion, main idea, cause and effect, inference, and drawing conclusions.
- References And Reproducibles 162
   Ready reference lists of capitalization rules, punctuation rules, plurals, contractions, compound words, prefixes, suffixes, homophones, synonyms, and antonyms; patterns for activities included.

Writing 171
Journal topics and ideas on important skills such as writing paragraphs, topic sentences, friendly letters, outlines and story maps, and poetry.
- References And Reproducibles 183
   Ready references for proofreading marks, synonyms for commonly used words, and writing terminology; patterns and reproducibles for activities included.

W9-AGU-668

Literature **191**
Activities that can be used with any story, alternatives to book reports, ideas to motivate students to read,
and reproducible forms.
- References And Reproducibles 199
    Ready references for grade-appropriate storybooks, chapter books, teacher read-alouds, and Caldecott
    winners; patterns for activities included.

Math **209**
Ideas and reproducibles for the major skill areas:
- Computations 210
- Place Value 214
- Measurement 216
- Graphing 218
- Geometry 220
- Fractions 222
- References And Reproducibles 223
    Ready reference for math-related literature; patterns for activities included.

Social Studies **231**
Ideas, literature lists, and reproducibles for teaching about:
- United States Heritage 232
- Native American Cultures 234
- Communities Of The Past And Present 238
- Economics 242
- Map skills 244
- Reproducibles 248
    Reproducibles and patterns for activities included.

Science **253**
Simple high-interest activities, experiments, reproducibles, and literature lists on these topics:
- Solar System 254
- Earth 258
- Rocks 264
- Earth's Moon 266
- Weather 268
- Plants 270
- Reproducibles 273
    Patterns to accompany your studies of the topics listed above.

Health And Safety **275**
Activities, reproducibles, and literature lists for teaching basic health and safety concepts such as:
- Nutrition 276
- Dental Health 278
- Fire Safety 280
- Identifying Safety Risks 282
- Character Education 284
- Reproducibles 286
    Patterns and forms to accompany your studies of the topics listed above.

Holiday And Seasonal **289**
Ideas and reproducibles for the seasons and major holidays.
- Fall 290
- Winter 292
- Spring 294
- Summer 296
- Holiday And Seasonal Reproducibles 298
    Seasonal reproducibles to help reinforce basic skills.

Answer Keys **319**

The MAILBOX® SUPERBOOK

GRADE 3

Your complete resource for an entire year of third-grade success!

Editors:
Cynthia Holcomb and Thad H. McLaurin

Contributors:
Lisa Allen, Elizabeth Chappell, Martha Cheney, Stacie Stone Davis, Brenda Dunlap,
Julie Eick-Granchelli, Cynthia Holcomb, Nicole Iacovazzi, Susie Kapaun, Lisa Kelly,
Martha Kelly, Kathleen Kopp, Susan Kotchman, Rosemary Linden, Leigh Ann Newsom,
Patricia Pecuch, Cheryl Sergi, Kim Sheppard, Susan Hohbach Walker

Art Coordinator:
Cathy Spangler Bruce

Artists:
Jennifer Bennett, Cathy Spangler Bruce, Clevell Harris,
Sheila Krill, Mary Lester, Rebecca Saunders, Barry Slate, Donna K. Teal

Cover Artist:
Jim Counts

The Education Center, Inc.
Greensboro, North Carolina

ABOUT THIS BOOK

Look through the pages of *The Mailbox® GRADE 3 SUPERBOOK*, and discover a wealth of ideas and activities specifically designed for the third-grade teacher. We've included tips for starting the year, managing your classroom, maintaining parent communication, and motivating your students. In addition, you'll find activities for reinforcing the basic skills in all areas of the third-grade curriculum. We've also provided reference materials for every subject, literature lists, arts-and-crafts ideas, holiday and seasonal reproducibles, and bulletin-board ideas and patterns. *The Mailbox® GRADE 3 SUPERBOOK* is your complete resource for an entire year of third-grade success!

Library of Congress Cataloging-in-Publication Data

The mailbox superbook : grade 3 : your complete resource for an entire
    year of third-grade success! / editors, Cynthia Holcomb and Thad H.
    McLaurin ; contributors, Lisa Allen ... [et al.] ; art coordinator,
    Cathy Spangler Bruce ; artists, Jennifer Bennett ... [et al.].
        p.   cm.
    ISBN 1-56234-199-5
    1. Third grade (Education)—Curricula.   2. Education, Elementary—
Activity programs.   3. Teaching—Aids and devices.   4. Elementary
school teaching. I. Holcomb, Cynthia. II. McLaurin, Thad H.
III. Mailbox.
LB1571 3rd.M35   1997
372.24'1—dc21   97-32811
                                                              CIP

Manufactured in the United States
10 9 8 7 6 5 4 3 2

BACK TO SCHOOL

BACK TO SCHOOL

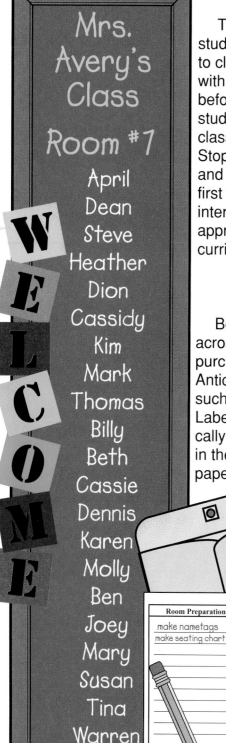

Mrs. Avery's Class

Room #7

April
Dean
Steve
Heather
Dion
Cassidy
Kim
Mark
Thomas
Billy
Beth
Cassie
Dennis
Karen
Molly
Ben
Joey
Mary
Susan
Tina
Warren
Patty
Austin

WELCOME

All Aboard!

This welcome-back idea is right on track for making students eager for the first day of school. Invite students to climb aboard the "Third-Grade Express" with the patterns on page 12. A week before the big day, mail each of your new students a special boarding pass to your classroom. Enclose a list of "Scheduled Stops"—a preview of projects, themes, and events that will take place in the first few weeks of school. Students' interest will be piqued, and parents will appreciate the information about your curriculum plans.

Boarding Pass
For The
Third-Grade Express
signed *Amanda Lipscomb*
Welcome Aboard!

Boarding Pass
For The
Third-Grade Express
signed *Mark Williams*
Welcome Aboard!

Organized Information

Be prepared for the many types of communications that will come across your desk in the beginning days of school. Prior to the first day, purchase a large three-ring binder and a package of pocket-type dividers. Anticipate the types of papers you need to keep on file during the year, such as faculty memos, parent correspondence, schedules, and policies. Label a divider page for each section and arrange the sections alphabetically in the binder. When important information arrives at your desk, file it in the appropriate divider section. You'll keep track of all your important papers and have a comprehensive record of the school year.

Room Preparations		Teacher Preparations	
make nametags	✓	copy math lesson	✓
make seating chart		make spelling list	✓
		get reading books	

Communications (office, parent...)
run copies of information packet

Check The Details!

The first few days before school can be a flurry of activity as you attend to the many details of getting your room ready, making lesson plans, and securing materials. Stay on top of things with the checklists on pages 13 and 14. Duplicate a copy of each list and fill in the tasks you need to accomplish. With a glance you will be able to see what progress you have made, and what tasks still lie ahead as the big day draws near!

Setting The Stage

Each school year brings with it new beginnings, new students, and new adventures in learning. Set the stage for back-to-school fun with a special look for your classroom. Peruse the list below for theme ideas; then put your imagination to work in designing a door decoration, a welcome-back bulletin board, a student-helper chart, a birthday display, and nametags that incorporate the theme.

"Stepping Into A New Year"
A kicky display of all types of footwear will help students make steps in the right direction.

"Making A Splash!"
Incorporate a fishy cast of characters to decorate your room in a theme from the deep, blue sea.

"Tracking Down A Great Year"
A safari scene amidst a tangle of vines will inspire your students to begin the year with a roar.

"It's Going To Be A 'Purr-fect' Year!"
Cuddly kittens and cool cats are the perfect teacher's pets for welcoming new students.

"Wanted—A Class Of Super Students"
Round up a rootin'-tootin' bunch of students with a display of star-shaped badges, a lasso-twirlin' sheriff, and a posse of Wild-West characters.

"Welcoming A Bright Bunch Of Students"
An animated array of lightbulb characters sporting sunglasses will get your year off to a shining start.

"Starting The Year On The Right Note"
Music notes, treble clefs, and a band of bouncy musicians will get students in tune for a great new year.

Birthday Graph

This first-day activity will also serve as a birthday-graph display. Before the first day of school, draw a blank graph on bulletin-board paper. Label the bottom of the graph with the months of the year. Staple the graph to a bulletin board and add a decorative border. Duplicate a class supply of the cupcake patterns on page 15 and place a pattern on top of each student's desk. As each student arrives on the first day, instruct him to complete the information on the pattern, color it, and then cut it out. Have the student staple his completed cupcake to the appropriate section of the graph. Extend the activity by asking students to volunteer information about the results of the graph.

Get To Know Us!

Combine photographs with a writing assignment to create an album your students will cherish. Prior to the first day of school, send each student a letter requesting that she bring a photograph of herself to be used for a special project. On the first day of school, distribute a copy of the form on page 15 to each student. Have the student complete the information, then turn in the form and her photograph to you. Compile the photos and forms in a picture album. Send the album home with a different student each night. Then keep the album on hand to share with new students who join the class later in the year.

TEACHER TRIVIA

WELCOME YOUR NEW STUDENTS WITH A DISPLAY THAT LETS THEM GET TO KNOW YOU. CREATE A DISPLAY OF FAMILY PICTURES, CRAFT PROJECTS, AWARDS, AND OTHER PERSONAL INFORMATION ON A SHEET OF POSTER BOARD. WRITE A QUESTION UNDER EACH ITEM, SUCH AS "WHAT KIND OF DOG DO I OWN?" OR "WHERE DID I GO ON VACATION THIS SUMMER?" AFTER STUDENTS HAVE HAD TIME TO EXAMINE THE DISPLAY, ASK THEM TO VENTURE A RESPONSE TO EACH QUESTION. VERIFY THE CORRECT ANSWER TO EACH QUESTION; THEN ASK STUDENTS TO CONTRIBUTE A LITTLE INFORMATION ABOUT THEMSELVES. WITHIN MINUTES STUDENTS WILL FEEL COMFORTABLE HAVING SOME BACKGROUND INFORMATION ABOUT THEIR NEW TEACHER AND CLASSMATES.

It's In The Bag!

Pair students in a get-acquainted activity in which two minds are better than one! Provide each pair of students with a bag filled with die-cut letters of the words "Third Grade." Instruct students to rearrange the letters to spell as many words as possible while recording their answers on a sheet of paper. After a designated time period, compare the word lists that the pairs have created.

Summer Sentences

Greet students on the first day of school with thoughts about their summer activities. Duplicate several copies of the form on page 16. As each student enters the room, ask him to write a sentence telling about his vacation on a form. (Remind the student not to include his name on the form!) After all students have written sentences, duplicate a class supply of the forms. Hand each student a copy and have him determine which sentence each classmate wrote. The student may gather clues about the sentences by asking each classmate three yes-or-no questions about his summer. After the third question, the student pencils in the classmate's name beside a sentence choice. After a designated time, read each sentence aloud. Ask the student who wrote the sentence to stand up. By the end of the activity, everyone has had a chance to share something about themselves!

Scrambled Rules

One challenge children face every fall is learning the rules of their new classroom. Make this task an enjoyable activity by creating a list of scrambled rules. Rearrange the words in each classroom rule so that the words are in random order. Write each scrambled rule on a sentence strip or on the board for students to decipher. After a designated time period, ask student volunteers to rewrite each rule correctly. Discuss each rule with your students. Then add a twist to the activity by asking students to create a list of rules for teachers to follow.

before hand your raise speaking

do best always your

everyone with treat respect

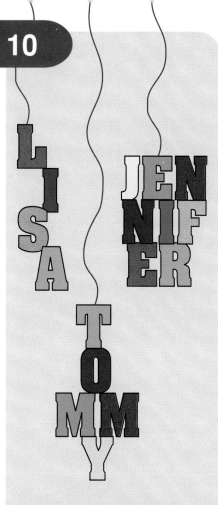

Name-Droppers

This first-day art project will not only decorate your classroom, but also help students learn one another's names as well! Provide a set of tagboard die-cut letters for students to use as stencils and an assortment of colored construction paper. Instruct each student to trace the letters of her name onto different colors of construction paper. Have the student cut out the letters and glue them together in an arrangement that spells her name. Use a length of yarn to suspend the personalized project from the ceiling above the student's desk. These colorful creations will have your students name-dropping in no time!

Students can use items on their school-supply list to create shapely works of art. Provide a supply of bright-colored construction paper. Instruct each student to select five or six of his school supplies and trace their outlines onto different colors of construction paper. After tracing around the items, have the student cut out each shape. Have each child glue the shapes onto a 9" x 12" sheet of black construction paper. Mount the completed projects on a bulletin board titled "We're In Shape For School!"

High-Flying Students

The year will be off to a soaring start with these personalized kite projects. Distribute a copy of the kite pattern on page 17 to each student. Have the student complete each section of the kite with information about himself. The student then colors the kite, cuts it out, and attaches a length of yarn as a tail. Provide time for each student to share his creation with the class. Display these high-flying projects in the classroom to help students become better acquainted.

Homework Hang-Ups

Promote the importance of a proper homework setting with an activity that reinforces good study habits. Have your students brainstorm a list of habits for homework time, such as working in a well-lighted place, avoiding distractions like television and radio, keeping necessary supplies on hand, ⋯ ⋯on. Dis-⋯ to ⋯e a ⋯with ⋯cre-⋯at ⋯s

before sending them home with your students.

please
plate
player
plane
plain

Stick With Spelling

Students will be more likely to study their spelling lists at home when they have a special place to keep the word list. Prior to sending home the first spelling list of the year, have each student make a special magnet for attaching the list to the refrigerator at home. Provide students with squares of poster board and an assortment of markers. Have each student decorate a poster-board square with brightly colored designs. Cover the square with clear Con-Tact® paper for durability; then attach a strip of magnetic tape to the back of the square. Send the magnets home with the first spelling list, reminding students to study the list every time they walk by the refrigerator.

Watch Us Grow

Students make so much progress throughout their third-grade year. Keep track of the growth and many changes each student experiences with the form on page 20. Distribute a copy of the form to each student on the first day of school. Have the student complete the first section of the form and draw a self-portrait in the picture-frame oval. Collect the forms for safekeeping. During the course of the school year, hand the form back to the student to complete other sections. The last section should be completed shortly before the end of the year. Students will enjoy comparing the information in the different sections, and will be amazed by the changes they have made!

Boarding Pass For The Third-Grade Express

signed _____

Welcome Aboard!

Scheduled Stops For The Third-Grade Express

During the next few weeks, we will:

- _____
- _____
- _____
- _____

Glad To Have You Aboard!

Room Preparations	Teacher Preparations
_____ ☐	_____ ☐
_____ ☐	_____ ☐

_____ ☐	_____ ☐
_____ ☐	_____ ☐
_____ ☐	_____ ☐
_____ ☐	_____ ☐
_____ ☐	_____ ☐

Communications (office, parents, etc.)

_____ ☐

_____ ☐

_____ ☐

_____ ☐

_____ ☐

Note To The Teacher: Use with "Check The Details!" on page 6.

M

_____
_____
_____
_____

☐
☐
☐
☐

T

_____
_____
_____
_____

☐
☐
☐
☐

W

_____
_____
_____
_____

☐
☐
☐
☐

T

_____
_____
_____
_____

☐
☐
☐
☐

F

_____
_____
_____
_____

☐
☐
☐
☐

Comments

_____
_____
_____
_____
_____

Note To The Teacher: Use with "Check The Details" on page 6.

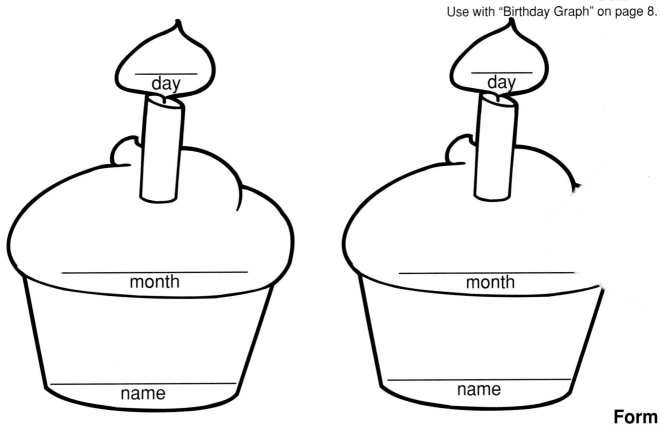

_____
day

_____
month

_____
name

_____
day

_____
month

_____
name

 **Get To Know Me!**

My name is _____

My birthday is _____

Three things about me:

1. _____

2. _____

3. _____

Some of my favorite things:
food _____
movie _____
book _____
game _____
color _____
school subject _____

Something I want to learn this year: _____

What Did You Do This Summer?

This summer, I _____

_____ .

This summer, I _____

_____ .

This summer, I _____

_____ .

This summer, I _____

_____ .

This summer, I _____

_____ .

This summer, I _____

_____ .

This summer, I _____

_____ .

This summer, I _____

_____ .

This summer, I _____

_____ .

This summer, I _____

_____ .

©1997 The Education Center, Inc. • *The Mailbox® Superbook • Grade 3* • TEC452

Note To The Teacher: Use with "Summer Sentences" on page 9.

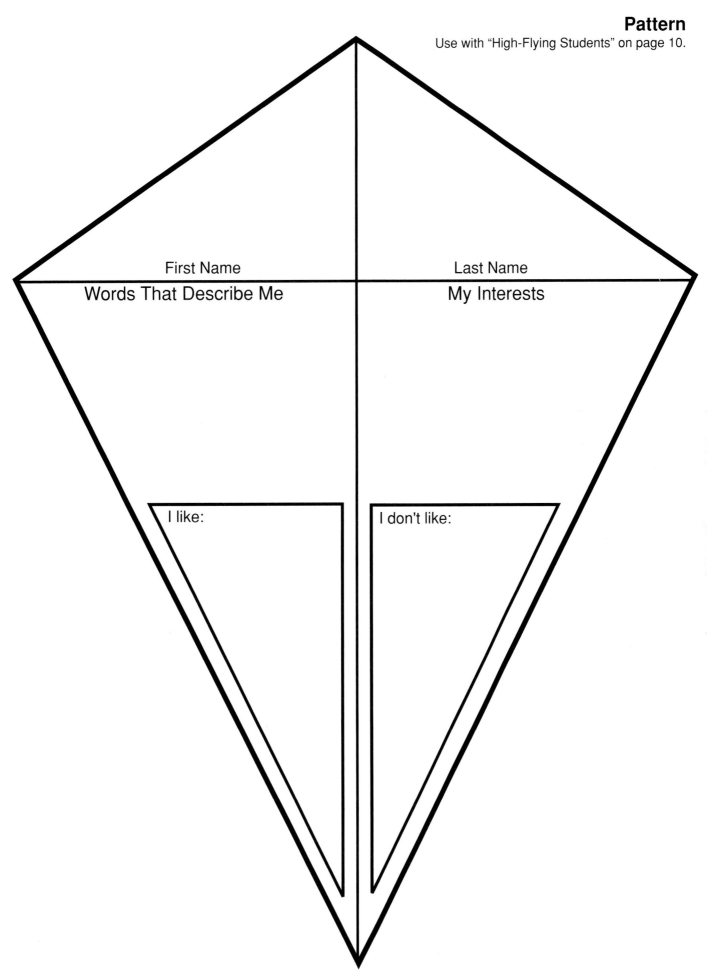

First Name

Last Name

Words That Describe Me

My Interests

I like:

I don't like:

Homework Plan

Homework is important.
This is my plan for completing my homework:

This is my plan for returning my homework to school:

This could happen if I follow my plan:

This might happen if I don't follow my plan:

Homework Plan

Homework is important.
This is my plan for completing my homework:

This is my plan for returning my homework to school:

This could happen if I follow my plan:

This might happen if I don't follow my plan:

©1997 The Education Center, Inc. • *The Mailbox® Superbook* • *Grade 3* • TEC452

 Note To The Teacher: Use with "Homework Hang-Ups" on page 11.

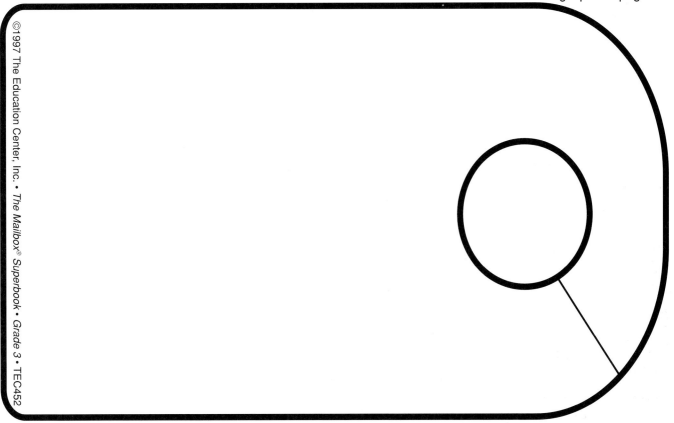

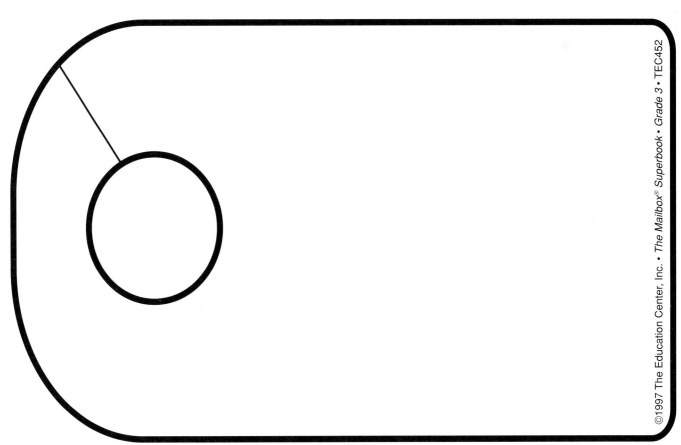

Watch Me Grow!

Date: _____

My favorite TV
show is _____.

My favorite game
is _____.

My best school subject is
_____.

I am proud of _____.

My goal is to _____.

My signature: _____

Date: _____

My favorite TV
show is _____.

My favorite game
is _____.

My best school subject is
_____.

I am proud of _____.

My goal is to _____.

My signature: _____

Date: _____

My favorite TV
show is _____.

My favorite game
is _____.

My best school subject is
_____.

I am proud of _____.

My goal is to _____.

My signature: _____

Date: _____

My favorite TV
show is _____.

My favorite game
is _____.

My best school subject is
_____.

I am proud of _____.

My goal is to _____.

My signature: _____

BULLETIN BOARDS

BULLETIN BOARDS

Bulletin-Board Bonanza

Bulletin boards are a vital part of the classroom. In addition to adding a decorative touch, bulletin boards can also be used to exhibit good work, as informative displays, and as interactive teaching tools. Try some of the following suggestions to create distinctive displays in your classroom.

Background Paper With Pizzazz

Let the theme of your bulletin board inspire your choice of background paper. Gift wrap comes in a variety of designs that can enhance a bulletin-board display. Use birthday wrap to cover a board that features students' birthdays, or holiday wrap to add spark to a seasonal display. Wrapping paper also comes in many colors and patterns that are not available in standard background-paper choices.

Create other interesting displays with the following background-paper ideas:

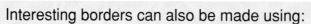

newspaper	wallpaper
road maps	colored cellophane
calendar pages	plastic tablecloths
fabric	bed sheets

Borders That Beautify

If you're looking for just a touch of color to add to a bulletin board, use items from the above list to create a border for a board covered with a solid-colored background. Make your own border by tracing several strips of precut border onto the new material. Laminate the strips before cutting them out for added durability.

Interesting borders can also be made using:

doilies	dried leaves
cupcake liners	die-cut shapes
adding-machine tape that students have decorated	

Distinctive Lettering

The title on a bulletin board can be a work of art in itself! Try cutting letters from these materials:

wallpaper samples	magazine pages
sandpaper	posters
greeting cards	paper bags
foil	

Keep It On File

Take a picture of each bulletin board before you take it down. Store the photos in an album or in an appropriate file. You'll have a wonderful collection of bulletin-board ideas to choose from in the coming years, as well as a handy reference showing the completed displays.

This first-day activity will have students working together to put the pieces in place for a great year. Supply each student with a marker and a square of white paper for each letter in her first name. Instruct the student to print one letter of her name on each square. Then have students work together to arrange their names in a cross-word-puzzle format. Help them staple the arrangement to a bulletin board. Add the title and the display is complete!

Calling all students...for an interactive bulletin-board display! Enlarge the telephone pattern on page 36 and staple it to the center of a bulletin board covered with pages from an old phone book. Provide each student with a copy of the calling card on page 36. Instruct the student to complete the information requested on the card. If desired, laminate the cards for durability before attaching to the display. Complete the board with the title and a colorful border.

Is it starting to feel like fall? It will with this hands-on display! Ask each student to bring to school an object that relates to fall, such as an acorn, a pinecone, or a maple leaf. Place each item inside a brown paper lunch sack. Arrange the sacks on a bulletin board covered with yellow background paper. Add a fall border and the title; then invite students to reach inside each bag to feel the object. Each student guesses the object by its feel, then checks his answer with a key provided on the board. What does fall feel like? Your students will know!

Set sail with Columbus on a sea of good books. Enlarge the Columbus pattern on page 37. Color the pattern and attach it to a bulletin board covered in blue background paper. Have each student add to the display by completing a copy of the ship pattern on page 37 with information about a book. Have students color the ships, then staple them to the board. Invite students to discover new books by reading their classmates' reports.

Treat your students to a safe Halloween by reinforcing some safety rules for the event. Have students brainstorm rules for safe trick-or-treating; then distribute a copy of one candy pattern from page 38 to each student. Instruct the student to write a safety rule on the candy before coloring and cutting out the shape. Attach the finished patterns around the border of a bulletin board. Attach a colorful trick-or-treat sack to the center of the board. Arrange black and orange tissue paper inside the sack as shown; then add the title. Happy trick-or-treating!

Let's talk turkey with these fine-feathered fowl! Provide a copy of the turkey pattern on page 38 for each student to color and cut out. Then create a colorful tail for each turkey by placing red, yellow, orange, and brown crayon shavings atop a circle of waxed paper. Cover the shavings with a second circle of waxed paper. Melt the shavings by placing several sheets of newspaper over the project and pressing with a warm iron. Allow to cool, and then staple the tail to the turkey's body. When displayed on a bulletin board, these fancy birds look good enough to eat!

Set the stage for holiday magic with a display of wish-filled stockings. Cover your board with red background paper. Use a black marker to draw a brick design on the paper so that it resembles a fireplace mantel. Provide each student with a copy of the stocking pattern on page 39. Have each student write her name at the top of the stocking, write a holiday wish on the lines, and then add decorative designs. Hang the completed stockings on the mantel along with the title and a string of garland. And the stockings were hung…with holiday wishes!

What does Christmas mean to your students? Focus on holiday happiness with family and friends in this pictorial display. Ask each student to supply a photograph of himself with family or friends. Mount the photo on a construction-paper copy of the package shape on page 40. Have the student use a fine-tipped marker to write a sentence about the picture on the gift-tag pattern. Connect the tag to the package with a length of ribbon. Staple the packages to a bulletin board covered with a holiday gift-wrap background. Add the title and a border, and your display is all wrapped up!

Celebrate Hanukkah with a star-studded display. Have each student cut two 6-inch triangles from aluminum foil. Arrange the two triangles to create a Star Of David. Lay the star on the adhesive side of a piece of clear Con-Tact® paper. Sprinkle a layer of glitter around the outside edge of the star, and then place another piece of Con-Tact® paper on top (adhesive side down). Trim around the star shape, leaving a one-inch border of Con-Tact® paper around the star. Mount the completed stars on a bulletin board for a sparkling holiday display.

Just as each snowflake is unique, so is every student! Create a winter display that reinforces that differences are special. Cover a bulletin board with dark-blue background paper. Distribute a sheet of white paper to each student. Have her fold and cut the paper to create a snowflake shape. Spread a thin coat of glue on the shape and sprinkle with iridescent glitter. Glue a photo of each student in the center of each shape before attaching the shapes to the display. The result—a beautiful arrangement of unique creations!

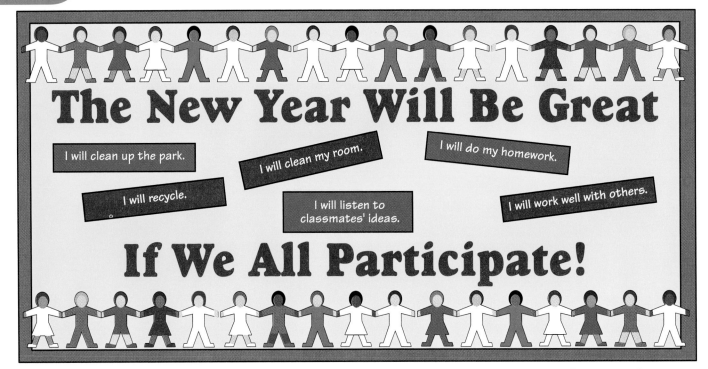

Bring in the new year with this student-created bulletin board. Give each child a copy of a pattern from page 41. Instruct the child to trace the pattern on a sheet of accordion-folded construction paper. Cut along the pattern and unfold the resulting paper-doll chain. Have each student decorate his chain of dolls to resemble members in the community. Staple the completed projects to a bulletin board to create a border. Then have each student compose a New Year's resolution telling how he will participate in the community. Mount the resolutions and the title, and you're ready to welcome the new year!

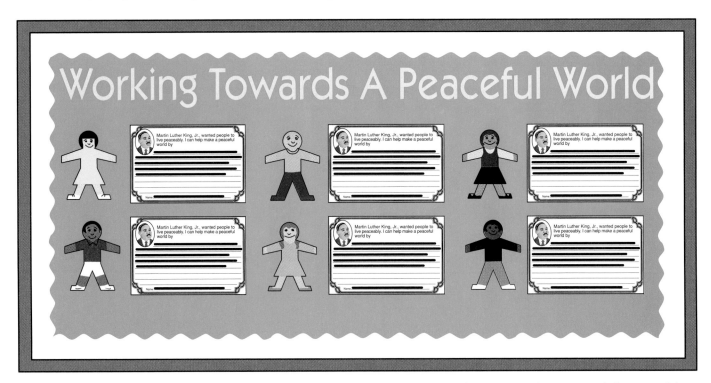

Honor the memory of Dr. Martin Luther King, Jr., with a display that features students' creativity. Provide each student with a copy of one pattern from page 41 and the form on page 42. Instruct the student to decorate the pattern in her own likeness, then complete the form with her thoughts on creating a peaceful world. Display the completed projects and the title on a bulletin board in honor of Dr. King.

Celebrating Afro-American History Month

February

Sunday	Monday	Tuesday	Wednesday	Thursday	Friday	Saturday
	1 Marian Anderson	2 Jesse Jackson	3 Martin Luther King, Jr.	4 Ray Charles	5 Alex Haley	6 Maya Angelou
7 Shirley Chisholm	8 Mary Macleod Bethune	9 George W. Carver	10 Colin Luther Powell	11 Paul L. Dunbar	12 Walter Payton	13 Bill Cosby
14 Josephine Baker	15 Michael Jordan	16 Malcolm X	17 Jackie Joyner-Kersee	18 Nat Love	19 Thurgood Marshall	20 Muhammad Ali
21 Billie Holiday	22 Carol Moseley-Braun	23 Louis Farrakhan	24 Nat "King" Cole	25 Harriet Tubman	26 Alice Walker	27 Sidney Poitier
28 Sojourner Truth						

This bulletin board will do double duty as an Afro-American History Month Calendar. Cover the board with background paper, and illustrate it with a calendar grid and the title. Program each square of the grid with the appropriate date and the name of a famous Black American. Assign each student a name on the calendar to research. Have him record information about the assigned person on a copy of the form on page 42. Provide time for each student to present the information to the class on the day designated on the calendar. After each presentation, staple the form to the calendar display. By the end of the month, your bulletin board will boast a wealth of information!

This Valentine's Day bulletin board provides a wonderful way to display student poetry! Provide each student with a six-inch paper plate. Instruct her to fold the plate in half and trim it to form a heart shape. Unfold the shape and add a red sponge-painted border around the edge. After the paint has dried, have each student compose a valentine couplet and write it in the center of the heart. Mount the completed projects on a board covered in pink background paper. Add the title and a border made from valentine cards. What a sweetheart of a display!

Create this star-studded interactive display for Presidents' Day. Distribute the name of a different U.S. president to each student. Provide a variety of resources for students to use as they research information about the presidents. Duplicate a supply of red and blue stars, and distribute a star to each student. Instruct each student to write his assigned president's name on the front of the star and a fact about him on the back. Attach a loop of yarn to each star and attach the stars to a bulletin board covered in white background paper. Encourage students to visit the display to learn more about presidents, past and present.

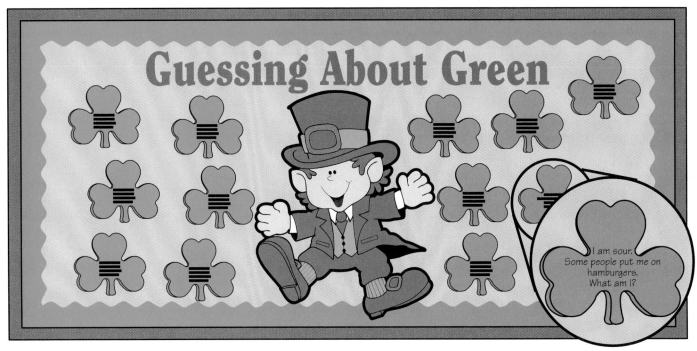

Present a puzzling project for St. Patrick's Day with a focus on green. Provide each student with a piece of green construction paper and a copy of the shamrock pattern on page 43. Instruct him to fold the construction paper in half and place the pattern on the fold as indicated. Have him trace and cut out the shape. Challenge the student to write a riddle about something green on the front of the shamrock, then write the answer to the riddle inside. Mount the riddles and a colored, enlarged copy of the leprechaun on page 43 on a bulletin board. Add the title and a bright green border, and invite students to solve each riddle with guesses about green.

A basketful of bunnies,
"Egg-cited" to be here,
Wish you Hoppy Holidays
As Easter time draws near.

This basket of bunnies will cause plenty of Easter "egg-citement"! Construct the basket by cutting nine 9-inch purple triangles and six 9-inch yellow triangles from construction paper. Staple each triangle to the board as shown. Create the handle and base of the basket from purple construction-paper strips. Fill the basket with student-made bunnies from the " 'Hoppy' Easter" activity described on page 103. Then place some Easter grass around the bunnies, add the verse, and your display is complete!

Welcome spring into your classroom with a striking display of butterflies. Have each student lightly sketch a butterfly on a sheet of black construction paper. The student then squeezes liquid glue onto the lines. After the glue has dried, the student colors in each section with brightly colored chalk. Spray the butterfly with a fixative before mounting it on a bulletin board covered in blue paper and titled "Welcome, Spring!"

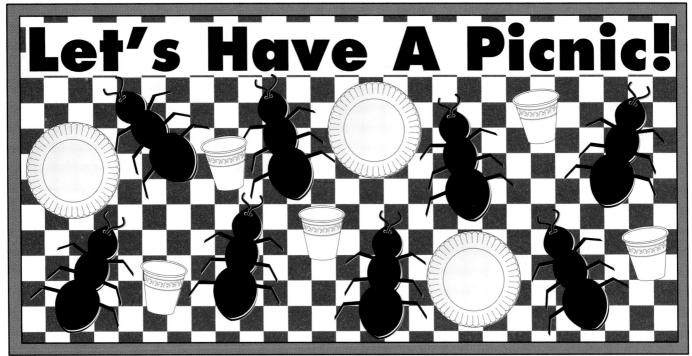

What is summer without a picnic, complete with ants? Set up a summery display by covering a bulletin board with a checkered tablecloth. Then give each student a copy of the ant pattern from page 44. Instruct the student to trace two copies of the pattern on black construction paper, and three copies of the pattern on white paper. The student writes a summertime story on the white shapes, then staples them in between the heads of the two black cutouts. Punch two holes under the staple and thread a black pipe cleaner through as antennae. Add six black legs to the back cover, and then mount on the board with paper plates and cups to complete the display.

End the year with a cool collection of third-grade memories. Provide each student with a copy of the pattern on page 45. Have each student write her favorite memory of the third-grade year on the pattern before coloring it and cutting it out. Decorate a bulletin board with the completed patterns, and have a cool summer!

Motivate students to soar to new heights with a display that shows off good work. Enlarge the airplane pattern on page 46. Color, cut out, and laminate the pattern before mounting it on a bulletin board covered in blue background paper. To display students' papers, have each student cut out and personalize a white construction-paper cloud. Staple the clouds to the bulletin board, and then attach samples of the students' work. Add the title and a border, and you have a high-flying display!

Serve a scoop of positive reinforcement with this display of student work. Enlarge the clown pattern on page 46. Color, cut out, and laminate the pattern before mounting it on the board. Attach a sample of each student's best work to the board. Have each student create an ice-cream cone out of colored construction paper. Program a student's name on each cone; then write a comment praising the student's handwriting, quality of work, or area of improvement. Staple the cone beside the student's paper. When it's time to replace the work on the board, attach the cone to the paper for the student to take home.

This motivational display will be a hands-down favorite! Post the title on a bulletin board covered with yellow paper. Staple an example of each student's best work on the board. Then have each student make a paper topper by placing her hand, palm down, in poster paint and pressing it on a sheet of white construction paper. When dry, trim around the handprint. Attach the print to the top of the student's paper. Now that's a hands-on display!

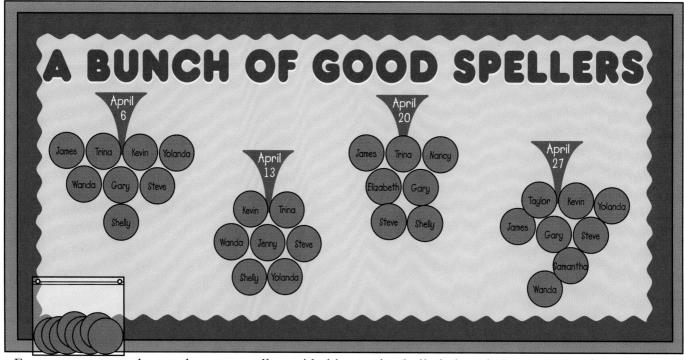

Encourage your students to be super spellers with this ongoing bulletin board. Cut a supply of three-inch circles from purple construction paper and store them in a resealable bag stapled to the board. Attach a stem programmed with the date of the weekly spelling test to the board. When a student scores above a predetermined grade on his weekly test, he writes his name on a circle and staples it to the board as shown. When the board is full, have each student collect all the circles with his name on them to redeem for minutes of free time.

Our Work Is On Target!

Students will aim for the best with this display of good work. Create a target design in the center of the bulletin board. Post examples of each student's best work around the target. Then cut out an arrow shape for each paper on display. Cut the arrow in half and attach it to the paper as shown. Students will be proud to make their mark with good work!

Step up to good habits with this record of class progress. Create a ladder from brown construction paper and attach it to a bulletin board. Label the top of the ladder with a classroom goal, such as turning in homework on time. For each day the class achieves the goal, move a paper cutout of the school mascot up one rung of the ladder. When the mascot reaches the top, celebrate your class's success with a special reward.

Patterns

Use with "Calling All Third Graders Back To School" on page 23.

Third-Grade Calling Card

Name:

Phone Number:

What do you like to be called?

Third-Grade Calling Card

Name:

Phone Number:

What do you like to be called?

Use with "Discover A Good Book" on page 24.

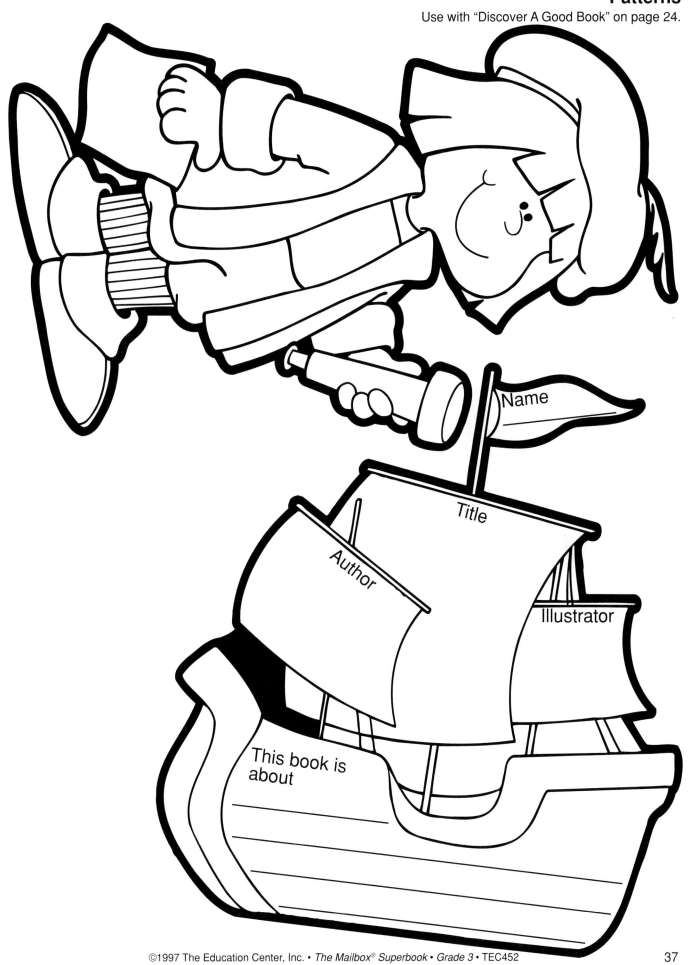

Name

Title

Author

Illustrator

This book is
about

Patterns
Use with "Treat Yourself To A Safe Halloween" on page 25.

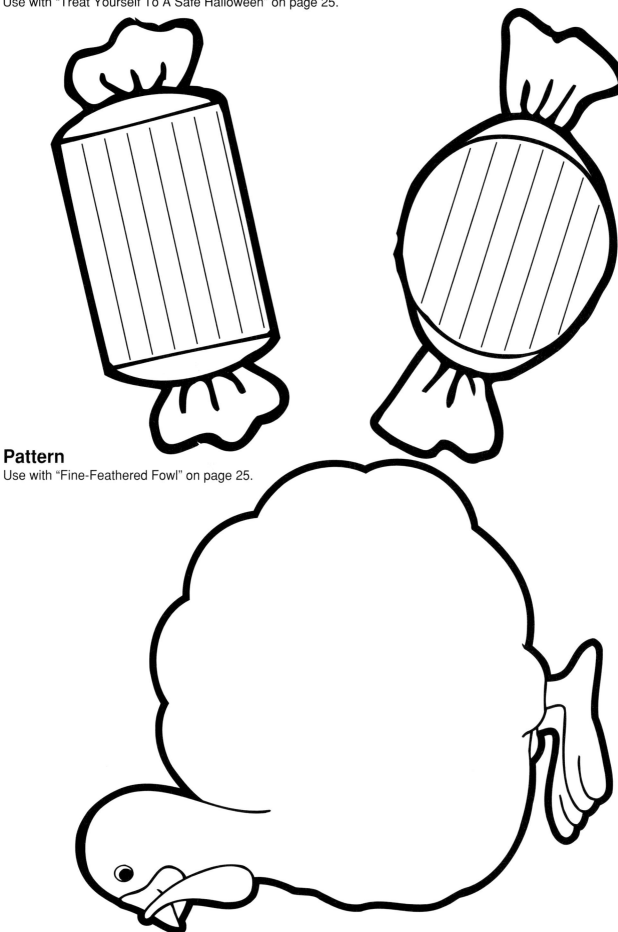

Pattern
Use with "Fine-Feathered Fowl" on page 25.

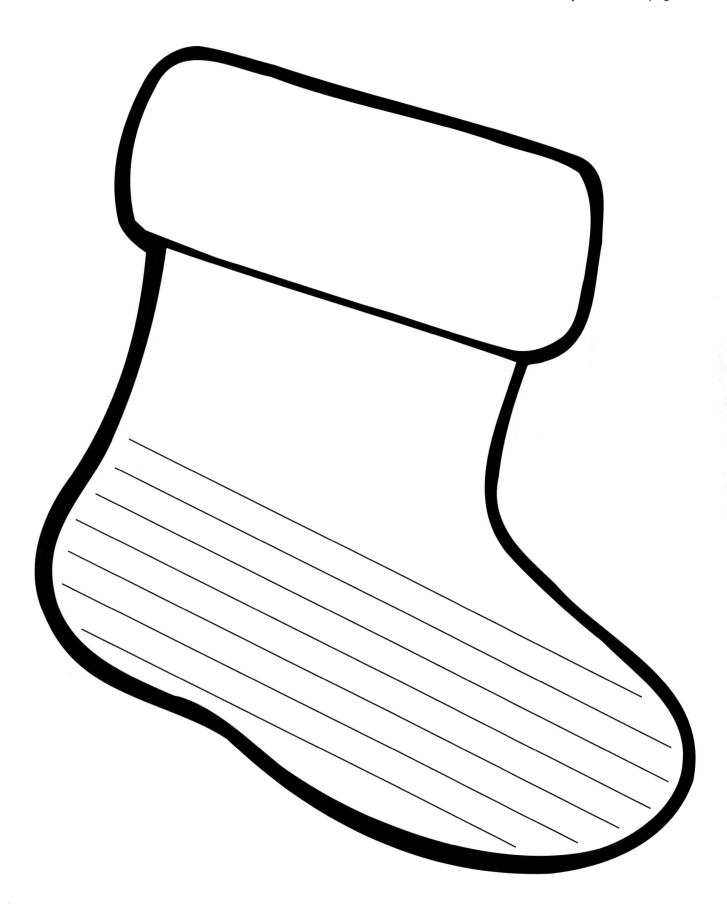

Patterns

Use with "Celebrate The Gift…" on page 26.

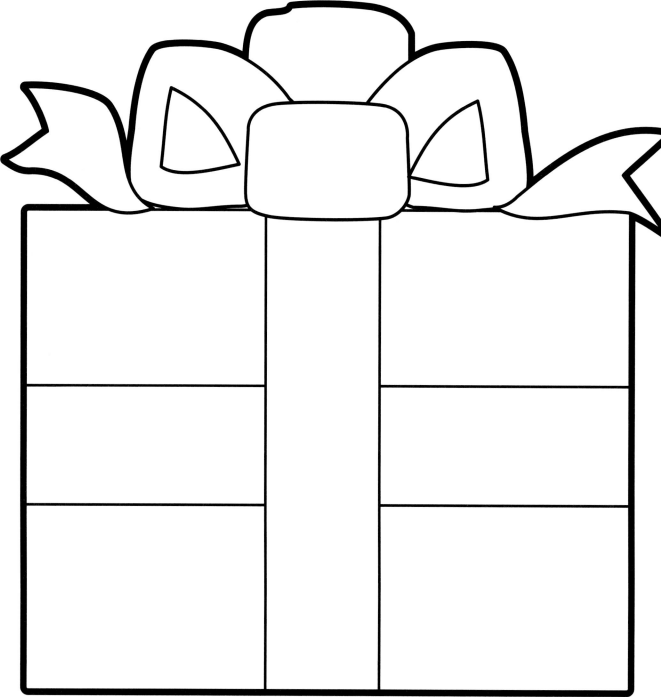

Use with "The New Year Will Be Great…" and
"Working • Towards A Peaceful World" on page 28.

Place on fold.

Place on fold.

Place on fold.

Place on fold.

Form

Use with "Working Towards A Peaceful World" on page 28.

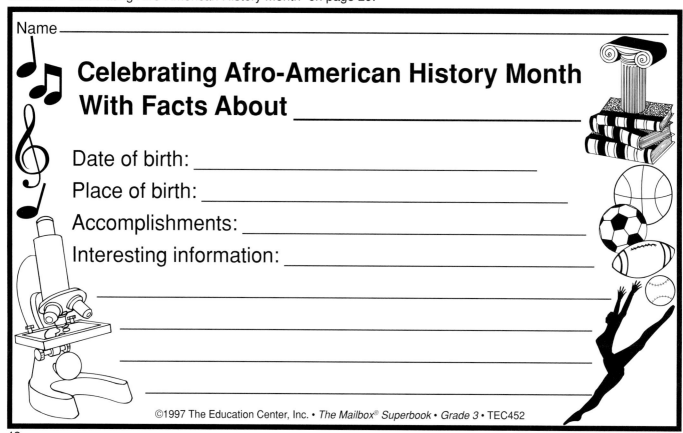

Martin Luther King, Jr., wanted people to live peaceably. I can help make a peaceful world by

_____

_____

_____

_____

_____

_____

_____

_____

Name _____

Form

Use With "Celebrating Afro-American History Month" on page 29.

Name _____

Celebrating Afro-American History Month With Facts About _____

Date of birth: _____

Place of birth: _____

Accomplishments: _____

Interesting information: _____

_____

_____

_____

Place on fold.

Pattern

Use with "Let's Have A Picnic!" on page 32.

Pattern
Use with "High-Flying Work" on page 33.

Pattern
Use with "Here's The Scoop…" on page 33.

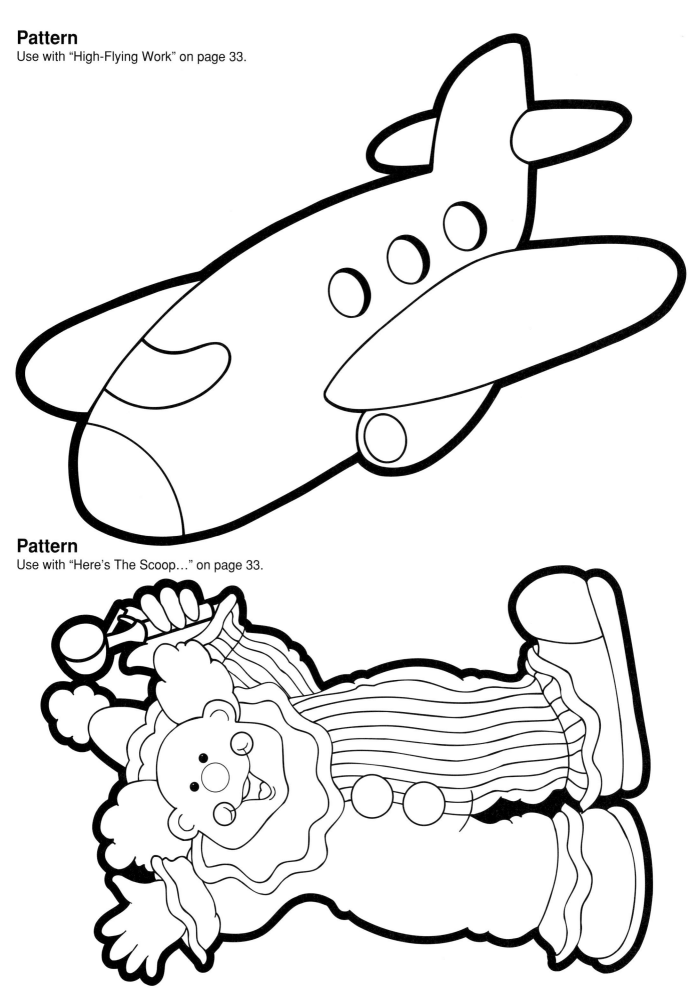

CLASSROOM MANAGEMENT

Classroom Management

Be Prepared!

Be prepared for unexpected situations by keeping an emergency kit on hand. In addition to the basic first-aid kit, stock a drawer or box with the following items:

* a sewing kit
* a screwdriver
* a hammer
* a package of assorted nails
* resealable plastic bags in assorted sizes
* a flashlight
* nail scissors and clippers

* tweezers
* a smock or old oversized shirt
* safety pins
* an emery board or a nail file
* matches or a lighter
* a ball of string
* packing tape

Planning Ahead

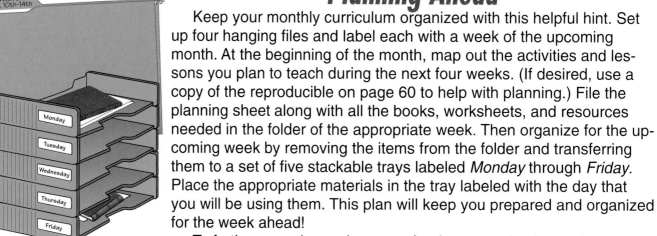

Keep your monthly curriculum organized with this helpful hint. Set up four hanging files and label each with a week of the upcoming month. At the beginning of the month, map out the activities and lessons you plan to teach during the next four weeks. (If desired, use a copy of the reproducible on page 60 to help with planning.) File the planning sheet along with all the books, worksheets, and resources needed in the folder of the appropriate week. Then organize for the upcoming week by removing the items from the folder and transferring them to a set of five stackable trays labeled *Monday* through *Friday*. Place the appropriate materials in the tray labeled with the day that you will be using them. This plan will keep you prepared and organized for the week ahead!

To further organize and prepare for the next school year, keep a copy of each week's planning sheet. Clip copies of worksheets, overhead transparencies, book lists, and other information pertinent to the lessons to each plan sheet. When the next school year rolls around, you will have copies of your previous lesson plans to refer to, as well as a resource for all the materials needed for each lesson.

Recycled File Storage

Check your attic for the best file-folder rack yet! Use old metal record-album holders to store file folders in your classroom. Students can easily remove and replace their folders in the wire slots, and the folders stay neatly and securely in place.

File-Folder Storage

For a simple way to keep track of file-folder games or centers, store the contents of each activity in a manila envelope. Label the envelope to identify the contents; then file it with the appropriate month or unit it is used with. This serves as excellent storage when the activity contains separate pieces or cards, and it will be easy to locate the materials when you are ready to set up the center.

Pocket Organization

A pocket folder is the perfect tool for helping you keep track of which activities and reproducibles you have used. Purchase a two-pocket folder for each of your thematic files. Label one pocket of each folder "Activities To Use" and the other pocket "Completed Activities." Store your ideas, activities, and worksheets in the first pocket. When an activity has been used, transfer it to the other side of the folder. At the end of each unit, transfer all pages back to the first pocket, and you'll be ready to go for the next year.

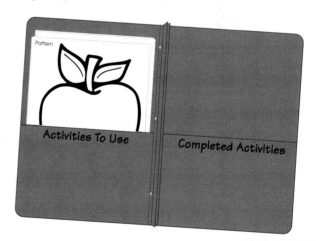

Handy Supply Boxes

Be on the lookout for plastic videocassette cases. The cases are the perfect size for holding pencils, crayons, and scissors, but take up very little desk space. These storage containers are also great for housing math manipulatives, science materials, art supplies, and learning-center items. See-through cases are especially handy since the contents can be identified at a glance.

Extra Storage Space

Create additional storage space in closets and cabinets by attaching stick-on pockets to the insides of the doors. These see-through pockets are great for storing flash cards, lunch forms, tardy slips, and daily reminders. You'll have access to the items you use most in a space-saving place!

Super Hang-Ups!

Store posters, maps, charts, and bulletin-board displays by using this simple and accessible method. Separate the items into the desired categories (by months, topics, or themes) and place each group in a see-through trash bag. Fold the top of each bag over a wire hanger and secure it with clothespins. Hang the bags in a closet or storeroom. When looking for a particular item, you'll be able to spot it hanging neatly in a bag.

Additional Storage Ideas

There is no end to the number and types of items that need to be organized in the classroom! Keep your classroom clutter-free by utilizing some of the following storage ideas:

Use a silverware tray to hold paintbrushes, colored pencils, and markers in your art center.

Ice-cube trays and egg cartons make handy organizers for storing tiny craft items or game pieces. They also work well for holding small amounts of tempera paints.

Cardboard tubes from wrapping paper or paper towels are perfect for storing charts, maps, and posters. Roll up each poster and place it inside a tube. If desired, label the tube's contents before putting it away.

Use margarine tubs and whipped-topping tubs to hold paints, clay, or small manipulatives.

Cardboard shoe organizers are just the thing for holding sets of papers or serving as cubbyholes.

Check craft stores for plastic, multidrawer containers. Use the drawers for holding sequins, buttons, pom-poms, beads, and other small craft items.

Clever Clothespins

Keep a supply of spring-type clothespins handy. They can be used in a variety of ways in the classroom.

Use a clothespin when a paper clip is too small for the job. A clothespin can hold a large stack of papers, a supply of lunch tickets, or a set of flash cards.

Display a chart or poster in a jiffy by using clothespins and a wire clothes hanger. Clip the poster to the clothes hanger; then hang it from the corner of the chalkboard or from a small nail placed in the wall.

The UNITED STATES OF AMERICA

Suspend several lengths of monofilament line from the ceiling. Attach a clothespin to the end of each length. Use the clothespins to hold student art-work or decorative displays.

Who has a ...
cat
dog
both

Program clothespins with students' names. Use the pro-grammed clips as emergency nametags, labels for art projects and materials, and manipulatives in graphing activities.

Glue magnets to the backs of several clothespins. They can be placed on filing cabinets as message holders or attached to magnetic chalkboards to hold posters, charts, and displays.

Jason leaves today at 2:00.

Some art projects require that pieces be held in place while the glue dries. Use a clothespin to hold the pieces in place, allow-ing you to attend to another task.

Program a set of clips to be used as passes to the office, nurse, and rest room. When a student needs to leave the room, he clips the appropriate clothespin to his shirt.

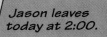

Super Shoe Bags

Clear, plastic, multipocket shoe bags have several uses in the classroom. Look for inexpensive bags at discount stores and put them to work in your classroom.

Hang a clear, multipocket shoe bag by your desk to organize the basics that you need every day. Place the following items in the pockets, and you'll have your necessary materials on hand in one central place:

- lunch tickets
- medical forms
- office passes
- overhead transparency markers
- extra chalk
- reward stickers
- grading pens
- scissors that students may borrow
- rubber bands
- index cards
- a calculator
- a bottle of glue

A see-through shoe bag can also serve as a classroom job chart. Use a permanent marker to label each pocket of the organizer with the title of a classroom job. Program a class set of index cards with your students' names. To assign jobs, place a name card in a pocket. Jobs can easily be reassigned by removing the card from the pocket and replacing it with another card.

Place a shoe bag in your art center and stock it with supplies needed for the current project. It will be easy for students to find each item, and cleanup will be a simple task as well.

Store laminated, die-cut letters in the pockets of the shoe bag. Each pocket will hold a generous supply of letters, and will protect the letters from becoming crumpled or bent.

Library Organizer

Keep your classroom library shelves in order with this simple organizing method. Distribute a paint-stirring stick (available at hardware stores) to each student. Have the student write her name on the stick with a permanent marker, then place the stick in a container atop the library shelf. When a student borrows a book, she removes her stick from the container and uses it to mark the place on the shelf where her selection belongs. When it's time to return the book, the student finds the stick with her name on it and places the book back in its correct order on the shelf. With minimal effort, your library will remain in good shape!

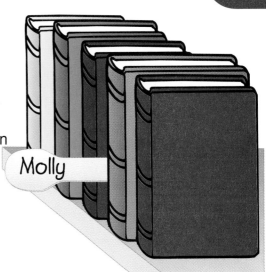

EXIT BOARD

Stay on top of the comings and goings in your classroom with a nametag charting system. Attach self-adhesive hooks to a bulletin board, and label each hook with a title such as rest room, speech class, library, and office. Distribute to each student a cardboard tag with a metal ring attached. Have him personalize the tag and keep it at his desk until he needs to leave the classroom. Before leaving the room, the student places his tag on the appropriate hook. When he returns, he removes the tag and stores it at his desk.

Traveling Nametags

If your grade level is departmentalized, use traveling nametags to help identify students during the first few weeks of school. To make a nametag, fold a large index card in half to create a tent shape. Write a student's name on both sides of the nametag, then place it atop the student's desk. When it's time to change classes, the student carries the nametag with her and places it on her desk in the next classroom. Have students carry their nametags to music class and the cafeteria as well, so that everyone on staff can become familiar with students' names.

Personalized Pencils

Put an end to misplaced pencils with personalized name flags. Print each student's name on a piece of masking tape and attach it to his pencil as shown. When a wayward pencil is found, it can quickly be returned to the rightful owner.

Book-Order Box

Student book clubs provide a wonderful way for students to purchase quality books at reasonable prices. But often the process of collecting the orders and keeping track of the forms becomes a burdensome task. Create a system for collecting the orders with a Book-Order Box placed on your desk. Instruct students to clearly label all book orders and money envelopes before placing them in the box. After you send the order, return the forms to the box for safekeeping until the shipment arrives.

Everything In Its Place

This management technique will ensure that all classroom materials are returned to their proper places. As you set up centers or free-time activities, trace the shape of each item that will be used in the activity on a sheet of construction paper. When a student is through using the materials for an activity, he places them back on the outlines that match their shapes. You will be able to make sure at a glance that all items have been returned to their proper places. (This method also works well for keeping track of the stapler, tape dispenser, and other items on your desk that students are apt to borrow!)

Incoming Mail

The morning rush of students wanting to hand you notes, return forms, and converse with you can be a bit overwhelming. Get your mornings off to a smoother start with a system for receiving all the information. Purchase an inexpensive mailbox to place on your desk. When students arrive in the morning with notes, permission slips, and other papers, instruct them to put the items directly in the mailbox. You can sort through the mail as soon as students have started on a morning task.

The beginning of your school day will be reserved for greetings and conversation.

Absences/Tardies

Pam	9/6	(9/7)						
Greg	9/2							
Katie								
Tim								
Ashton								
Paul								
Carly								

Attendance Made Easy

Make attendance-taking an easy task with this quick tip. Instead of marking each student present in your grade book each day, write down only the dates each student is absent. Place the date in a blank square by the name of the absent student. If the student comes in late, draw a circle around the date to indicate a tardy. Absences and tardy marks will be easier to count, and your daily record keeping will be much more simple.

Lesson-Plan Checklist

A checklist is the perfect way to keep your daily plans within reach. Make a generic schedule of your daily routines and duplicate several copies. Use a copy to fill in your specific plans for the day and attach it to a clipboard. Cross off items as they are completed. Make notes next to activities that went well or concepts that need to be reviewed. At the end of each day, look over the checklist. Any unfinished items can simply be clipped to the next day's planning sheet.

Class Information

Have a list of important details ready when you need it by creating a class information list. Duplicate one copy of the form on page 61. Program it with the desired information, such as students' birth dates, parents' names, and phone numbers where parents can be reached. Attach the completed list to your attendance or lesson plan book for easy access after making a copy of the list to take home with you.

COLOR-CODED Grade Book

This system for color-coding your grade book will allow you to see at a glance which scores are daily grades, homework assignments, or test scores. Select a different-colored highlighter for each type of grade to be recorded. Before recording a set of grades, use the appropriate highlighter to color in the column in your grade book. The color-coded page will help you evaluate students' progress and simplify grade averaging.

MATH	p. 13	p. 14	p. 15	quiz	p. 16	test 1	project				
Mary	✓+	95	95	91	✓+	93	A+				
Tina	✓	90	90	94	✓+	94	A				
Miguel	✓	90	90	86	✓	90	A-				
Eric	✓+	85	85	91	✓+	89	B+				
Tanya	✓	88	88	89	✓+	86	B				
Andrew	✓+	93	93	94	✓	95	A				

☐ = daily homework grade   ☐ = quiz grade   ☐ = test grade   ☐ = project grade

Anecdotal Notecards

Have anecdotal records right at your fingertips with this easy idea. Begin by labeling a large index card with the name of each student in the lower right-hand corner. Next tape the top of the cards to a clipboard as shown, overlapping the cards until each student's card is attached. Tape a blank card at the top to keep your notes private. When you need to assess a skill or make note of a behavior, flip your records open to the appropriate student card. The cards will quickly fill up with comments to share on report cards, at parent conferences, and with students.

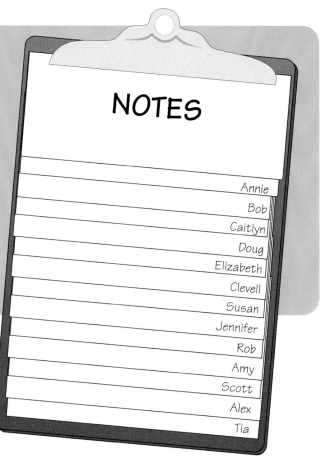

NOTES

Annie
Bob
Caitlyn
Doug
Elizabeth
Clevell
Susan
Jennifer
Rob
Amy
Scott
Alex
Tia

Note-Taking Tip

Have a simple record-keeping system ready with this reusable note-taking form. List your students' names in a column on the left-hand side of a sheet of notebook paper. Create several untitled columns by the list of names. (A copy of the "Class Information" sheet on page 61 can be reprogrammed for this purpose.) Laminate the sheet of paper; then attach it to a clipboard. Use a wipe-off marker to jot down oral test scores, flash-card results, behavior notes, academic concerns, or checklist information. At the end of the day, transfer the information to your grade book or to the appropriate file. Wipe the page clean, and it's ready to use for another day.

READY REINFORCEMENT

Have a supply of encouragement on hand with preprogrammed sticky notes. Use a rubber stamp to create a positive remark on each sheet of a small sticky-note pad. Keep the pad in your pocket or on your desk. When you see an opportunity to praise a student, hand her a sheet from the pad. The notes can also be attached to papers that show praiseworthy work!

YOU'RE A SUPER STAR!

JOB WELL DONE!

Absentee Assignments

When a student is absent, use this simple system for collecting class work that he has missed. Program a folder with the absent student's name and place it on his desk. As papers are passed out during the day, have a designated classmate place a copy of each assignment in the student's folder. At the end of the day, the folder will contain all the day's work and be ready to send home to the student. If desired, have classmates sign the folder and add get-well wishes and hopes for a speedy recovery.

If you are going to introduce a new concept, begin a new unit, or give an oral test when a student is absent, you may want to tape-record the lesson. The tape can be sent home with the student so he can be kept up-to-date on the information discussed in the lesson. When he returns to school, the student can make up any oral testing by listening to that portion of the tape.

Color-Coded Groups

Add a little color to the classroom as you place students in cooperative seating groups. Purchase a small plastic caddy and code it with a different-colored dot for each group. Fill each caddy with necessary materials such as glue sticks, markers, and scissors. If desired, color-code these supplies as well. Choose a group captain each week to distribute and gather supplies for his group. The captain is also responsible for collecting papers from his group when assignments are complete. Make sure everyone in the group has the opportunity to be the captain, promoting a sense of leadership and responsibility for everyone.

Helping Hands

Create a system so students can let you know when they need help or have a question about an assignment. Have each student trace, cut out, and personalize his handprint from a piece of construction paper. When the student needs your assistance but sees that you are already occupied, he places his handprint on your desk, signaling that he needs your attention. He then quietly reads a book or works on another assignment until you are free. Return the handprint to the student as you assist him with the assignment. This routine will help prevent interruptions as you help others in the class.

The Name Cup

For a great time-saver, program a class set of wooden tongue depressors or craft sticks with your students' names. Store the sticks in a decorated cup or tin. When it becomes time to randomly draw a student's name, place students in small groups, choose partners or teams, or select a student to go first in an activity, simply pull the names from the cup. Students will know that the selection was done fairly, and you won't have the burden of making a decision!

Timely Tip

Keep a kitchen timer on hand to help students use their time wisely. When students are having a difficult time staying on task, set the timer for the length of time needed for students to complete half of the assignment. When the timer rings, check each student's progress. Then set the timer again and let students know that they should complete the assignment in the allotted time. When used periodically, the timer is a great reminder for students to stay focused on their work.

Thrifty Containers

When distributing small game pieces, manipulatives, or food items to your students, coffee filters serve as inexpensive, one-time containers. Place a filter on each student's desk to prevent rolling or misplaced pieces, or to contain messy crumbs. When it's time to clean up, the scraps, crumbs, and leftovers can be neatly disposed of inside the filter. Used filters that are still clean can be recycled for another activity.

Monday	Mary Joel
Tuesday	
Wednesday	Tammy
Thursday	Sarah
Friday	Joan Derrick

The Sharing Board

To avoid the confusion and time it often takes for students to share or tell something special, design a classroom sharing board. Use a marker to visually divide a large piece of poster board into five sections. Label each section with a day of the school week. Attach a wipe-off marker to the board using a length of string or a Velcro® fastener. When students enter the room in the morning with news or items they would like to share, they must sign up on the board. Encourage students to share with their classmates at least once a week.

Student Helper Chart

Keeping track of student helpers is an easy task with this management system. List each student's name on a piece of poster board. Program several clothespins with the titles of classroom jobs, such as plant monitor and line leader. To assign a student a job, clip a clothespin beside her name. When it's time to reassign jobs, move each clothespin down to the next name. This will guarantee that every student has an equal opportunity to participate as each type of helper.

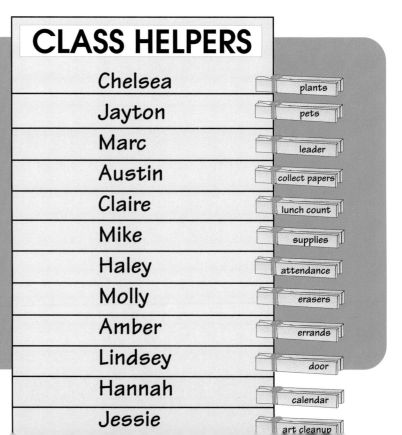

CLASS HELPERS

Chelsea	plants
Jayton	pets
Marc	leader
Austin	collect papers
Claire	lunch count
Mike	supplies
Haley	attendance
Molly	erasers
Amber	errands
Lindsey	door
Hannah	calendar
Jessie	art cleanup

"CARROT" Conduct

Teach classroom expectations with the help of Captain Carrot, a cute character that promotes positive classroom conduct. Create a display using an enlarged copy of the pattern on page 66. Use die-cut letters to spell the word *carrot*. Arrange the letters in an acrostic form; then copy the word that corresponds with each letter as shown. Discuss the expectations with your students. When you are ready to take down the display, keep Captain Carrot close at hand. Have him pay an occasional visit to reinforce positive classroom behavior.

Cooperation

Attitude

Respect

Responsibility

Organization

Teamwork

Handy Reminders

Students will have a reminder of the classroom rules on hand with this activity for reinforcing good conduct. Distribute a piece of colored construction paper to each student. Instruct her to trace her hand on the paper and then cut out the shape. On each of the fingers, have her copy a classroom rule, such as "Respect others," "Keep hands and feet to myself," "Use self-control," "Raise my hand to speak," and "Be responsible for my belongings." Write the title "Handy Rules" in the center of the palm. Tape the completed projects to each desk for a visual reminder of behavioral expectations.

Respect others
Keep hands and feet to myself
Raise my hand to speak
Be responsible for my belongings
Use self-control
Handy Rules

Expect The Best

Expect the best from your students by letting them know what you expect in your classroom. Post a copy of your daily schedule, a copy of the classroom rules, and a list of your policies regarding homework and discipline. (If desired, use copies of the forms on pages 62–65. Enlarge a copy of each form; then program it with the desired information.) When students are aware of the standards that are set, they will be able to respond in an appropriate manner.

Shared Responsibility

Help students keep up with homework assignments with "Buddy Books"—small spiral notepads for keeping track of homework information. Provide time at the end of the day for each student to copy the necessary homework information in her Buddy Book. The book is then read by a classmate buddy who checks the information for accuracy. After any corrections have been made, the buddy initials the notepad and passes it back to its owner. Students have the information they need to complete their assignments, and they develop a feeling of teamwork as well.

Lesson Plans For The Month Of _____
Week # _____

Subject	Topic/Skill	Materials

Note To The Teacher: Use with "Planning Ahead" on page 48.

Class Information

	Name				

Note To The Teacher: Duplicate this page, then program it with the desired information. (See "Class Information" on page 55.)

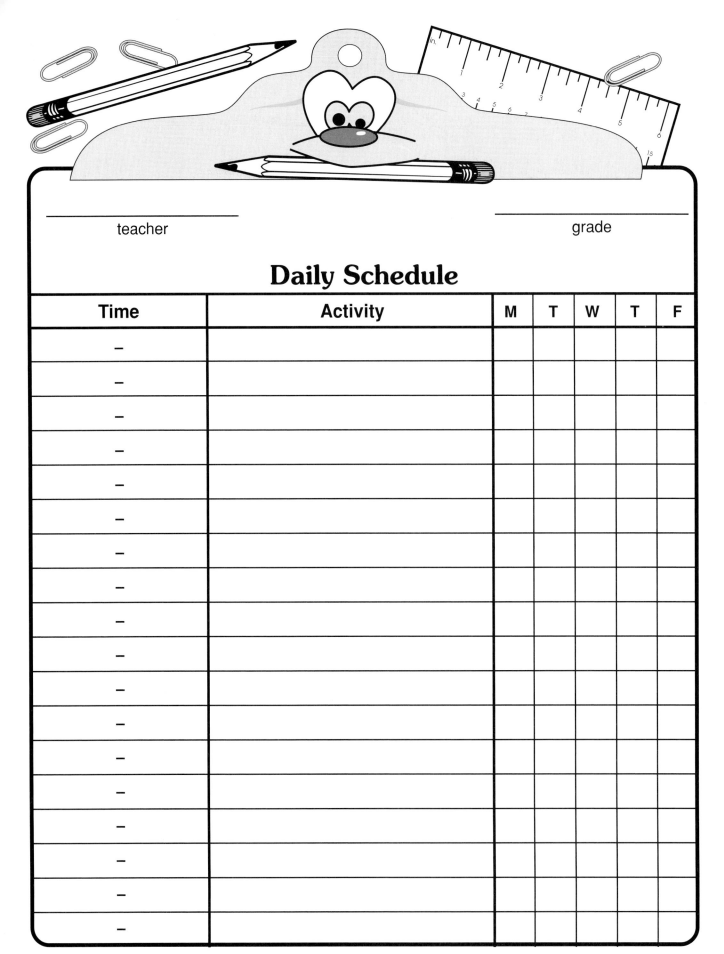

_____ teacher   grade

Daily Schedule

Time	Activity	M	T	W	T	F
–						
–						
–						
–						
–						
–						
–						
–						
–						
–						
–						
–						
–						
–						
–						
–						
–						
–						

- -

Note To The Teacher: Duplicate this page; then program it with the necessary information. If desired, enlarge and color the page before displaying it.

Our Classroom Rules

We have discussed the rules we need in
order to have a positive learning environment.
We agree to:

_____

_____

_____

_____

_____

_____

Note To The Teacher: Duplicate this page; then program it with the necessary information. If desired, enlarge and color the page before displaying it.

Homework Policy

_____

_____

_____

_____

_____

_____

_____

_____

Rewards:

_____

_____

_____

_____

Note To The Teacher: Duplicate this page; then program it with the necessary information. If desired, enlarge and color the page before displaying it.

Discipline Policy

Severe situations will be handled by:

Note To The Teacher: Duplicate this page; then program it with the necessary information. If desired, enlarge and color the page before displaying it.

Pattern

Use with " 'Carroty' Conduct" on page 59.

Note To The Teacher: Duplicate this page; then program it with the necessary information. If desired, enlarge and color the page before displaying it.

MOTIVATING STUDENTS

MOTIVATING STUDENTS

Marvelous Motivation

Set the stage for learning by creating a positive environment for your students. When students feel good about themselves, they are better equipped to learn. See the lists below for ideas about letting each student know how special she is. Use copies of the rewards and coupons on page 73 to recognize positive student behavior and encourage each student to do her best.

Recognize Students For:

- helping a classmate
- making a new student feel welcome
- encouraging a fellow student
- acting cooperatively
- using nice handwriting
- turning in neat work
- treating others with respect
- learning math facts

- being a careful proofreader
- learning the weekly spelling words
- consistently turning in homework assignments
- keeping an orderly work space
- perseverance with a difficult assignment
- consistently following classroom rules
- a good attendance record
- efforts as well as for good grades

10 Ways To Reinforce Positive Behavior

Program copies of the coupons to be redeemed for:

- the opportunity to sit by a friend during a lesson
- choosing a classroom job for the week
- being first in line for a day
- designing a bulletin board
- choosing a game for the class to play
- selecting bonus words for the spelling list
- skipping a homework assignment
- selecting a musical tape to be played during art time
- eating lunch with the principal or another member of the faculty
- sitting at the teacher's desk for the day

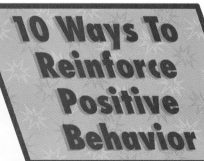

Dressed For Success

Rather than spending a lot of money on candy, treats, or material rewards, recognize your students' outstanding behavior and work habits with a special privilege. Invite students who have exhibited desired behaviors to participate in a special dress-up event such as hat day, sunglasses day, or pajama day. Provide a special table in the cafeteria for these well-attired students to eat their lunch. Then take pictures of the students in their special garb. Display the photographs as a reminder of what fun good behavior can be!

Book Order Incentives

Student book order forms can be an incentive to encourage proper classroom behavior. Post a list of books from the current order that could be purchased with bonus points for the classroom library. When you see a student modeling good conduct, allow her to cast a vote for one of the books on the list by making a tally mark beside it. As an extra bonus, reward students who have earned the most tally marks by giving them first opportunities to read the new books when they arrive.

Reward Raffle

Encourage students to maintain good conduct with a classroom raffle. At the beginning of each week, enlist students' help to create five certificates for classroom privileges. Have students suggest the types of rewards, such as a no-homework pass, the chance to eat lunch in the classroom, or the chance to choose a free-time activity. Program each certificate with one reward privilege. Then, each time a student displays outstanding behavior during the week, write his name on a slip of paper and place it in a raffle jar. At the end of the week, draw five names from the jar. Present each winner with a certificate, redeemable anytime in the following week.

Conduct Celebration

Motivate the class to work together to earn a special reward. Plan an event, such as a popcorn party, a video showing, or an extra recess to celebrate classwide behavior. On the chalkboard, write a blank for each letter in the name of the reward. For each day the class works together to maintain good conduct, fill in a blank with a letter of the reward. When all the blanks have been filled in, it's time to celebrate!

Sticking With Good Behavior

Students love to collect the stickers they receive for good grades, nice manners, and overall effort. Provide a place for each student to display her stickers by covering a small area of her desk with a square of clear Con-Tact® paper. This adhesive paper allows the students to affix the stickers to her desk without placing them directly onto the furniture. The stickers will easily peel away from the Con-Tact® paper, enabling students to periodically take stickers home.

Choose a sticker from your teacher.

Be the leader in line.

Encouraging Organization

For an easy and effective way to encourage students to keep their desks in tip-top order, cut out a supply of seasonal shapes. On each shape, write a reward such as being first in line, using a colored pen on an assignment, or spending extra time at a learning center. Choose a time when the students are out of the room to inspect each desk for being neat and orderly. If a student has a well-organized desk, leave a reward shape on his desk. When students return to the room, they will be surprised to find rewards on some of the desks. Continue to make random inspections to encourage students to keep their desks orderly at all times.

Spend ten extra minutes in any learning center.

It's In The Cards

Add a spark of excitement to positive reinforcement. Purchase a deck of playing cards and divide it into the four suits. Place two of the suits in a container. When you notice a student displaying positive behavior, allow the student to reach into the container and draw out two cards. If the cards are a matching pair, the student may take a prize from the prize box. If the cards do not match, offer a smaller prize such as a sticker or bookmark. Aside from the treat, the element of chance will make reaching into the jar a special reward of its own.

Stamps Of Approval

As the school year progresses, it becomes apparent that each student has certain strengths and weaknesses. Use an individualized progress card to motivate each student to work on a specific area of improvement while reinforcing her strengths. Meet with each student to discuss both strong points and areas that need to be improved. Personalize an index card for each student and write a goal for the student. At the end of each day, stamp the card with a motivational rubber stamp if progress has been made towards the goal. After a predetermined number of stamps have been earned, reward the student with a special treat or privilege.

Ann
Use your best handwriting all week.

WOW!

#1

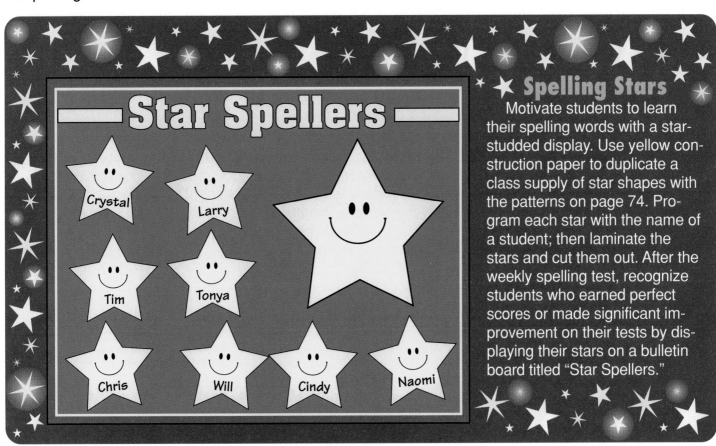

Star Spellers

Crystal

Larry

Tim

Tonya

Chris

Will

Cindy

Naomi

Spelling Stars

Motivate students to learn their spelling words with a star-studded display. Use yellow construction paper to duplicate a class supply of star shapes with the patterns on page 74. Program each star with the name of a student; then laminate the stars and cut them out. After the weekly spelling test, recognize students who earned perfect scores or made significant improvement on their tests by displaying their stars on a bulletin board titled "Star Spellers."

Conduct Magnets

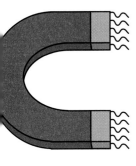

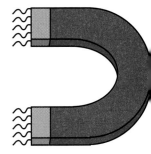

If free time is on your students' list of favorite things, allow them the opportunity to earn it with positive behavior. Keep a supply of magnet shapes in an upper corner of your chalkboard or dry-erase board. Under the magnets draw a square and label it "Free Time." When the class demonstrates appropriate behavior, place a magnet inside the square. If behavior does not meet expectations, remove a magnet from the square and place it back in the corner. At the end of the week, award the class five minutes of free time for every magnet in the box. This concrete reminder will help students stick to appropriate conduct!

In The Spotlight

This esteem-boosting display allows every student to have her turn in the spotlight. Decorate a bulletin board with colored background paper, a shiny border, and the title "Student Spotlight." Every week select a student to be featured in the spotlight. Encourage the student to bring from home photographs, hobby samples, artwork, and other items that tell about her. Display the items on the bulletin board. Set aside time during the week for the student to tell about the items on display. Then take a picture of the featured student standing in the spotlight (in front of the display).

Special Awards

The end of a grading period is often the time when achievement awards are handed out. Why not choose a special time to recognize students for nonacademic accomplishments? Set aside time every month for a celebration of all the good qualities your students possess. Duplicate copies of the invitation and award patterns on page 76. Have each student fill out an invitation for his family members to attend the ceremony. Then complete an award for each student applauding characteristics such as a cooperative attitude, a willingness to help others, an improved behavior, and an artistic ability. On the day of the awards ceremony, present each child with a certificate while his family and friends look on. Then toast your students with juice or punch, and conclude the event with refreshments.

Self-Esteem Supply

Stock your classroom with a supply of self-esteem! Distribute a copy of the jar pattern on page 75 to each student. Instruct the student to cut out the shape and write her name on the label. Collect the patterns and redistribute them in random order. The student reads the name on the jar she receives, then writes a positive comment about that student on the pattern. Continue collecting and redistributing the jars until each jar is full of favorable comments. Provide time for each student to read the statements written about her; then display the jars on a bulletin board decorated with a construction-paper shelf.

Chris is a good sport.

Chris is good at math.

Chris has cool shoes.

Chris

Chris uses his manners.

Chris knows a lot about snakes.

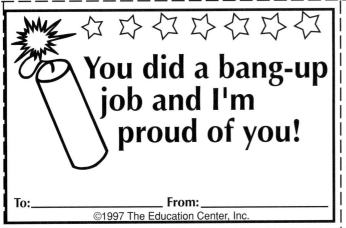

You did a bang-up job and I'm proud of you!

To:_____ From: _____
©1997 The Education Center, Inc.

Award-Winning Efforts

#1

Presented to:

_____

Keep up the good work!
©1997 The Education Center, Inc.

Three Cheers For_____!

Hip, Hip Hooray!
©1997 The Education Center, Inc.

You're On A Roll!

To:_____

From:_____
©1997 The Education Center, Inc.

This coupon is good for

_____
_____
_____
©1997 The Education Center, Inc.

This coupon is good for

_____
_____
_____
_____
©1997 The Education Center, Inc.

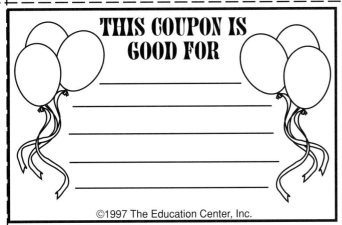

THIS COUPON IS GOOD FOR

_____
_____
_____
©1997 The Education Center, Inc.

THIS COUPON IS GOOD FOR

_____
_____
_____
_____
©1997 The Education Center, Inc.

Patterns

Use with "Spelling Stars" on page 71.

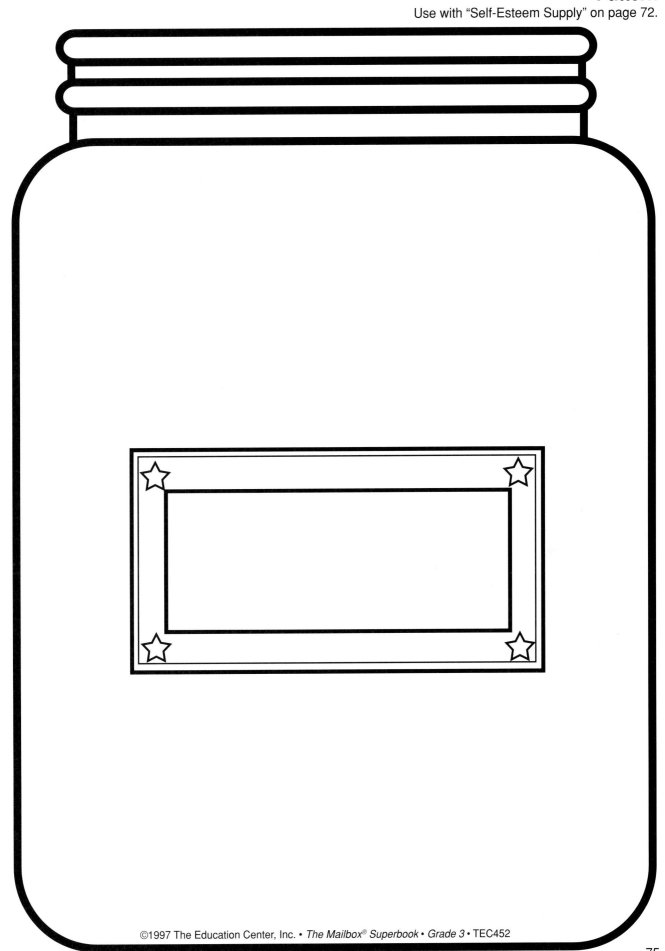

Invitation

Please come . . . to a celebration of super students!

Date:_____

Time:_____

Place:_____

Award

In Recognition Of

_____
(Student)

For

_____

_____

_____

What A Super Student!

GREAT! FANTASTIC! HOORAY!

GREAT! FANTASTIC! HOORAY!

PARENT COMMUNICATION

Parent Communication

Keeping In Touch

Strengthen communication between home and school with the reproducible forms on pages 83–86. You'll find forms for making parents aware of homework and discipline policies, party information, and special project supplies requests. In addition, there are forms for requesting school supplies, alerting parents of missing assignments, obtaining permission for field trips, and sending out special reminders. Reproduce the forms as needed to help maintain the vital parent-communication link in your classroom.

Calling All Volunteers

To remind parents that they are a very important part of the learning process, invite them to volunteer for various tasks in the classroom. Even if parents work, they may be able to take on some of the responsibilities listed below. Parents will feel as though they are making significant contributions, and you will have much-needed help with classroom duties!

- chaperone field trips
- assist students in the library
- prepare art projects (at school *or* at home)
- organize class parties
- supply materials for special projects, events, and celebrations
- read a story to the class
- share a skill or information with the class
- work with students in class
- create a bulletin-board display
- assist students with computer skills

Classroom News

A classroom newsletter is the perfect tool for letting parents know all the happenings in your classroom. Use the newsletter form on page 87 combined with the writing talents of your students to produce a periodical for parents to enjoy. Each week assign each newsletter topic to a different student. Encourage the student to interview classmates, talk with the school secretary, or confer with school staff members to gather information about his topic. After the student writes his article, have him copy the information onto the newsletter form. When all sections are complete, duplicate a copy for every student to take home.

Open House

Open House provides a wonderful occasion for parents to get to know you and to observe your classroom. Encourage parents to attend Open House by sending the student-made pop-up invitations described below. The " 'Class-y' Door Display" on page 80 will extend a warm welcome as parents enter your classroom. Then capture parents' interest with the "Cozy Corner" project (see page 80) that shows off both writing and artistic efforts. You can also use Open House as an opportunity to enlist parents to help out in the classroom—be sure to check out "Calling All Volunteers" on page 78 for ideas on encouraging parents to become partners in your classroom.

Pop-Up Invitations

Parents will be eager to attend the Open House celebration when they receive these clever invitations! To make a pop-up invitation, duplicate a construction-paper copy of the card pattern on page 88. Cut out the pattern on the solid lines around the edges. Fold the resulting card on the dotted line marked "fold 1." Cut on the solid lines in the center of the card, and push the tab in the center through the inside of the card as shown. Crease the tab on the dotted fold lines and on the earlier fold.

To add the finishing touches, glue the card inside a folded 6" x 9" piece of construction paper, taking care to leave the tab unattached. Color a copy of the schoolhouse pattern on page 88 and glue it to the pop-up tab in the center of the card as shown. Then add the necessary information about the date, time, and place inside the card. Decorate the front cover with a welcoming message, and your invitation is complete!

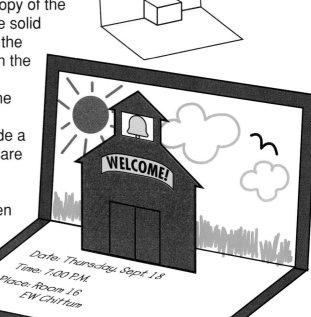

Date: Thursday, Sept. 18
Time: 7:00 P.M.
Place: Room 16
EW Chittum

"Class-y" Door Display

This door display offers a special welcome to parents at Open House. Prior to the event, take a picture of each student. Have the student cut around her likeness in the photo and glue it to a copy of the schoolhouse pattern on page 88. The student also writes a sentence stating one of her strengths at school. Tape the completed projects to your door. As families arrive for Open House, each student removes her schoolhouse from the display and gives it and a pin to a parent to wear as a nametag. This will help you associate each parent with the right student, and parents have a special keepsake of the event.

Cozy Corner

A student usually has a favorite place in the classroom. Have each student construct a model of his favorite place to show his parents at Open House. Provide each student with a copy of the trirama pattern on page 89 that has been duplicated onto heavy paper. Cut out the shape on the solid lines; then fold and crease on the dotted lines. Overlap the two bottom triangles as shown, and glue to form the base.

Provide a supply of construction paper, scissors, glue, and colored markers for students to use in decorating their triramas to look like favorite areas in the classroom. (If desired, the students may decorate the models before gluing the bottom sections together.) Then have each student write a paragraph describing his favorite place in the classroom. Place the completed triramas and paragraphs on the students' desks for parents to observe at Open House.

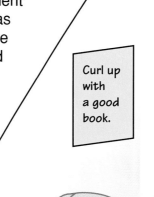

Curl up with a good book.

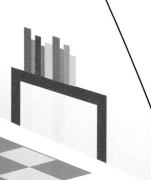

Conference Scheduling

Open House can be a good time to set up parent conferences. Post a sign-up sheet so that parents know they can schedule a time to talk to you in a conference setting, and not during Open House when you have so many people to visit with. You can also distribute preconference forms at this time, so that parents will have a chance to reflect on topics that they wish to discuss at the conference. See pages 90–91 for a reproducible preconference form, reminder notice, and conference record.

Conference Preparations

Set the stage for parent conferences by having each student fill out a copy of the checklist on page 92 for his parents to see. Have the student also write a few sentences on the lines provided to describe his feelings about his school performance. Ask each student to select several examples of his work for his parents to observe at the conference, attaching a self-stick note to each page explaining why he selected the paper.

Finally have each parent complete a copy of the form on page 92 at the end of the conference, praising the student's strong points and offering encouragement in other areas. Distribute these notes to the students the day after the conferences to show that everyone has the child's best interests in mind.

Management Tips

Take a few extra steps to ensure that each conference is as smooth as possible. Keep the following tips in mind when planning your conferences:

▶ Prepare a conference schedule for the school secretary. She will be able to confirm appointments if parents call the office, and will also know not to disturb you if you are currently engaged in a conference.

▶ Limit the number of conferences you schedule in one day. Don't tire yourself by trying to fit too many meetings into a short time period. Parents will be more receptive when you have the energy to be enthusiastic during the conference.

▶ If you know in advance that you have lengthy concerns to discuss with parents, save the conference for the end of the day and allow plenty of time. When there are special matters to discuss, parents may need extra time to ask questions, and you will not want to rush or have a time constraint.

▶ Have copies of lists of grade-appropriate books, web sites, library programs, and recreational activities to give to parents. They will appreciate having the resources to take home with them, as well as the extra interest you show in their child.

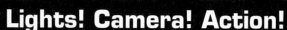

Lights! Camera! Action!

Make use of a video recorder to record special events in your classroom. Record class plays, book reports, music programs, and presentations. Also capture on film candid activities, such as art time, small-group work, and recess footage. Send the tape home with a different student every night. Parents will enjoy seeing the many activities their child participates in throughout the school day.

Family Night Fun

Invite parents to join in a special Family Night in your classroom. Use the opportunity to show parents how to use math manipulatives with their children, how to promote good work habits, and how to constructively help a child correct a missed problem on a paper. Other topics can include simple science experiments, fun ways to practice spelling words, and tips for helping with writing assignments. Parents will feel like partners in the classroom when you share your experience with them!

Thank You!

Take an opportunity during the year to thank parents who have donated their time and materials, and participated with students. Host a special Thank-You Brunch, inviting parents to join you for fresh fruit, muffins, and juice. Have the students decorate your room with giant thank-you notes that can be awarded to the parents at the end of the event.

To create a giant card, fold a sheet of construction paper in half. Have each student dip her thumb into a shallow dish of tempera paint, then create a flower-petal design on the front of the card. Next the student dips her pinkie into a second color of paint and presses her fingerprint in the center of her flower. Allow the paint to dry; then use a green marker to draw stems and leaves. Have each student write a thank-you message on the inside of each card. Don't forget to add your signature to each card before displaying it in the room!

Homework Policy

Dear Parent,
  Homework is an important part of your child's learning experience. Your child will benefit greatly from your support and encouragement of good work habits at home.
  Please read the homework policy below and discuss it with your child. Then sign the lower portion of the form and return it to school with your child. Be sure to keep this portion of the form for future reference.

Homework Policy:

_____
_____
_____

                                    Sincerely,

                                    _____
                                    teacher signature

                                    _____
                                    date

I have read and understand the homework policy. I have also discussed the policy with my child.

_____   _____   _____
parent signature   date   student

Behavior And Discipline Policies

Dear Parent,
  Your child's success is very important. To create and maintain a positive learning environment for all students, I will follow the behavior and discipline policies below.
  Please read the policies and discuss them with your child. Then sign the lower portion of the form and return it to school with your child. Be sure to keep this portion of the form for future reference.

Behavior Policy:

_____
_____
_____

Discipline Policy:

_____
_____
_____

                                    Sincerely,

                                    _____
                                    teacher signature

                                    _____
                                    date

I have read and understand the behavior and discipline policies. I have also discussed these policies with my child.

_____   _____   _____
parent signature   date   student

It's A Celebration!

Dear Parent,

We are celebrating _____ at _____
time

on _____, _____.
day   date

You can help with the celebration by _____

_____

_____

_____.

Thank you for your help!

Sincerely, _____
teacher signature

Special Project Supplies

Dear Parent,

We are working on a special project related to _____.

Your child needs to bring the following items by _____ :
date

- _____

- _____

- _____

- _____

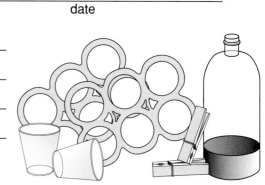

Thank you for helping!

Sincerely, _____
teacher signature

Date: _____

Dear Parent,
Your child needs the following school supplies:

_____ pencils

_____ paper

_____ crayons

_____ glue

_____ scissors

_____ other: _____

_____

_____

_____

Thank you!

_____
teacher signature

- -

Date: _____

Dear Parent,
Your child needs to complete the following assignments:

_____

_____

_____

_____

_____

This work is due by _____.

Please sign and return this form.
Thank you for your help and support!

_____
teacher signature

_____
parent signature

We're Going On A Field Trip!

Dear Parent,
   We are planning a trip to _____ on _____, _____ .
                                                          day   date
Your child will need to bring:

   • field-trip permission form (below)

   • _____

   • _____

   • _____

   • _____

Keep this note at home and post it as
a reminder.
   Thank you!

_____
teacher signature

- -

_____ has my permission to attend the field trip on _____.
        student   date

_____
parent signature

Just A Reminder!
To:
From:

Don't Forget!
To:

From:

The Classroom Gazette

Teacher_____ Date_____

What We're Learning

Notes Of Interest

Upcoming Events

Students In The News

What's New Around School

Odds And Ends

Note To The Teacher: Use with "Classroom News" on page 78.

Card Pattern
Use with "Pop-Up Invitations" on page 79.

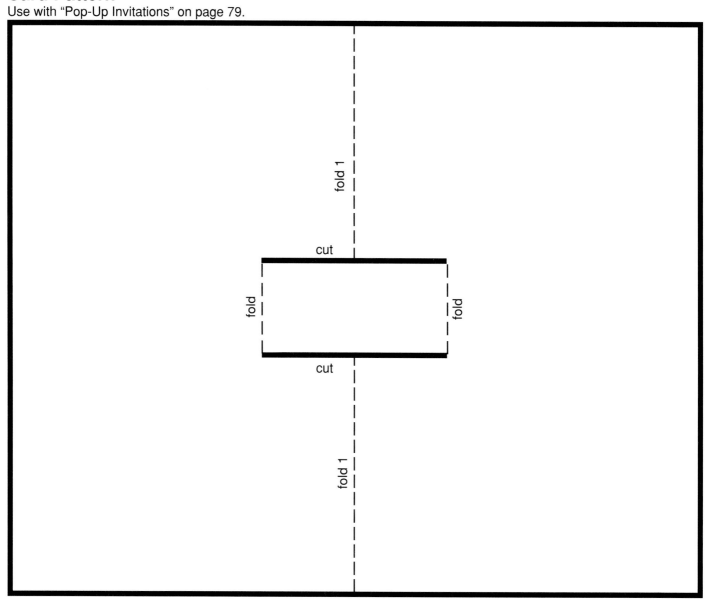

Pattern
Use with "Pop-Up Invitations" on page
79 and " 'Class-y' Door Display" on
page 80.

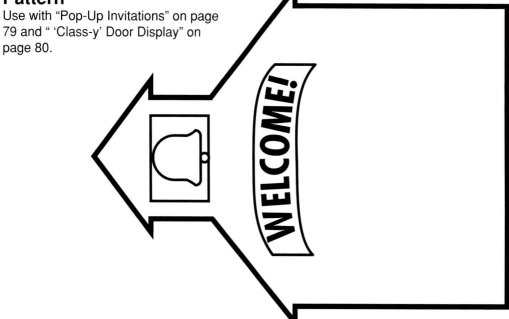

©1997 The Education Center, Inc. • *The Mailbox® Superbook* • *Grade 3* • TEC452

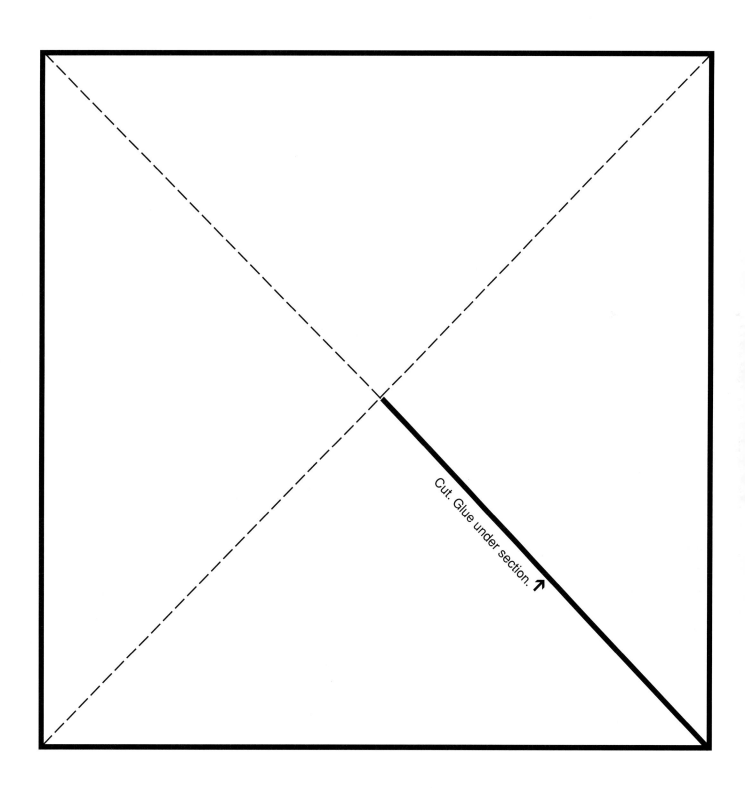

Cut. Glue under section.

Preconference Form

Student's Name _____

Parent's Name _____

Date _____

My child's attitude about school is:

_____

I see strengths in my child's progress in these areas:

_____

I have concerns about my child's progress in these areas:

_____

Topics I would like to discuss:

_____

©1997 The Education Center, Inc. • *The Mailbox® Superbook • Grade 3* • TEC452

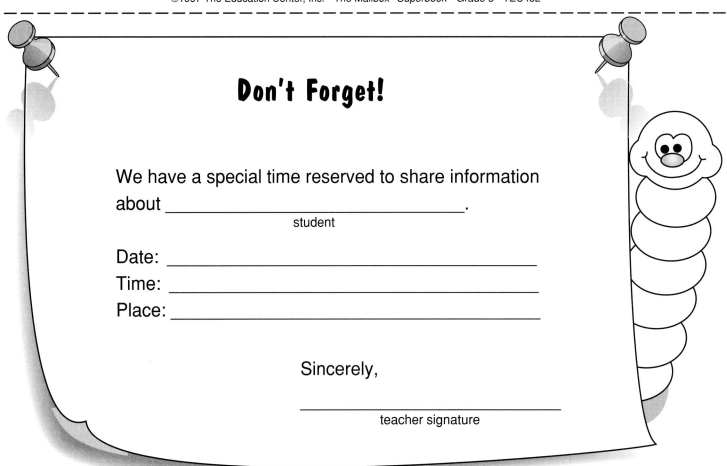

Don't Forget!

We have a special time reserved to share information
about _____.
                     student

Date: _____

Time: _____

Place: _____

Sincerely,

_____
teacher signature

Conference Record

Student: _____

Date: _____

Persons In Attendance:

_____

_____

Student's Strengths:

_____
_____
_____
_____

Areas For Improvement:

_____
_____
_____
_____

Parent's Concerns:

_____
_____
_____
_____

Follow-up Plan:

_____
_____
_____
_____

Progress And Comments:	
Reading	
Spelling	
Writing	
Grammar	
Math	
Science	
Social Studies	
Work Habits	
Social Skills	

Additional Information
(tests, cumulative record, observations, etc.):

_____
_____
_____
_____

Actions/Suggestions:

_____
_____
_____

signed _____
(teacher)

_____
(parent)

Note To The Teacher: Use with "Conference Scheduling" on page 81.

Parent Conference Forms

My Conference Checklist

Name_____

	Excellent	Satisfactory	Needs Improvement
I listen and follow directions.	☐	☐	☐
My work is neat and easy to read.	☐	☐	☐
I finish my work on time.	☐	☐	☐
I show respect to others.	☐	☐	☐
I always try to do my best.	☐	☐	☐

At school, I am proud of _____.

One thing I would like to improve is _____

_____.

- -

Dear _____,

   Your teacher has shared some information about your schoolwork. We think that you are doing very well in

_____

_____

   We are going to help you improve

_____

_____

   I also want to let you know that

_____

_____

_____

Love,

_____

Note To The Teacher: Use with "Conference Preparations" on page 81.

ARTS & CRAFTS

Arts and Crafts

Tricks & Tips

Many art projects involve a variety of materials, and organizing the supplies can be a challenge. Arrange your materials in easy-to-use ways to help make art time more enjoyable for you and your students.

▶ Keep balls of yarn and string tangle-free with a plastic funnel. Place the ball inside the funnel and pull the string out through the spout.

▶ Use baby-wipe containers to hold cotton balls, sponge shapes, paintbrushes, and craft sticks. The containers will stack neatly in your closet or cupboard.

▶ Make individual sets of paint by pouring leftover tempera paint into the cups of a Styrofoam® egg carton. Allow the paint to dry. Reuse the paint by moistening a paintbrush with water and running it over the desired color.

▶ Store seasonal craft supplies in see-through plastic shoeboxes. Felt, pipe cleaners, and glitter in seasonal colors will be easier to locate when grouped together.

Stock up on project materials when you find them on sale. Some items to keep on hand are:

clothespins	coffee filters	cotton balls
doilies	paper cups	paper lunch sacks
paper plates	pipe cleaners	wiggle eyes

Other materials can be obtained by asking parents to send specific items to school. Use a copy of the form on page 106 to request donations for special projects.

Personalized Posters

Student individuality will shine with this colorful poster project. Give each student a sheet of art paper. Instruct him to wet the paper using a sponge. While the paper is still wet, have him paint designs on the paper with watercolors, allowing the colors to bleed and run. After the paper is dry, have each child trace the letters of his name with stencils. Then have him cut out the letters and glue them to a sheet of colored construction paper. Have students cut additional shapes from any leftover painted paper and add them to the poster. Hang the posters in your room for a colorful display.

Amazing-Me Collage

Students will love creating these distinctive collages to describe themselves. Provide each student with a sheet of construction paper, scissors, glue, markers, and a supply of magazines. Instruct each student to look through the magazines for words that describe his appearance, personality, hobbies, and talents. Have each child cut out 20–25 words, then glue them on the construction paper in a unique pattern or design. Using markers, have each child add details to his design. The result? A very descriptive work of art!

Student Mobiles

Students will share information about themselves as they create these decorative mobiles. Ask each student to bring an empty, plastic, two-liter bottle to school. Use an X-acto® knife to cut off the top of the bottle, and punch 8–10 holes around the edge of the piece as shown. Have each student draw or cut out pictures of objects that tell about her, such as illustrations of pets, hobbies, favorite foods, and interests. Have the child mount each picture between pieces of clear Con-Tact® paper, and trim around each picture, leaving an edge of film. Instruct each student to punch a hole in each picture and attach it to the bottle with a length of string. To hang each mobile, punch two holes near the neck of the bottle and thread a loop of yarn through the openings. Suspend the mobiles from the ceiling for a "class-ic" display.

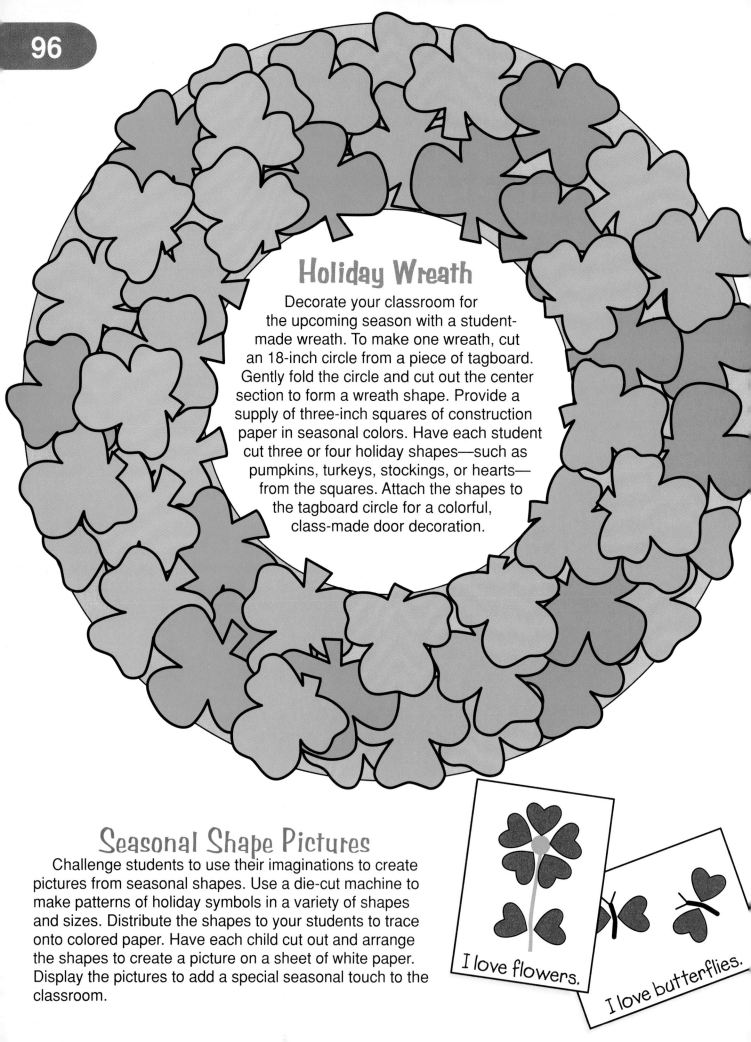

Holiday Wreath

Decorate your classroom for the upcoming season with a student-made wreath. To make one wreath, cut an 18-inch circle from a piece of tagboard. Gently fold the circle and cut out the center section to form a wreath shape. Provide a supply of three-inch squares of construction paper in seasonal colors. Have each student cut three or four holiday shapes—such as pumpkins, turkeys, stockings, or hearts— from the squares. Attach the shapes to the tagboard circle for a colorful, class-made door decoration.

Seasonal Shape Pictures

Challenge students to use their imaginations to create pictures from seasonal shapes. Use a die-cut machine to make patterns of holiday symbols in a variety of shapes and sizes. Distribute the shapes to your students to trace onto colored paper. Have each child cut out and arrange the shapes to create a picture on a sheet of white paper. Display the pictures to add a special seasonal touch to the classroom.

I love flowers.

I love butterflies.

MERRY Mobiles

Suspend some seasonal fun from your classroom ceiling by hanging these student-made holiday mobiles. Enlarge a seasonal pattern from the clip art on page 107. Duplicate a copy of the pattern for each student to color and cut out. Then provide colored construction paper for the student to cut out appropriate holiday shapes to hang from the pattern. Decorate your room with scarecrows holding pumpkins, turkeys dropping feathers, elves clutching ornaments, snowmen dangling snowflakes, Cupids grasping hearts, leprechauns bearing shamrocks, or bunnies suspending eggs.

Pretty Prints

Students can design holiday prints for a variety of projects with this easy, seasonal stamp activity. Have each student draw a simple seasonal shape on a square of poster board. Then have him glue a length of yarn onto the shape as shown. After the glue is dry, have each student brush poster paint onto the yarn and press the design onto a piece of paper. Students can use the stamps to decorate artwork, gift wrap, stationery, or holiday cards.

Autumn Leaves

Bring the beauty of fall leaves into your classroom with this autumn scene. Create a set of leaf stencils from the patterns on page 108. Have each student trace and cut out 12 leaf shapes from yellow or orange construction paper. Have each student curl the leaves slightly by wrapping the ends around a pencil. Next have him use pastel watercolors to lightly stroke the leaves with a touch of color. While the paint is drying, have each student cut out a tree trunk from brown construction paper. Finally have each student arrange and glue the leaves on the branches. Tape the trees to the windows or to a wall for a burst of fall color.

GLOWING "Ghosties"

Set up a "spook-tacular" display with these glowing "ghosties"! Give each student a sheet of black construction paper. Instruct her to lightly sketch a ghost shape onto the paper. Tape the paper to a piece of cardboard; then have each student use a thumbtack to punch holes on the pencil outline. When the entire shape has been punched, remove the cardboard and tape the paper to a window. As the light shines through the tiny holes, the ghosts will appear to glow!

COLORFUL Corn

These Indian corn projects will fill your room with a harvest of fall colors. Have each student trace a copy of the corn pattern on page 109 onto a piece of tagboard, then cut it out. Then have each student trace the leaf patterns on page 109 onto a brown paper grocery sack. Have her cut out the leaf shapes and set them aside.

Place several shallow dishes of tempera paint on a table. Have students take turns dipping their pinkies into a color and pressing it onto their tagboard ears of corn. Have your students repeat this step using different colors until the ears of corn are covered. While the paint is drying, have each child crumple her leaves into a ball, then unfold them. To complete the project, have each child attach her leaves to the bottom of the corn using a brad. Use these colorful creations to decorate a bulletin board or door display.

Shining Stars

Celebrate Hanukkah with a display of sparkling stars. Show your students how to make the shape of the Star Of David by overlapping two large triangles. Give each student a piece of waxed paper, and have him draw the star shape on the paper with liquid glue. After each student sprinkles his design with glitter, let it dry for an hour. Have each student add another line of glue to the project to thicken the outline, and sprinkle again with glitter. Let the designs dry overnight; then gently peel the waxed paper away from the shapes. Create a hanging loop for each star using metallic thread. Suspend the stars from the ceiling for a shimmering display.

Holiday Bookmarks

This simple project is perfect for holiday giftgiving. Purchase several designs of seasonal ribbon and felt squares in coordinating colors from a craft store. Cut the ribbon into ten-inch strips. To create a bookmark, have each student trace a holiday shape onto one half of a felt square, then fold the felt in half and cut the shape so that two identical pieces are created. Have each child place the ribbon between the two felt shapes and secure with fabric glue. Have your students give the bookmarks to friends or family members during the holiday season.

Framed Photographs

Class photographs will become treasured keepsakes when presented as holiday gifts. Take a picture of your class and have a copy made for each student. Help each student glue her photo in the center of a piece of construction paper. (Allow at least a 1/2-inch border to show around the picture.) Have each student sign and date the back of her project. Then have each child decorate the border by gluing on holiday-shaped confetti or sequins. If desired, have each student pass her picture around and have her fellow classmates sign their names in the border. Laminate the pictures for durability and attach a piece of magnetic tape to the back of each project. Students will take delight in presenting these picture-perfect gifts to their families!

Honest Abe Mobiles

Have your students make this whimsical mobile to celebrate Presidents' Day. Each student will need glue, scissors, two 12" x 18" pieces of black construction paper, one 12" x 18" piece of brown construction paper, scraps of manila paper and red construction paper, and several pieces of yarn. Use the patterns provided on page 110 to make tagboard stencils for the students to trace. Have each student trace the patterns on the color indicated on each shape, and then cut them out. Have each child cut a 2" x 15" section from each side of both sheets of black construction paper as shown.

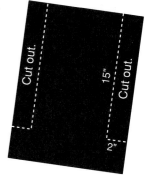

To assemble the mobile, have each student follow these steps:

1. Fold the 12" x 18" sheet of brown construction paper in half lengthwise. Place the bottom of the beard pattern along the fold. Trace the pattern then cut it out. Unfold and glue the top of the beard to the bottom edge of one of the hat pieces.

2. Cut two 4-inch pieces of yarn and glue to the bottom of the hat as shown.

3. Attach the eyebrows and eyes by gluing the corresponding shapes together with the yarn pieces between them as shown.

4. Glue a 7 1/2" length of yarn to the center of the hat brim.

5. Attach the nose and mouth by gluing the shapes on each side of the yarn piece, as done with the eyes and eyebrows.

6. Glue the second hat shape on top of the first hat shape so that the ends of the yarn pieces are in-between the two shapes.

7. Punch a hole in the top of the hat and thread with a loop of yarn for hanging.

Pretty Page Holders

Have each of your students create this simple Valentine's Day project to give to family members, friends, or special someones. Provide each student with a white, business-size envelope, and have him sketch heart shapes at the bottom corners of the envelope as shown. Have each child decorate the heart shapes with colored markers. Then have him cut the heart shapes from the corners so that the tips of the hearts are still joined together. Each heart shape can slip over a page corner to mark a valentine's place in a book!

March Weather Windsocks

Show students that March comes in like a lion and goes out like a lamb with this wild and woolly windsock project. Each student will need scissors, glue, a 12" x 18" sheet of yellow construction paper, a length of yarn, and assorted colors of crepe-paper streamers. To decorate the windsock, supply each child with 9" x 12" sheets of light brown, dark brown, white, and black construction paper. Provide copies of the pattern pieces on page 111 for students to trace.

To make a lion, have each student trace and cut the face pattern from light brown construction paper, and attach ears cut from dark brown paper. Have her glue strips of dark brown paper behind the face to create a mane.

To complete the windsock, have each student roll the yellow sheet of construction paper into a cylinder and staple it together. Have each child glue the faces on opposite sides of her cylinder. Create a handle by having each child staple a length of string to the top as shown. Provide crepe paper for students to add streamers to the bottoms of their socks, and they're ready to sail in the March breeze.

To make the lamb, have each child trace the face pattern on black paper, and attach ears cut from white paper. Have the student glue strips of white paper that have been curled around a pencil behind the face.

Using scraps of paper, have each student add eyes, a nose, and a mouth to each face.

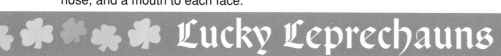

Lucky Leprechauns

Combine an art project with a writing assignment to create some very lucky leprechauns. Duplicate a copy of the form on page 112 for each student. Have each child write a paragraph telling about his luckiest day. Then distribute to each student one nine-inch paper plate; one 9" x 11" sheet of green construction paper; scraps of pink, white, yellow, and black construction paper; and a supply of orange yarn. Students will also need access to glue, scissors, a hole puncher, and a black marker.

To assemble the leprechaun, have each student follow these steps:
1. Punch two rows of 20 holes each along the bottom edge of the plate.
2. Cut the yarn into eight-inch pieces. Tie a piece through each hole to form a beard.
3. Cut the eyes, nose, and ears from colored construction paper and glue to the plate as shown. Use a marker to draw a mouth.
4. Cut a hat from the green construction paper. Glue the paragraph to the top of the hat. If desired, create a band and buckle for the hat with colored construction paper.
5. Glue several strands of yarn to the back side of the hat brim. Then glue the hat to the paper plate.

My luckiest day was when... I found five dollars on the playground...

After your students create these bunnies from handprint patterns, use them to decorate your classroom, or add them to the Easter bulletin board described on page 31. To make a bunny, have each student trace one of your hands twice on a sheet of manila construction paper. (The project is easier to make with an adult-sized hand.)

To complete the project, have each student follow these directions:

1. Cut out both handprints. The index and middle fingers need to be cut off one of the hands. (Make a peace sign to show students which two fingers on the handprint need to be cut.)

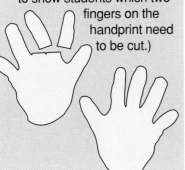

2. Place the three-fingered hand under the five-fingered hand so that the thumbs point out in opposite directions. Glue the palms and wrists together, leaving the fingers apart.

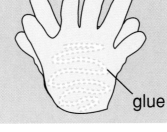

glue

5. Complete the bunny by coloring the center of the remaining two fingers pink to make ears.

3. Bend the thumbs in towards the middle and glue the tips together. Repeat with the fingers directly above the thumbs. Secure with a paper clip until the glue dries.

4. Add a pink pom-pom nose, construction-paper eyes, and teeth to the figure as shown.

Mother's Day Magnets

This scented kitchen magnet will make a sweet Mother's Day surprise. Mix dough from 2 cups of applesauce and 12 ounces of cinnamon. Roll out the dough on a sheet of waxed paper. Have each student cut out a shape by tracing around duplicates of the butterfly patterns on page 112 with a plastic knife. Place the cutouts on a wire rack. When dry, have each child decorate his butterfly with touches of paint (do not varnish them). Attach a magnet to the back of each shape. Have each student present the magnet to his mother, explaining that it should be attached to the metal hood over the stove. While dinner is cooking, the heat from the stove will release the cutout's spicy scent.

RECIPES

Create a variety of art materials for your classroom with the following collection of recipes for glue, dye, paints, dough, and papier-mâché.

SPARKLE PAINT

light corn syrup
food coloring
glitter

In each of several small containers, mix corn syrup, a few drops of food coloring, and glitter. Have students use the mixture to paint on construction paper, paper plates, tagboard, or other heavy paper. Allow several days drying time.

PASTEL PAINT

evaporated milk
food coloring

Pour evaporated milk into several small containers. Add a few drops of food coloring to each container and mix. When painted on construction paper, the paint has a creamy, pastel appearance.

EASY DYE

rubbing alcohol
food coloring

Use this simple method to color pasta, rice, seeds, or dried flowers. Put a small amount of rubbing alcohol into a container with a tight-fitting lid. Add the desired amount of food coloring. Place the objects to be dyed inside the container and secure the lid. Gently shake the container for one minute. Spread the objects on paper towels to dry.

COLORED GLUE

white glue
food coloring

Pour glue into a small container and add the desired amount of food coloring. Stir until the glue is blended. Have students apply the colored glue with a paintbrush to a variety of materials.

WET-LOOK PAINT

1 part white liquid glue
1 part tempera paint

Mix the paint and glue together, and apply to paper with a paintbrush. This paint retains a shiny, wet appearance when dry.

SIMPLE PAPIER-MÂCHÉ

1 part liquid starch
1 part cold water
newspaper torn into strips

Mix together the starch and water. Have students dip strips of newspaper into the mixture before applying to a balloon, chicken wire, or other form.

EDIBLE DOUGH

2 cups creamy-style peanut butter
1 cup honey
3 cups instant dry milk

Stir together the peanut butter and honey; then add the powdered milk a little at a time. When the mixture becomes stiff, knead it with your hands until it is thoroughly blended. Refrigerate the dough overnight. Provide each student with a piece of waxed paper and a small amount of dough. After the dough is molded into shape, students can eat their creations.

COOKED PLAY DOUGH

1 cup flour
1/2 cup salt
2 teaspoons cream of tartar
1 cup water
1 teaspoon vegetable oil
food coloring

Mix the dry ingredients. Stir in the water, oil, and food coloring. Place the mixture in a heavy skillet and cook over medium heat for two or three minutes, stirring frequently. Knead the dough until it is soft and smooth. Store in an airtight container.

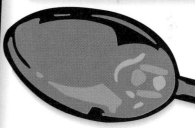

NO-COOK MODELING DOUGH

2 cups flour
1 cup salt
water
tempera paint powder

Mix the ingredients, adding enough water to make the dough pliable. This dough will air-dry to harden, or can be baked at 300°F for an hour, depending on the thickness of the object.

DEAR PARENT,

For our upcoming art projects, we will need the supplies indicated below. If you are able to donate any of these items, please send the materials to school with your child. We appreciate your help!

___ aluminum foil

___ baby food jars

___ buttons

___ cardboard tubes from paper towels or toilet tissue

___ coat hangers (metal)

___ craft or Popsicle® sticks

___ empty coffee cans

___ cotton balls

___ egg cartons

___ empty plastic milk jugs

___ fabric scraps

___ glitter

___ magazines or catalogs

___ newspapers

___ paper plates

___ paper sacks

___ pipe cleaners

___ empty plastic margarine containers

___ plastic six-pack rings

___ empty plastic soft-drink bottles

___ ribbon

___ sandpaper

___ plastic drinking straws

___ Styrofoam® packing pieces

___ clean Styrofoam® meat trays

___ sponges

___ wallpaper samples

___ wrapping paper

___ yarn

Other:

___ _____

___ _____

___ _____

___ _____

Patterns

Use with "Autumn Leaves" on page 98.

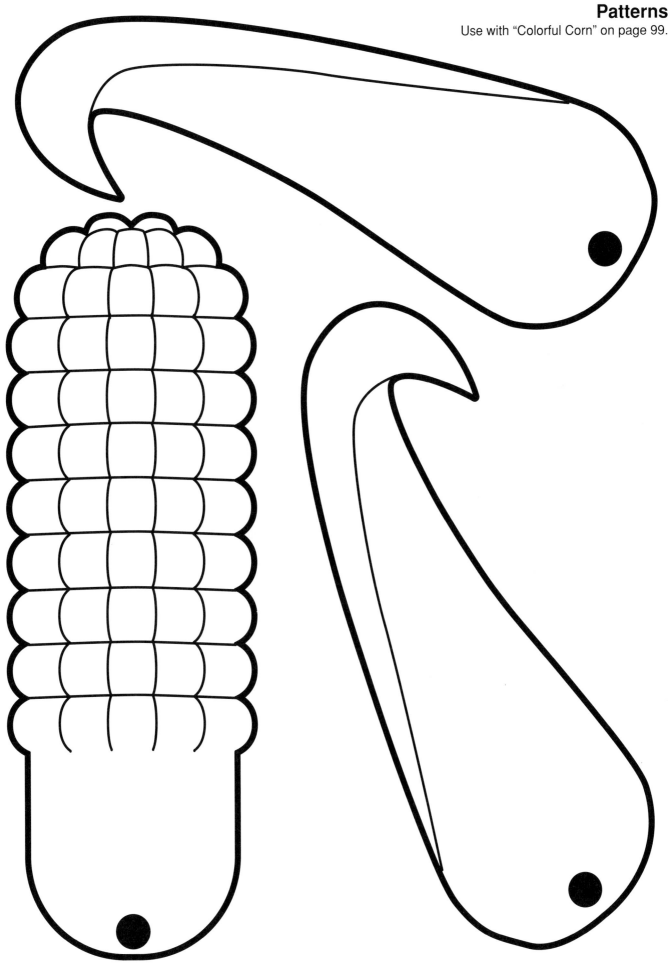

Patterns

Use with "Honest Abe Mobiles" on page 101.

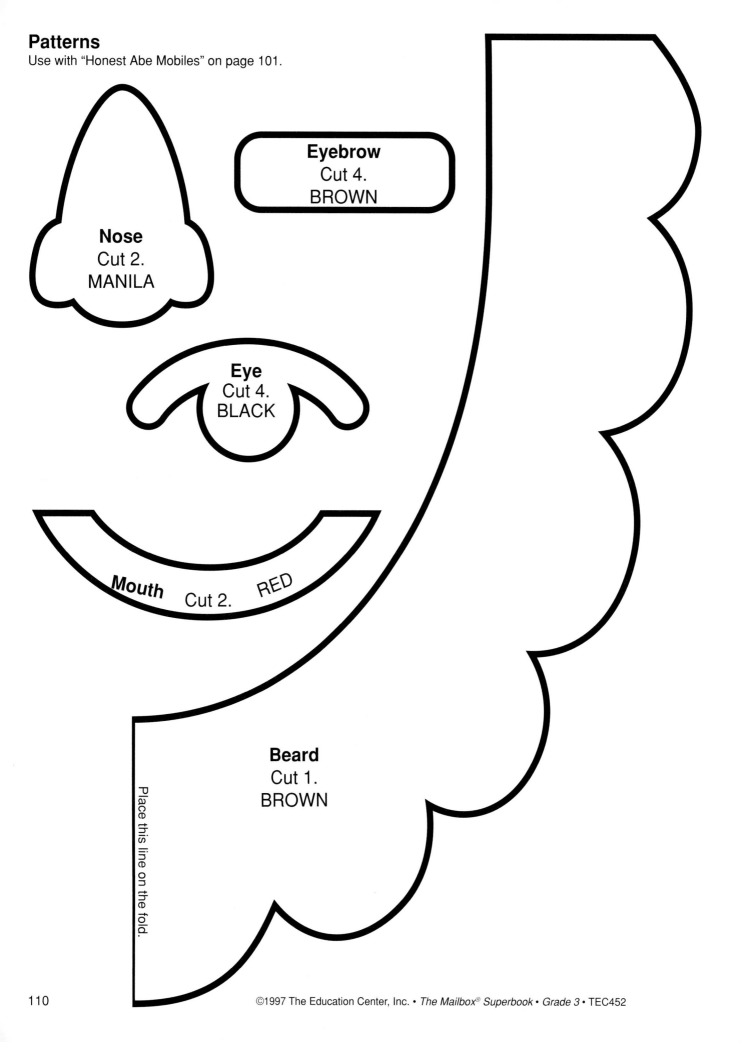

Eyebrow
Cut 4.
BROWN

Nose
Cut 2.
MANILA

Eye
Cut 4.
BLACK

Mouth   Cut 2.   RED

Beard
Cut 1.
BROWN

Place this line on the fold.

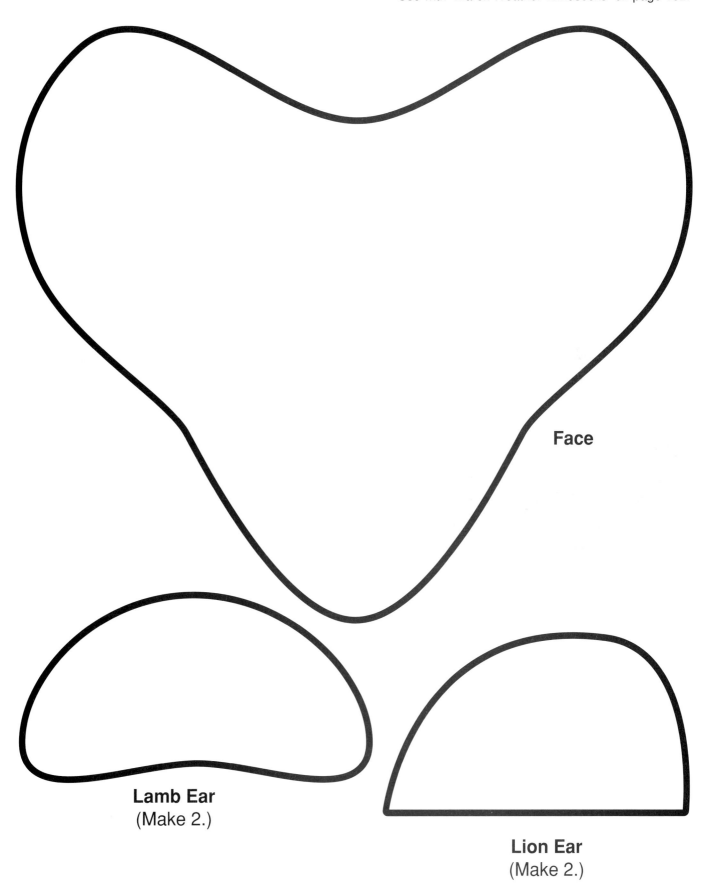

Face

Lamb Ear
(Make 2.)

Lion Ear
(Make 2.)

Form

Use with "Lucky Leprechauns" on page 102.

My luckiest day was when...

Patterns

Use with "Mother's Day Magnets" on page 103.

CENTERS

CENTERS

HOW TO USE CENTERS

1 Learning centers provide excellent opportunities for students to practice a variety of skills in kid-pleasing ways. Every area of the curriculum and almost any skill can be reinforced through file-folder games, puzzles, partner activities, small-group projects, or individual tasks.

2 As you set up a center, decorate the area so that it is inviting to students. Place a sign or poster explaining the steps or rules of the activity. Centers should be designed so that students can complete the activity with little or no help from you. Have all the materials the student will need at the center. Include a method for students to check their own work and make any necessary corrections.

3 Design some centers for students to use during their free time. Encourage students to visit the center to complete an art project, explore a topic of study, or work a puzzle. Make these open centers available to students at any time.

4 Design other centers for additional skills practice and reinforcement, and have students visit the centers as part of an assignment. Schedule a time for each student or group of students to visit each center once a week. (If desired, provide each student with a learning center rotation schedule or contract so that everyone is accountable for visiting the centers.) Or create a simple chart similar to the one shown for students to refer to each day. Reprogram the chart each week or at the beginning of the center rotation cycle. Students can tell at a glance which activity they are scheduled for each day.

Materials List For Making Centers

- Scissors
- Glue
- Paste
- Construction Paper
- Paint
- Counting Markers
- Buttons
- File Folders
- String-Tie Envelopes
- Crayons
- Newspapers
- Magazines

Center Schedule	Mary, Sue Paul, Mike	Amy, Jane, Harry, John	Gina, Rachel, Bob, David	Wendy, Joe, Rose, Roger
Monday	math	writing	spelling	language
Tuesday	writing	language	art	spelling
Wednesday	language	art	math	writing
Thursday	art	spelling	writing	math
Friday	spelling	math	language	art

Let's Get STARTED!

Center activities should be designed to meet the needs and curriculum of your classroom. Basic centers can be set up at the beginning of the year. As the subject matter and skill levels progress, adjust the activities accordingly. Include some of the following centers in your classroom:

✳ **Science:** Provide students with the opportunity to use microscopes, hand lenses, scales, and other equipment.

✳ **Listening:** Have students use headphones to listen to classical music, a set of taped directions, or recorded stories. Drawing activities, writing assignments, or skill sheets can accompany each recording.

✳ **Math:** Encourage students to use manipulatives or play games that reinforce basic skills.

✳ **Reading:** Place a collection of books, magazines, newspaper articles, and poetry selections at the center. The collection may enhance a unit of study, spotlight a featured author, or promote seasonal selections.

✳ **Game:** Keep a supply of purchased games, jigsaw puzzles, word searches, crossword puzzles, and game pieces at the center. Remember that many games help students develop problem-solving strategies.

✳ **Art:** Use seasonal themes, curriculum tie-ins, and a variety of materials for students to use in creative expression.

✳ **Writing:** Supply students with writing prompts, journal topics, vocabulary lists, and supplies for creating student-made books. References such as dictionaries, thesauruses, and encyclopedias should also be included at the center.

Try This!

This is an easy way to keep tabs on which students have visited a center. Place a colorfully decorated can in each center. Program a craft stick with each student's name and the number or name of the center, and place the sticks in the can. When the student visits the center, she removes her stick from the can and places it in a designated container on your desk. After all students have visited the center, transfer the sticks back to the original can. You'll be set to monitor attendance for the next center activity.

Devon Center #27

Connect-The-Dots

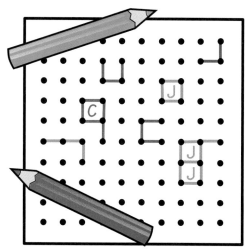

Looking for an easy way to review any skill? Students connect the dots to show their mastery. Create a set of programmed index cards for the desired skill such as identifying parts of speech, math facts, vocabulary words, or fact and opinion statements. Place the set of skill cards, a supply of colored pencils, and several copies of the game pattern on page 122 in a learning center. Two to four students may play the game at one time. To play, each student selects a colored pencil to use during the game. Instruct each student to take a turn drawing one vertical or horizontal line to connect two adjacent dots. If a student draws a line that completes a square, he earns the opportunity to claim the square by correctly answering a skill card. If he answers correctly, he writes his initials in the square. He may also take another turn. If he answers incorrectly, the square is left blank. The game ends when all the dots have been connected. (The skill cards can be shuffled and reused if necessary during a game.) The player with the most initialed squares is declared winner of the game.

Skill Swatters

Create swat teams of three students to practice a variety of skills. Cut two simple paddle shapes from different colors of construction paper. Attach each paddle to a craft stick to use as swatters in the game. Duplicate the fly patterns on page 122; then color, cut out, and glue them to the inside of a file folder. Make a self-checking list of comparative skills for students to practice, such as odd and even numbers, nouns and verbs, singular and plural words, or correct and incorrect spellings. Designate each fly as one category of the review. As a swat team visits the center, one student is the caller and reads each item on the list to the other players. As each item is called out, the players swat the fly that represents the correct answer. The player whose swatter is first to hit the correct fly is awarded one point. Play continues until all the words on the list have been called out. Players tally their scores to determine the winner of the game.

Punctuation In A Cup

Students can review punctuation with this low-cost, easy-to-make activity. Program three plastic cups with ending punctuation marks. Then write sentences on a supply of craft sticks. If desired, program the sticks for self-checking. A student reads the sentence, then places the stick in the cup programmed with the correct ending mark. For additional practice, have students copy five of the sentences on paper, adding the appropriate punctuation. The center can be adapted to practice place value; to identify parts of speech; or to recognize synonyms, antonyms, and homophones.

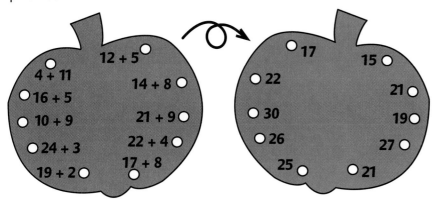

Punch And Poke

Provide individual skills practice for students with these clever shapes. Select a page-size pattern to color, cut out, and mount on heavy tagboard. Use a hole puncher to make 10 to 12 holes around the edge of the shape and number each hole. If desired, laminate the shape for durability. Program the shape by writing a math problem (or other skill) by each hole. Turn the shape over and write the answer to each problem by the corresponding hole. A student answers each problem on paper; then he checks his work by poking his pencil through a hole, turning the shape over, and checking the answer by the hole.

Vocabulary Hangman

Students enjoy reviewing vocabulary when it involves this version of Hangman. To set up this center, place a list of vocabulary words, a die, a pencil, paper for score-keeping, a student-sized chalkboard, and a piece of chalk at a desk or table. Invite groups of two to four students to visit the center to play the game. One student who acts as the host secretly selects a word from the list, then draws on the chalkboard a blank line for each letter of the word. In turn, each remaining student rolls the die to determine the point value of his turn, and then guesses a letter in the puzzle. If he correctly guesses a letter, he is awarded the points indicated on the die. If the guess is incorrect, the host draws a section of the hangman on the chalkboard and no points are awarded. A student may try to guess the word at the beginning of his turn. If his guess is correct, he can gain ten bonus points by giving the correct definition of the word. When the word has been correctly identified, students add up their points to determine the winner. The person with the highest score acts as host for the next game.

Just The Facts!

Invite students to discover new and interesting information all year long with an ongoing research center. Supply numerous nonfiction and factual books related to a topic of study, as well as a stack of blank index or shape cards. Challenge each student to visit the center and find three new facts about the topic. Have her write each fact on a blank card. Collect the cards each day and post them on a bulletin board titled "Just The Facts!" As students visit the center, they must first check the bulletin board to prevent repeating a fact.

Poetry In Motion

Provide the opportunity for poetic expression at this adaptable writing center. Post a topic in the center, and provide a supply of blank paper and an assortment of patterns in shapes related to the topic. Each student brainstorms a list of words about the topic. He then selects a shape pattern and places it on top of a blank sheet of paper. Next he copies words from his list around the outline of the shape. When the student is finished, he has a poem in the shape of the pattern. If desired, provide colored pencils for each student to decorate the remainder of his paper. Display the poetic work in the hallway for all to enjoy, or compile it into a class-created poetry book.

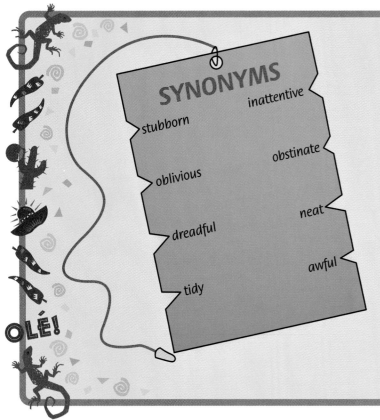

"NOTCH-O"

Recycle empty cereal cartons to make these individual practice cards. Cut out the front and back panels of the cereal box to make two cards. To complete one card, cut five small V-shaped notches at equal intervals along each side of the panel. Program the plain side of the panel with the desired skill, writing one set of words or math problems on the left side and the matching answers on the right side. (See the example.) Attach a length of yarn to the top of the card. Students use the yarn to connect the words on the left to their match on the right. Mount an envelope containing an answer key to the back of each card.

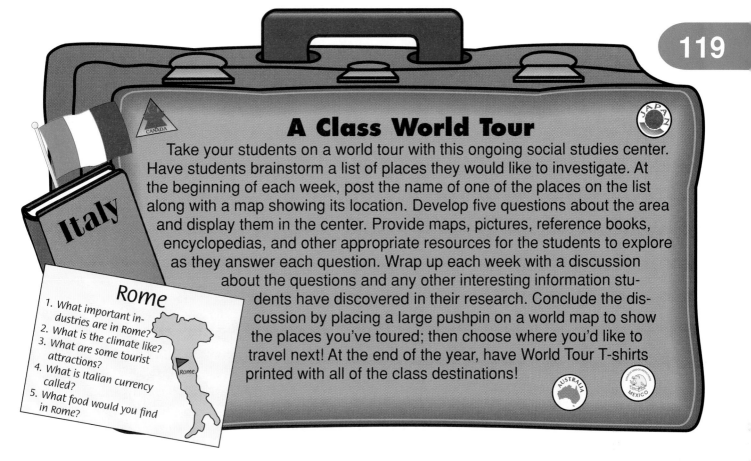

A Class World Tour

Take your students on a world tour with this ongoing social studies center. Have students brainstorm a list of places they would like to investigate. At the beginning of each week, post the name of one of the places on the list along with a map showing its location. Develop five questions about the area and display them in the center. Provide maps, pictures, reference books, encyclopedias, and other appropriate resources for the students to explore as they answer each question. Wrap up each week with a discussion about the questions and any other interesting information students have discovered in their research. Conclude the discussion by placing a large pushpin on a world map to show the places you've toured; then choose where you'd like to travel next! At the end of the year, have World Tour T-shirts printed with all of the class destinations!

Rome

1. What important industries are in Rome?
2. What is the climate like?
3. What are some tourist attractions?
4. What is Italian currency called?
5. What food would you find in Rome?

Artist Of The Week

Develop your students' art appreciation with this interactive center. Feature a different artist in a learning center each week. Gather books about the artist, copies of his work, and a description of his technique. Provide materials for students to experiment with the artist's style. Display the students' creations in a Young Artists' Art Gallery. If desired, challenge a group of student volunteers to research an artist independently and prepare the next art center for their classmates.

Scrabble® Spelling

Enhance spelling skills by introducing Scrabble® at your spelling center. Have students follow the rules of the game with these added scoring bonuses: If a student spells a word from a previous spelling-word list, she doubles her points for that word. If she spells a word from the current list, her points for the word are tripled. Post a list of past and present spelling words at the center for players to refer to during the game. Then ask students to bring copies of Scrabble® games from home before each semester review test. Hold a Scrabble® Spell-a-thon to help students prepare for the test.

The Life Of Alexander Calder

Paint

Spelling Words For September 8-12

Spelling Words For September 15-19

Spelling Words For September 22-26

1. mad
2. stock
3. flock
4. lamp
5. stamp
6. cramp
7. cost
8. blast
9. plant
10. chant

TRIPLE POINTS!

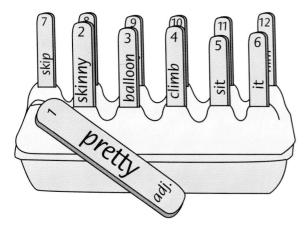

Egg-carton Parts Of Speech

Reinforce the parts of speech with this self-checking center activity. Program a dozen numbered craft sticks, each with a word in the middle. Write the word's part of speech on the other end of the stick. (See the example.) Insert the sticks into an egg carton as shown, so that the parts of speech are hidden. Have each student number his paper from 1 to 12. Then he selects a stick, reads the word, and writes down its part of speech on his paper next to the corresponding number. He removes the stick to reveal the correct response. Provide a new set of words each week, or program the sticks with math problems for students to solve.

Scrambled Eggs

This center works well as a review of spelling and vocabulary words. Gather a supply of plastic, snap-apart eggs. Fill each egg with squares of paper that have been programmed with the letters of the desired word. Store the eggs in an egg carton and place the carton in a center. When a student visits the center, she "cracks" open an egg, dumps out the contents, and arranges the letters to spell a word. She writes the word on her paper before replacing the letters in the egg and returning it to the carton. Have the student repeat the procedure until she has "cracked" all of the eggs. Provide an answer key for students to check their work.

An "Egg-stra" Idea!

Adapt the center to reinforce math facts by placing three numbers from a family of facts in each egg. After opening the egg, have the student arrange the numbers to create the family of facts. The student must write down all four facts before returning the numbers to the egg.

Sippin' Center

This review center will quench a thirst for word skills! Write each word of a synonym pair on a separate slip of paper. Then obtain several fast-food cups with lids and straws. Tape one word of a synonym pair to each cup before stapling the cups to a bulletin board and replacing the lids. Tape the matching synonyms on the straws. Have each student match the synonyms by placing the straws in the correct cups. Provide an answer key for students to check their work. The center can also be programmed with homophones, antonyms, rhyming words, or math problems.

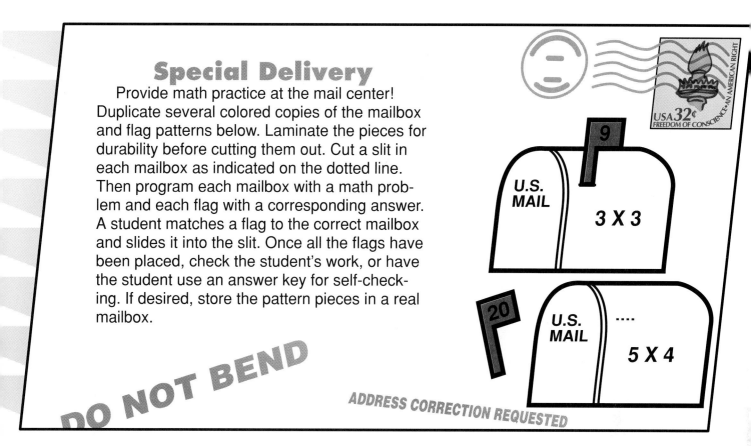

Special Delivery

Provide math practice at the mail center! Duplicate several colored copies of the mailbox and flag patterns below. Laminate the pieces for durability before cutting them out. Cut a slit in each mailbox as indicated on the dotted line. Then program each mailbox with a math problem and each flag with a corresponding answer. A student matches a flag to the correct mailbox and slides it into the slit. Once all the flags have been placed, check the student's work, or have the student use an answer key for self-checking. If desired, store the pattern pieces in a real mailbox.

Patterns

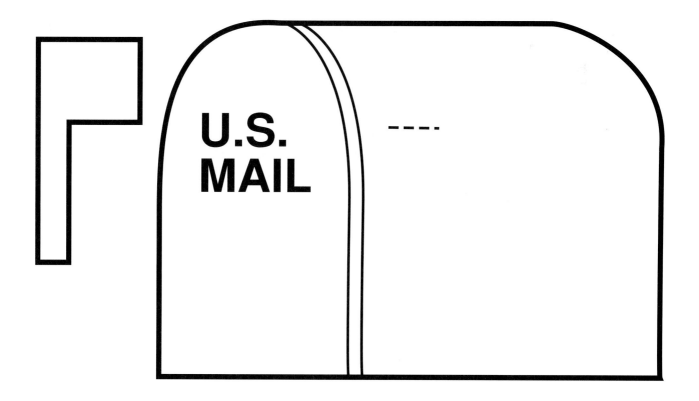

Patterns

Use the flies with "Skill Swatters" on page 116.

Use the grid with "Connect-The-Dots" on page 116.

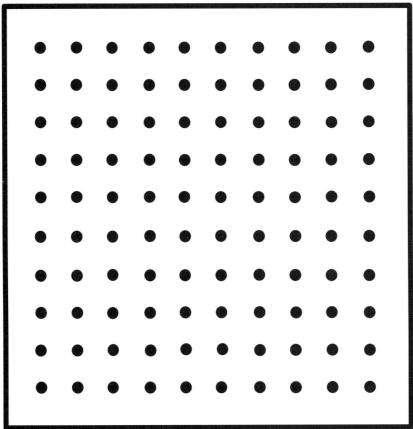

GAMES

Teaming Up

Having team captains choose teammates for a game can often result in hurt feelings or unequal teams. Try this approach to having students choose up sides. Select team captains for the desired amount of teams. Have each captain take turns choosing one student to join a team, continuing until all students have been selected. The twist is in the final decision; after the teams have been formed, the captains must then flip a coin to see which team *they* are on!

DICTIONARY RACE

This fast-paced word review will provide students with dictionary-skills practice. Have the students sit on the floor in two teams, with the members of each team sitting directly behind each other. Hand a dictionary to the first player in each row. Begin the race by writing a word on the board. The players with dictionaries race to look up the word. The first player to find the word reads the definition to the class, earning two points for his team. The other team has a chance to earn one point if the competing player can correctly use the word in a sentence. To begin the second round, the first players pass the dictionaries to the second players in each row, who will look up the next word you write on the board. Play continues until all students have had a turn.

Math-Review Relay

Math review will soon become a favorite activity when played as a relay game. To prepare for the relay, draw a line down the center of the chalkboard. Copy the same set of math problems on each side of the board, making sure that there is a problem for every student in the class. Divide the class into two teams and supply each with a piece of chalk and an eraser. At your signal, the first player on each team leaves a starting point and walks to the board while balancing the chalk on top of the eraser. When the student reaches his team's side of the board, he solves the first math problem, then carries the chalk on top of the eraser back to the next player on his team. Continue in this fashion until each player has had a turn. Determine the winning team by having the class check each answer on the board. Teams are awarded a point for each correct answer, with a bonus point given to the team who finished first.

$$\begin{array}{cc} 4 & 6 \\ \times 3 & \times 2 \end{array} \quad \begin{array}{cc} 4 & 6 \\ \times 3 & \times 2 \end{array}$$

$$\begin{array}{cc} 5 & 7 \\ \times 4 & \times 3 \end{array} \quad \begin{array}{cc} 5 & 7 \\ \times 4 & \times 3 \end{array}$$

$$\begin{array}{cc} 6 & 4 \\ \times 5 & \times 2 \end{array} \quad \begin{array}{cc} 6 & 4 \\ \times 5 & \times 2 \end{array}$$

Slapjack Review

Use the game of slapjack to review a variety of classroom skills. Create a deck of cards for the game by programming index cards for the desired skill. Each card should match at least one other card in the deck; for example, program two cards with synonyms so that each card contains one word of the synonym pair. To play, have a group of two to four students divide the deck into equal stacks and keep each stack facedown. Players sit facing each other so that the discard pile will be between them. Each student takes the top card from his stack and turns it over as he places it in the discard pile. If two cards create a match, the first student to slap the cards wins the pile. If they do not make a match, the cards remain in the discard pile. The game ends when one player runs out of cards. The player holding the most cards at that time is declared the winner.

PREPOSITION TOSS

A game of toss provides the perfect opportunity to review prepositions. Divide students into two groups. Hand a foam ball to the first player in a group. The player tosses the ball and then makes a statement about where it lands, such as "The ball is under the desk," or "The ball is by the window." If desired, have the student write the statement on the board. A member of the other group must identify the preposition in the statement to earn a point for his side. The ball is then passed to the other group's first player, and the process is repeated. After each student has had a turn tossing the ball, add up the points each group has earned to determine the winner.

The ball is <u>under</u> the desk.

I rolled a 3, times the 7, equals 21!

7	6	10	5
8	5	4	7
4	3	6	3

On A Roll With Math

Students will be on a roll with math when they use this dice game to review facts. Program a class supply of index cards with numbers for the appropriate skill level. Tape the cards to the board. Have each student take a turn selecting a card, rolling a die, and then adding (or multiplying) the numbers together. If the student answers correctly, he removes the card from the board. Play several rounds during the week. Challenge students to earn a specified amount of cards each week, and reward those who meet the challenge with a coupon good for skipping one math homework assignment.

Card Capers

Purchase several decks of cards for a variety of skill-review games. Distribute a deck of cards to student partners. Call out a task for sorting cards, such as finding all even-numbered red cards, finding all cards with multiples of three on them, or arranging each suit in numerical order. Allow the students a time limit for finding the designated cards; then check each pair's work. Award each pair a point for every task it successfully completes.

STUDENT-CREATED GAMES

Provide students with the opportunity to create their own board games. Use copies of the reproducibles on pages 127 and 128 to supply students with dice, spinners, and board-game patterns. Also make available to students a set of assorted markers, index cards, and materials for making place markers. Once a student creates a game, have her write a list of rules and directions for play. Store the list and game pieces in a manila envelope that the student has decorated. Keep the games in a center for students to use during free time or for indoor recess.

Die Cube
Cut on solid lines.
Fold on dotted lines.
Glue tabs to form a cube.

Spinner
Cut out the spinner pieces.
Glue each piece on heavy paper.
Assemble pieces with brads.

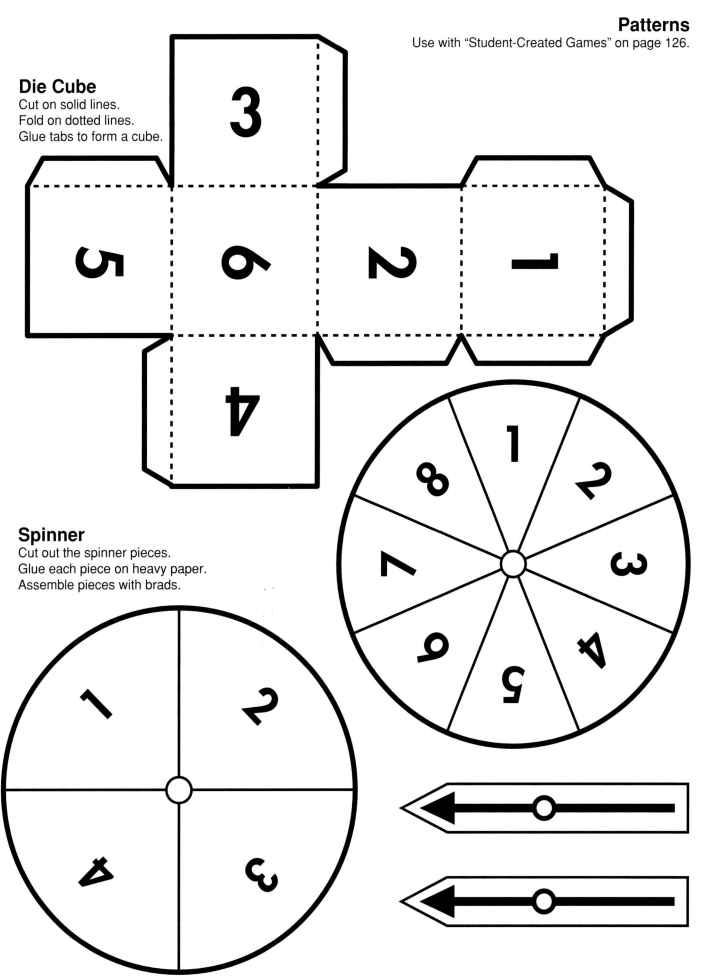

Pattern

Use with "Student-Created Games" on page 126.

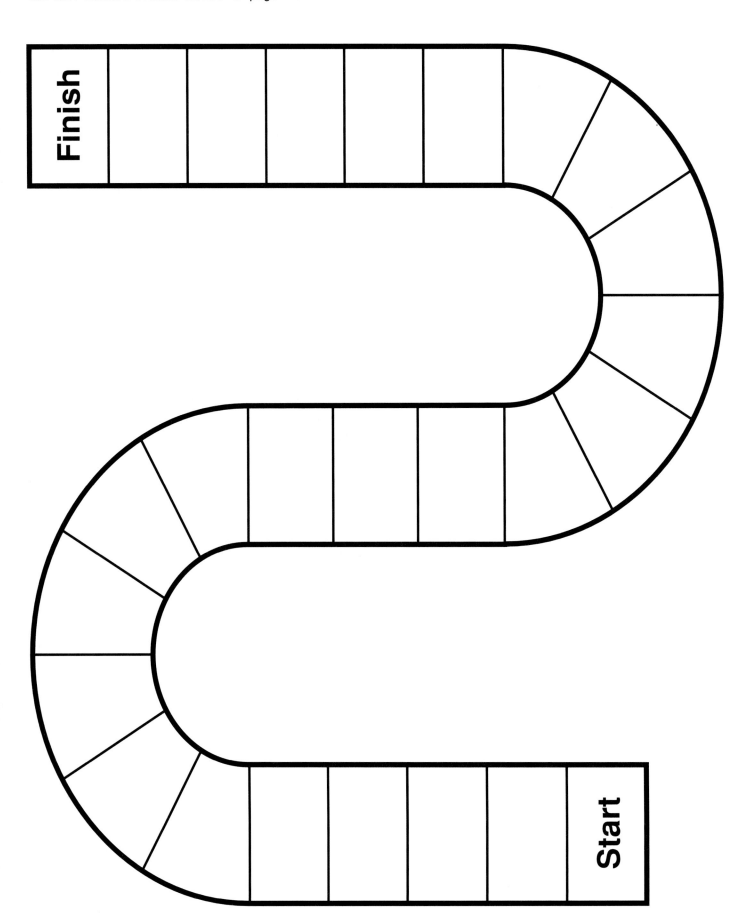

5-MINUTE FILLERS

5-MINUTE FILLERS

Phonics Filler

Provide phonics reinforcement with this easy filler idea. Write a spelling pattern—such as -ing, str-, or -each — on the board. Challenge students to write as many words as they can think of using the pattern. After a designated time period, ask for students to share their responses while you record their answers on the board.

str-

string	stripe	strong
street	strange	strap

5-MINUTE MATH

For an instant math review, keep a die or spinner handy. When there are a few minutes to fill, ask each student to write a numeral on her paper. Announce a math operation, and have each student write the sign for the operation by the numeral. Roll the die (or spin the spinner) to determine the second numeral for the problem. Allow time for students to solve the problem, then have them trade papers with classmates to check their work.

Spelling-Word Activities

Review spelling words in a variety of filler activities. To prepare for the activities, have each student copy his spelling words onto individual index cards. Have students store the cards in resealable plastic bags inside their desks. In spare moments between classes, ask students to take out their cards. Have students alphabetize the words, group them by vowel sounds, sort them by parts of speech, or follow other classifying directions.

Vocabulary Word Search

Students will have an activity at the ready with this weekly word-puzzle project. At the beginning of the week, distribute a blank centimeter grid to each student. When the student has a few spare minutes, have him create a word search by programming the grid with spelling words, vocabulary words, or words from a unit of study. Once the words are in place, the student fills the blank squares with random letters. Provide time at the end of the week for students to trade grids with their classmates and solve the puzzles.

Q	J	Y	X	L	R	A	L	G	J
Y	C	A	P	I	T	O	L	Y	D	M
O	B	L	R	E	O	T	R	O	B	P
S	H	X	E	F	S	Q	K	S	Y	E
H	W	A	S	H	I	N	G	T	O	N
U	K	V	I	C	K	L	F	K	E	Z
P	S	C	D	N	W	I	B	W	L	M
G	O	V	E	R	N	M	E	N	T	R
Z	J	E	N	M	K	H	T	K	P	I

LINE-UP LESSON

Students are lined up at the door, but there are still a few minutes before it's time to leave. Why not initiate a brainstorming session? Name a category that students are familiar with. Have students name an item in the category for each letter of the alphabet. By the time everyone has volunteered an answer, it will be time to go!

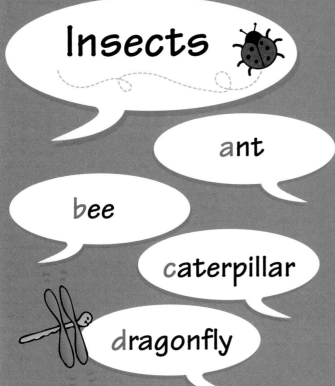

Insects

ant

bee

caterpillar

dragonfly

Number-Concept Practice

Students can practice number concepts in the extra minutes between classes. Write four numerals on the board. Call on volunteers to come to the board and write numbers that can be made using the four numerals. After several numbers have been made, ask students to identify the greatest number written, the least number written, or the number that has a certain numeral in a designated place-value position.

Operation, Please!

Use spare moments to reinforce problem-solving strategies. Distribute two index cards to each student. Instruct the student to write one of the four basic operation signs (addition, subtraction, multiplication, and division) on each side of the index cards. When a few extra minutes arise, read a story problem to the class. Each student holds up the sign for the correct operation needed to solve the problem. Not only will this provide extra practice, but you can also see at a glance who is having trouble with the concept.

Instant Graphing

Fill spare minutes with a graphing activity. Prepare for the activity by drawing a bar graph on poster board, then laminating it for durability. To use the graph, write the topic and categories of the graph on the poster board with a wipe-off marker. Then distribute a self-stick note to each student. The student writes his name or response on the note, then posts it in the correct column on the graph. If time allows, have students discuss the results, making comparative or observational statements about the findings.

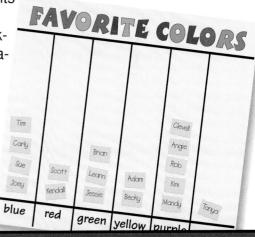

8	4	9	2
9,842	4,298		2,984
2,489	9,248		4,829
8,429	2,894		8,942

Word Challenge

Engage students in a word-building challenge during the transitional time between classes. Choose a vocabulary word from a current unit of study. Write the word on the board. Challenge students to use the letters in the word to create other words. As a student discovers a word, have him write it on the board.

kitchen

kit   nice   hen
chin   kite   tick
think   ten   ice

LINE-UP LESSON

Create a supply of riddles that reinforces a variety of skills. Compose riddles relating to the curriculum, such as "Can you think of a mammal with three syllables in its name?" or "Can you name a difference between Mercury and Jupiter?" Write each riddle on an index card. Store the cards in a file box or on a metal ring, and keep them in a handy location. When you need a time-filler, the riddles will be ready to go!

Can you think of a mammal with three syllables in its name ???

Can you name a difference between Mercury and Jupiter ???

Word-Skills Search

Review basic word skills with this easy activity. Announce a specific type of word, such as compounds, contractions, or four-syllable words. Have students look through their library books for examples of that type of word. When a student locates a word, ask her to write it on the board. Leave the list on the board for students to copy for handwriting practice.

Four-Syllable Words

elevator
interesting
situation
January
alligator
information

Wrap-Up Review

Students will be lined up and ready to go with this activity that reinforces lesson concepts. At the conclusion of a lesson, ask a question relating to the topic. If a student volunteer answers the question correctly, he may line up at the door. Continue asking questions until all students are in line.

MYSTERY STUDENT

Have each student write her name on a slip of paper. Collect the papers and place them in a container. Choose a student to draw a name from the container. Without revealing the person's name, the student makes three statements about the mystery student. His classmates have three chances to identify the mystery student. If the name is identified, the person who guessed correctly will draw the next name from the container. If no one guesses the name, the mystery student becomes the next player.

The mystery student has a brother.

He likes ketchup on his pizza.

He also plays the piano.

And The Answer Is...

Challenge students to practice math by having them create a list of problems. Designate a numeral that will be the answer to the problems and write it on the board. Then have students come up with as many problems as they can think of that yield that answer. If desired, specify an operation for students to use in creating the problems.

Vocabulary Booster

As new vocabulary is introduced throughout the year, copy each vocabulary word and its definition on an index card. Store the cards in a file box; then fill spare minutes with a vocabulary review. Randomly pull a card from the box and read aloud the vocabulary word. Award the student who can define the word with a sticker or a point towards a larger prize.

Memory Test

This activity will enhance students' observational skills. Write ten vocabulary words on the board in a random arrangement. Have students study the words for one minute. Then ask students to put their heads down while you erase two of the words. Have students study the remaining words and try to identify which two have been erased.

$$21$$

$$10 + 11 = \qquad 42 - 21 =$$

$$7 \times 3 = \qquad 15 + 6 =$$

$$29 - 8 = \qquad 21 \times 1 =$$

Twenty Questions

When it comes to polishing thinking skills, keep the game of Twenty Questions in mind. To guess the object you are thinking of, have students formulate questions that can be answered with *yes* or *no*. Keep track of the number of questions asked by having a student write tally marks on the board. If students identify the object before 20 questions have been asked, challenge them to supply five facts about the object. If the students are not able to identify the object after 20 questions, provide facts about the object until students are able to guess what it is.

> Is it alive?

> Is it smaller than a bread box?

SCHOOL MENU

sloppy joes
french fries
green beans
applesauce
milk

MENU ACTIVITIES

Use the school lunch menu for a variety of fast filler activities. Write the daily menu on the board and challenge students to:

✔ name an item from each food group

✔ alphabetize the items

✔ predict which item is the class favorite, then vote to determine the answer

✔ count the number of syllables in each item

✔ categorize the menu into solids and liquids

✔ name the ingredients in an item

✔ think of ways to categorize the items

VITAMIN D MILK VITAMIN D MILK

Student Similarities

Generate positive bonds between your students with an activity that focuses on similarities. Select a student to come to the front of the room. Have each classmate identify one thing that he has in common with the student. If desired, have the student record the responses on the board. The students may be surprised at how much they have in common with their fellow classmates!

Following Directions

With a few extra minutes, you can provide students with an exercise in following directions. Have each student take out a sheet of paper, a pencil, and crayons. Call out a list of directions for the students to follow, such as "Draw a blue triangle in the center of the page. Draw a red circle inside the triangle." After you have called out ten directions, have students compare their papers with each other. Extend the activity with an exercise in giving clear directions by having student volunteers each give one direction for their classmates to follow.

SUBSTITUTE TEACHER TIPS

SUBSTITUTE-TEACHER TIPS

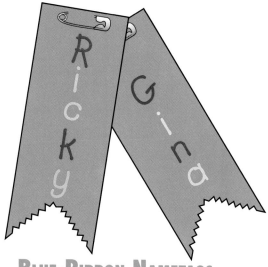

THE SUBSTITUTE FOLDER

If you are preparing for a substitute teacher, you will want to take necessary steps to ensure that things run smoothly. Use copies of the reproducibles on pages 137–140 to help organize important information into a substitute-teacher folder. Then use the following checklist to make certain that you have furnished the substitute with everything she needs for a successful day.

* Did I make complete plans, with no time left unaccounted for?
* Are all the materials needed for the activities listed in my plans available?
* Are all the photocopies needed for the day at hand?
* Did I stack all reproducibles, materials, and books in the order in which they are to be used during the day?
* Did I leave instructions for taking lunch count and roll call?
* Did I provide information about classroom discipline?
* Did I leave instructions for dismissal, the bus schedule, and after-school activities?

BLUE-RIBBON NAMETAGS

To provide fast and easy nametags for a substitute, purchase a roll of wide-width blue ribbon from a fabric store. Cut a six-inch length of ribbon for each student in the class. Use pinking shears to cut a V-shape from the bottom edge. Have each student write his name on a ribbon with a fabric pen. Keep the ribbons in an envelope labeled "My Blue-Ribbon Class." Store the envelope and a supply of safety pins with your substitute folder.

SUBSTITUTE KIT

Put together a special box full of items your substitute might need during the day. The box can include extra pencils, nametags, a small first-aid kit, index cards programmed with five-minute filler activities, stickers, and passes to the office or nurse. Place the box on your desk for easy access.

In addition, include the instructions and materials for an emergency lesson in the event that a scheduled library visit, P.E. class, or music class is canceled. Provide a file folder of reproducibles copied and ready to use, a book to read to the class, a cassette of sing-along songs, or directions and supplies for an easy art project. Be sure to note in your lesson plans that the kit is available for the substitute to use.

SIMPLE SEATING CHART

You'll want to give the substitute a seating plan for your classroom, but a chart drawn on paper will soon become obsolete. To maintain an up-to-date seating chart, use a small magnetic board and cardboard squares backed with magnets. Write the name of each student on a cardboard square. Each time you rearrange the desks, place the magnets in the corresponding places on the board. This chart can be used for years to come!

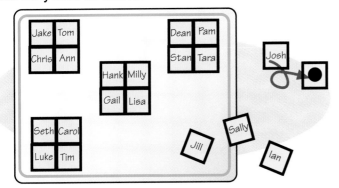

CLASSROOM CONDUCT

Classroom management can be a challenge for even the best substitute. If you have a detailed behavior management system, provide a simpler plan for the substitute to use for controlling discipline problems or rewarding positive behavior. Make the students aware of your expectations of them while a substitute is in the classroom. Provide a copy of the form below for the substitute to jot down behavioral concerns. Once you're back in the classroom, follow up on any problems that occurred while you were gone. Students will know that you are keeping tabs on their conduct even when you are away!

While You Were Away

Here are some of the problems I encountered:

Student	Behavior	Measures Taken

These students exhibited positive behavior:

Student	Behavior	Measures Taken

Signed,_____ Date _____

   substitute teacher

Setting The Stage For A
Substitute Teacher

Faculty Information:

Principal: _____

Secretary: _____

Custodian: _____

Aide(s): _____

_____

Helpful Teachers: _____

_____

Procedures For:

Start Of The Day: _____

_____

Attendance: _____

_____

Fire Drill: _____

_____

_____

Recess: _____

_____

_____

Lunch: _____

_____

_____

Behavior Policy: _____

_____

_____

Other: _____

_____

_____

Children With Special Needs:

Health: _____

_____

_____

Supervision: _____

_____

_____

Learning: _____

_____

_____

_____

Students Pulled Out For Special Programs:

Name	Class	Day/Time

Helpful Students:

_____

_____

_____

138

Daily Schedule

Time	Monday	Tuesday	Wednesday	Thursday	Friday

Free-Time Activities: _____

_____

_____

_____

Emergency Lesson Plans

Reading	Language	Math	Science	Social Studies	Other

LANGUAGE ARTS

GRAMMAR

Language On The Loose

Have your students hot on the trail of adjectives, adverbs, or other parts of speech. Provide each student with a copy of the same newspaper or magazine article. Ask students to list as many nouns, verbs, conjunctions, and prepositions as they can find in a designated time period. Have each student read his list to the class to confirm that each word is the correct part of speech. Then have students tally their answers to see which student tracked down the most words.

nouns	verbs	prepositions
rabbit	hop	around
carrot	jump	under
ears	nibble	by
bunny	twitch	

Grammar Baseball

Use the popular game of baseball to help your students review the parts of speech. Divide the class into two teams. Designate four areas of the room to be the bases. As the first team comes to "bat," say a word and use it in a sentence. The first player must identify the word as being a noun, a verb, or an adjective. If the player correctly identifies the part of speech, she may walk to first base. Repeat the procedure for the second player. Play continues until the first team has had three strikes, or incorrect responses. The first team then retreats to the bleachers (their desks) while the second team goes to bat. If desired, assign a scorekeeper to record tally marks for each player who advances to home plate. The game can become more challenging by increasing the difficulty of the words and asking batters if they would prefer a first-, second-, or third-base problem.

Hot-Potato Grammar

Make grammar a hot topic in your classroom with a game to review the parts of speech. Gather a set of beanbags and label each with a different part of speech. Then program slips of paper with words that are examples of the parts of speech labeled on the beanbags. (You should have as many s   tudents playing the game.) Place the slips of pape   dents to sit in a circle and pass the beanbags aro   ecording. When the music stops, draw a slip of pa   read it to the class. The students must identify t   person holding the bean- bag labeled with that pa   of the game. (If desired   dent to draw the next sli   when the music stops in the next round of play.) Continue playing until one student is left. That student must identify the last word in the container to be named the Hot Potato of the game.

moon
shiny
dance
quiet

Capital Letter Trivia

Play a game of Capital Letter Trivia. Divide students into small groups and have them brainstorm words for categories such as boys' names that start with the letter *M,* states that begin with *N,* or winter holidays. Each group earns a point for every reasonable answer that has been written with a capital letter.

Joe went to Texas in July.

Robert went to Anchorage, Alaska, last August.

Proper-Noun Poem

Provide a poetic reference list of rules for capitalizing proper nouns. Review several examples of nouns that are always capitalized. Then display this poem to remind students when a noun should be capitalized. Encourage students to add to the poem with couplets that reinforce capitalization rules.

CAPITALIZATION CHALLENGE

Use a roll of the die for an ongoing capitalization challenge. As part of a daily capitalization review, instruct each student to write a sentence containing proper nouns. Explain to students that the number on the die will determine how many capitalized words each sentence must contain.

Proper-Noun Poem

Every name is a proper noun,
So put a capital letter down.

Months and days are nice enough,
But capital letters make them big stuff!

States and towns across this land
Need capital letters to make them grand.

Abbreviations are surely neat.
Capital letters make them complete.

Titles are important in every way,
Except maybe words like *the, and,* and *a.*

Street names should not be forgotten.
Leaving those out would be just plain rotten!

A capital letter is the way to start
A proper noun. Now aren't you smart!

Seasonal Language

Have students brainstorm nouns and verbs associated with the current holiday or season. Give each student a sheet of drawing paper to illustrate and label the nouns and verbs. For an added challenge, ask students to label adjectives in their artwork as well. Display the creations for students to use as a reference for seasonal stories and journal writing.

Pantomine

Bring nouns and verbs to life with creative dramatics. Write a simple sentence on the board, omitting the noun and verb by drawing a blank where each word should go. Call on one volunteer to supply the noun and another volunteer to supply the verb. The volunteers do not say the words aloud, but rather pantomime the parts of speech. Call on students to guess the words being dramatized by the volunteers. Then write the correct responses in the blanks and have the class read the sentence together.

ILLUSTRATED Grammar

Have students look through old magazines for pictures that contain examples of nouns and verbs. Have them work individually or in pairs to create lists for their pictures. Challenge students to find at least ten nouns and ten verbs in each picture. For a variation, reverse the lesson by giving your students a list of nouns and verbs and having them create pictures showing examples of the words. Provide time for students to show their pictures to the class.

Playing With Words

Create a class book that encourages students to have fun with language. To begin, distribute two index cards to each student. Instruct the student to write a noun on one card and a verb on the other card. Collect the cards and place them into bags marked "Nouns" and "Verbs." Have each student draw one card out of each bag. Have the student compose a sentence using the words he selected from the bags. Give each student a sheet of drawing paper and have him illustrate his sentence. Compile the illustrated sentences into a booklet for the class to use in a variety of language activities.

mother

planted

My mother planted carrots in our garden.

*I better clean my desk. The inside looks **atrocious**.*

atrocious

Daily Challenge

Introduce an adjective a day to your students by writing an unusual or unfamiliar adjective on the board. Have students find the word in the dictionary. Challenge the students to use the word in conversation at least twice during the day. Give extra credit or a bonus to students who use the word in their journal writing, too.

Artistic Adjectives

Incorporate art appreciation into a reinforcement of adjectives. Display a copy of a famous work of art. Ask students to study the work, then list ten adjectives to describe it. Compare the students' lists, and discuss how the word choices might reflect their reactions to the art. If desired, ask student volunteers to display their own artwork for this assignment.

1. serious
2. famous
3. pleasant
4. interesting
5. attractive
6. graceful
7. unusual
8. lovely
9. calm
10. dark

Brainstorming

Place students in cooperative groups and challenge each group to list as many adjectives as possible to describe a topic, such as ice cream or feathers. After a designated time period, ask each group to share its list with the class, having the other students confirm that each word is an adjective. Extend the activity by having students group the words on the collective lists into categories describing touch, taste, smell, sound, or appearance.

Bountiful Adjectives

This partner activity will help your students become familiar with adjectives. Distribute a picture book to each pair of students. As the partners look through the pages, have them write an adjective to describe each illustration. After they complete the book, have the partners select five of the adjectives from their list. Instruct the pair to copy the adjectives onto colorful construction-paper shapes. Mount the words on a bulletin board titled "Bountiful Adjectives." Encourage students to refer to the display during writing assignments.

Sentence Skills

DESCRIPTIVE SENTENCES

Encourage students to use description in their writing with this write-and-draw project. Distribute a 12" x 18" sheet of drawing paper to each student. Tell students to make a crease down the middle of their papers. On the left side of the papers, have students copy and illustrate a simple sentence such as "The bear sat." Provide time for students to show their completed illustrations to the class. After everyone has had a chance to share, ask students why there was a wide variety in the pictures drawn for the same sentence. Discuss ways to improve the sentence by adding detail and description. Instruct each student to add to the sentence so that it tells more about the picture he has drawn. Encourage the student to use adjectives, prepositions, and adverbs to compose a descriptive sentence and write it on the right side of the paper. Share the illustrations once more, having students read their new sentences to the class.

The Official Daily Subject

Add interest to daily sentence-writing practice by using a personal approach. Select a student each day to be the Official Daily Subject. Have the class use the student's name as the subject for sentence-writing practice. Remind students to use positive messages in their sentences. Provide time for students to share the sentences aloud; then let the Official Daily Subject take the collection of sentences home.

Offical Daily Subject

Fact-Filled Sentences

Use sentence writing as part of a unit culmination. At the end of a unit of study, provide each student with a sentence strip. Have each student copy the phrase "I learned that…" onto the strip. Then have her complete the sentence with a fact she learned during the course of study. Post the completed strips on a bulletin board to create a fact-filled display.

I learned that Mercury is the closest planet to the sun.

FRAGMENT ALERT

Watch your words—and have students watch theirs, too! Increase students' awareness of sentence fragments by proposing a challenge. After a discussion on distinguishing a sentence fragment from a complete sentence, encourage students to speak only in complete sentences for a designated time period. During that time (can they make it an entire hour?), every utterance must have a subject and predicate and tell a complete thought. Have students keep track of how many times they hear an incomplete sentence (they will be listening to your sentences, too!) and discuss the results at the end of the time period.

"Hand-y" Sentences Practice

This "hand-y" activity reinforces the concept of a complete sentence. Have each student trace her hand on a piece of construction paper and cut it out. Next have the student write a phrase on each finger of the cutout, then turn it in to you. Redistribute the cutouts to the students and instruct them to write a complete sentence from each phrase on a sheet of paper. For an added challenge, encourage students to relate each sentence to a designated topic. Provide time for students to share their sentences with the class.

in the garden

a big, juicy carrot

down the bunny trail

fuzzy tails

rascally rabbits

SENTENCE DRAMA

Challenge students to practice the four types of sentences with a role-playing activity. Review the definitions of imperative, interrogative, exclamatory, and declarative sentences. Then place students in groups of four to create a Sentence Drama. Assign each group a situation to act out, such as Johnny trying to convince his mother to buy him candy, or three friends trying to equally share two apples. Each group must work together to write a script for the situation. The script should consist of four sentences, one of each of the types mentioned above. Provide time for each group to compose the script and rehearse the lines; then sit back and enjoy the shows! Hold the audience members accountable for identifying the types of sentences in each skit.

CLASS-CREATED SENTENCES

Reinforce sentence-writing skills with class-effort corrections. Review the procedure for restating the question when answering in complete sentences. Give students an assignment that requires them to use this skill. After collecting the papers, write on the board examples of sentence fragments found on students' papers. (Make sure to keep the examples anonymous.) Ask your students to determine which question the fragment was trying to answer. Then work as a class to restate part of the question to transform the fragment into a complete sentence. Repeat this strategy when you notice fragments appearing frequently on student papers.

Punctuated Pictures

After students complete this punctuation activity, you'll have a ready-made learning-center game! Provide a supply of magazines, drawing paper, scissors, glue, and a stack of index cards. Instruct each student to cut out a picture from a magazine. Have the student glue the picture to a sheet of drawing paper, then write a question and a statement relating to the picture on an index card. After checking the students' work, place the pictures and cards in a center. Challenge students to match the sentences to the correct pictures. If desired, program the back of the index cards for self-checking.

Literature-Linking Punctuation

Share a short story with your class; then have each student write three questions about the story. Tell each student to switch papers with a classmate and answer the questions on the traded paper. After the questions have been answered, have each child proofread the classmate's paper for punctuation errors before returning it to its owner.

What did the Velveteen Rabbit wish for?

Who did the rabbit belong to?

How did the story end?

PUNCTUATION PAIR-UP

Have students create a classroom punctuation challenge with this partner activity. Pair students and distribute two sentence strips and two index cards to each pair. Instruct the partners to look through a textbook or library book to find examples of sentences with different ending punctuation. Have each partner copy a sentence from the book onto a sentence strip, leaving off the ending punctuation. Have her write the correct ending punctuation on an index card. Ask students to take turns displaying the sentences to the class, calling on volunteers to name the correct ending punctuation. After several responses have been given, have the student display the index card to show the correct answer.

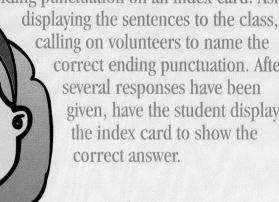

All afternoon the little boy played with his puppy

Daily Punctuation Review

Invite the student helper or daily leader to write three unpunctuated sentences on the board. Have her call on student volunteers to add the missing punctuation. Ask the class to show thumbs-up or thumbs-down in response to the answers. Then reinforce the correct responses before erasing the sentences.

Rabbits have long ears short tails and long legs

What do domestic rabbits eat

What is the difference between a bunny rabbit and a hare

Flash-It Review

Distribute an index card to each student. Have him write the word *question* on one side of the card, and the word *statement* on the other side. Read a sentence to the class. Ask students to identify what type of sentence it is. Have each student "flash" his answer by holding up the appropriate side of his index card. Announce the correct answer before reading the next sentence.

PUNCTUATION SIGNAL

Create this eye-catching display to remind students of the purpose of punctuation. Enlarge the stoplight pattern on page 167 and color it appropriately. In the red circle, use a marker to write a period, a question mark, and an exclamation mark. Explain to students that these marks tell us to come to a stop. Write a comma in the yellow circle, explaining to students that it is a signal to pause. Leave the green circle empty, as students should keep going when there is no punctuation mark. Post the stoplight in a prominent place in the classroom to remind students of the importance of punctuation.

WORD SKILLS

THE BUDDY SYSTEM

Have your students buddy up to practice their spelling words. Pair up students for an oral spelling review prior to the weekly test. One student quizzes his partner by calling out words from the list. If a student has trouble with a word, his partner gives him the correct spelling. The student writes the word before spelling it aloud again. Then partners trade roles for another round of practice. This teamwork approach provides students with additional practice and reinforces cooperative skills.

KEYBOARD SPELLING

Students practice their spelling words and their keyboarding skills with this activity. Photocopy a computer keyboard for each student in your class. If desired, laminate the copies for durability. Begin each spelling lesson by distributing a copy of the keyboard to each student. Call out a spelling word and have students say each letter as they "type" the word on the keyboard. Remind them to hit the return key before typing the next word!

Word Examinations

Help your students learn their spelling list by identifying familiar parts of each word. Model the process for the students the first time the activity is used; then allow students to complete the process on their own in the following weeks. Review the spelling list with the class. Ask a volunteer to select a word and identify letter combinations, prefixes, suffixes, or pneumonic devices that make the word easier to spell. Use a different color chalk to write the identified part of the word. Fill in the remaining letters with white chalk. Demonstrate a few examples; then have students try it on their own. Discuss the results with the class. Each student will find a way to remember the spelling of each word, and can compare his method with those of his classmates. Making each word more familiar will help students recall its correct spelling.

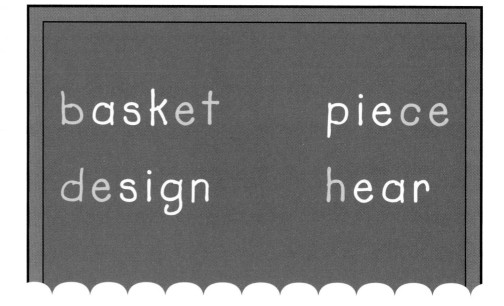

Outdoor Spelling

Take students outside for an alternative way to review spelling words. Have each student bring a ruler or find a sturdy stick to use to write his spelling words in the dirt. Call out a spelling word and provide time for each student to write the word in the dirt. Check the spellings before each child erases his work by rubbing his foot across the word. Continue calling out words from the list as students scratch out their way to spelling success.

SPELLING DICTIONARIES

Spelling lists will always be on hand when your students have their own personal spelling dictionary. To make a spelling journal, bind 26 pieces of lined notebook paper inside a letter-size manila folder. Provide markers or crayons for each student to decorate his covers. Then have him label each page with a letter of the alphabet. After a student is given a new list of words, have him copy each word onto the corresponding page in his dictionary. The dictionary should be kept in the student's desk for future reference during writing time, spelling games, and independent studying.

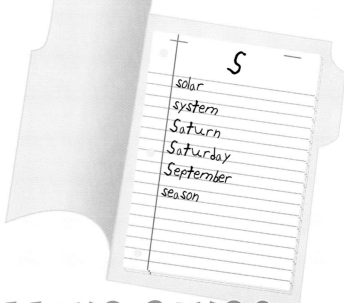

Spell-Tac-Toe

Try this spelling game to add spark to the traditional spelling practice. To play the game, draw a tic-tac-toe grid on the chalkboard. Divide the class into two teams. Assign one team to be *X*s and the other to be *O*s. Explain to students that their team earns the chance to place a mark on the grid by spelling a word correctly. Call out a word to the *X* team. The student who is first to raise his hand and announce the number of letters in the word may spell the word for his team. If he spells the word correctly, he marks his team's symbol on the tic-tac-toe grid. If he misspells the word, the other team has the opportunity to spell the word. Continue the game by alternating between each team using words from the list. Several tic-tac-toe games can be played so that all the weekly spelling words are reviewed.

SPELLING BINGO

A round of Spelling Bingo provides an enjoyable way for students to practice their spelling words. Each time a new spelling list is given, have students prepare a bingo card to correspond with the list. To make a bingo card, distribute a sheet of white paper to each student. Have students fold their papers four times to create 16 squares. Have them unfold the papers and trace over each crease with a pencil or a black crayon. The student writes his name in one square (to be used as a free space), and a spelling word in each of the other squares. (If the spelling list contains more than 15 words, allow each student to select which words he will leave out. If the spelling list is less than 15 words, add enough review words to the list to fill the squares.)

When the cards are complete, distribute beans, paper scraps, or chips to use as markers. Call out one of the spelling words and use it in a sentence. The student covers the word on his card. Continue to call out words until a student has four covered spaces in a row. The student must then spell each of his covered words. If he spells them correctly, ask him to be the word caller for the next round of play.

SEASONAL COMPOUNDS

Provide a vocabulary-building review of compound words with a learning center that changes with the seasons. Place a supply of seasonal cutouts, scissors, colored pencils, and a dictionary in a center. To use the center, a student brainstorms a list of compound words related to the season, checks the spellings of the words in the dictionary, and then writes each word on a seasonal cutout. The student illustrates each word on the back of the cutout. She then cuts apart the word in a puzzle-piece fashion, separating the individual words of the compound. Store the completed puzzle pieces in a decorated envelope at the center for students to assemble as they review the seasonal compounds.

Prefix Patrol

Send your students on a scavenger hunt for examples of prefixed words. Distribute a dictionary and assign a prefix to each pair of students. Have partners work together to find five words with the designated prefix. In addition, ask each pair to find two words that begin with the same prefixed letters, but are not a prefixed word. Instruct the pair to write each word on a notecard. When the class is ready, call on the pairs to share their findings. Have them display their cards for the class to observe. After announcing the letters of the prefix and its meaning, the partners call on volunteers to identify the two "outlaw" words in the group. Then have each pair code its word cards for self-checking, and store the cards in a center for students to use during free time.

WORD TRAINS

Put students on the right track to identifying word parts with this locomotive word display. Duplicate several sets of the train-car patterns on page 168 onto heavy tagboard. To make a word train, each student will need colored construction paper, crayons or markers, glue, and access to a dictionary. Have each student use the train patterns to trace each car onto his construction paper. Then the student peruses the dictionary for a word containing both a prefix and a suffix. Ask him to write the prefix on the engine, the root word on the boxcar, and the suffix on the caboose. After cutting out each piece, the student glues the cars together. Mount the completed word trains on a bulletin board titled "All Aboard The Word Express!"

re view ing use ness

ANTONYM BUDDIES

Pair each student with a buddy to test their knowledge of antonyms. Prior to joining his partner, have each student secretly compose a list of ten antonym pairs. Keeping his list a secret, he joins his partner. The first partner in the pair calls out a word from his list, and the second partner names an antonym for the word. If her response matches what was written, she is awarded one point. Extra points are added for each additional antonym she names. Then the roles are reversed, and the second partner calls out a word from her list. Play continues until both partners have called out each word on their lists. For an extra challenge, have the students play a second round using synonym pairs.

Opposite Tales

Incorporate creative writing into this antonym activity. Have your students brainstorm a list of antonym pairs while you record their responses on the board. Instruct each student to select one word from a predetermined number of the pairs to use in a story. After writing the story, each student underlines the words he chose from the list. The student then replaces each underlined word with its antonym. Provide time for students to share their "Opposite Tales" with the class.

Synonym Story

This class-created book provides plenty of practice with synonyms. Distribute a 9" x 12" sheet of construction paper to each student. Instruct each student to think of a synonym pair. Using one word of the pair, the student writes a sentence and creates an illustration for a topic such as "Guess What Happened At The Zoo!" or "If Everything Were Upside Down." The student underlines the word in the sentence, then rewrites the sentence on the back of his paper replacing the underlined word with its synonym. Collect the completed papers and compile them into a book. Read the resulting story to the class, pausing after each page for students to name the synonym for the underlined word in each sentence. Then turn the page to reveal the rewritten sentence.

WORD-PAIR SENTENCES

Homophone pairs double the fun of writing assignments! Have each student select ten homophone pairs to use in writing sentences. Each sentence must contain a homophone pair. Then have the student illustrate two of the sentences on his list. Did anyone think of a pair of pears?

1. We bought a sundae on Sunday.
2. Did the flea flee?
3. Come in to the inn.
4. Would you cut some wood?
5. We went to the sea to see a tuna boat.
6.
7.
8.
9.
10.

Homophone Humor

Introduce the humorous side of homophones with fun-filled books by Fred Gwynne. *The King Who Rained, A Little Pigeon Toad,* and *A Chocolate Moose For Dinner* (Simon & Schuster Children's Books, 1988) take a look at homophones while tickling the funny bone. Read each page aloud to your class before showing the illustrations. Discuss how each picture reflects the wrong word of a homophone pair. Then distribute a sheet of drawing paper to each student and challenge him to create a similar sentence and illustration. Compile the completed works in a class big book for students to enjoy.

TRACKING DOWN HOMOPHONES

Reinforce the correct meaning of each word in a homophone pair. Compose a paragraph that contains several homophones on an overhead transparency. Use the incorrect choice for several of the homophones. Display the paragraph for the class and have students identify which words were used incorrectly. Then have the class copy the paragraph making the necessary corrections.

Homophone Challenge

How many homophones can your class think of? Challenge your students to think of 100 homophone pairs! Place students in small groups to brainstorm as many pairs of homophones as possible. Compile the lists and delete duplicate entries. If the class is still a few shy of 100, extend the challenge for a week or two. Remind students to be on the lookout for more homophones to add to the list before the end of the time period.

RACING WITH CONTRACTIONS

Have students rev up their engines for a contraction review as they create words on wheels. Distribute several copies of the wheel and race-car patterns on page 168 to each student. Instruct the student to write a contraction on the body of each car, then write the two words forming the contraction on each wheel. After the student colors each car, display her work on a bulletin board titled "Racing With Contractions."

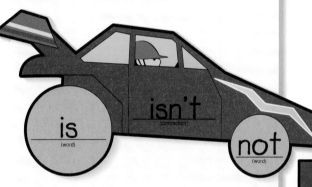

MORE CONTRACTION ACTION

Continue to reinforce contraction practice with these activities:

• Provide magazines and newspapers for a contraction hunt. Students find and circle as many contractions as possible, then write the two words that make up the contraction on a sheet of paper.

• Start a Contraction Club in your classroom. To qualify as a member, a student must use a predetermined amount of contractions in a writing assignment. Attach an Apostrophe Award to student papers that meet the criteria.

Adventures With Abbreviations

Provide practice with abbreviations by introducing the following partner activities in your classroom:

• Create a learning-center activity that focuses on abbreviations. Place a telephone book in the center. Have student partners visit the center together to look through the telephone book to find abbreviations. Challenge them to find and list at least ten.

• List some common abbreviations such as FBI, NBA, FYI, ASAP, and UFO. Have students work in pairs to guess what the abbreviations stand for. Ask each team to share its responses before you reveal the actual meanings.

• Have students learn the abbreviations for the states. Introduce three or four abbreviations each day. Provide time for students to pair up and quiz each other on the abbreviations. Then hold a contest (similar to a spelling bee) to see who can identify the most states by their abbreviations.

Reading

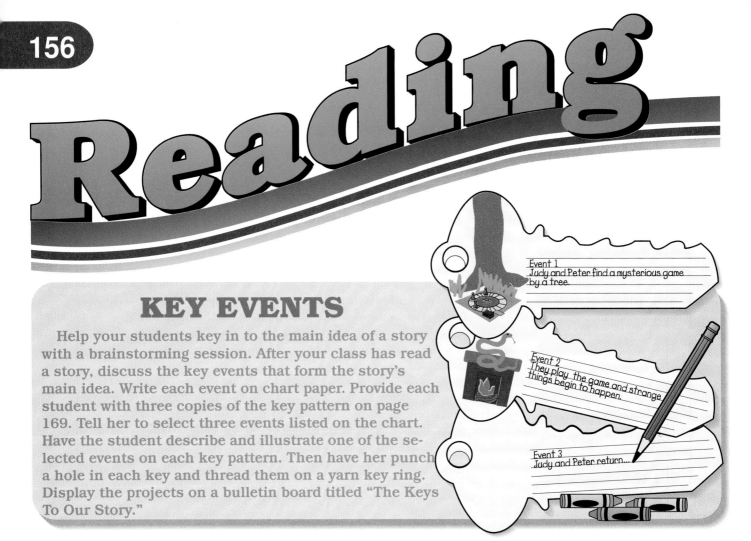

KEY EVENTS

Help your students key in to the main idea of a story with a brainstorming session. After your class has read a story, discuss the key events that form the story's main idea. Write each event on chart paper. Provide each student with three copies of the key pattern on page 169. Tell her to select three events listed on the chart. Have the student describe and illustrate one of the selected events on each key pattern. Then have her punch a hole in each key and thread them on a yarn key ring. Display the projects on a bulletin board titled "The Keys To Our Story."

Event 1
Judy and Peter find a mysterious game by a tree.

Event 2
They play the game and strange things begin to happen.

Event 3
Judy and Peter return...

Four-Star Stories

Capitalize on students' independent reading to reinforce the main idea. Have each student select a story he has read independently. Instruct the student to take on the role of a literary critic to review the story. On an index card, have each student list the title, author, and main idea of the story. Then ask the student to rate the book based on a four-star rating scale:

⭐ I can take it or leave it.

⭐⭐ It's good for a rainy day.

⭐⭐⭐ You have to read this one!

⭐⭐⭐⭐ It's one of the best books I've ever read!

Provide time for students to share their reviews with the class, or post the cards in your reading center for students to investigate.

Front-Page News

Challenge students to show their understanding of the main idea with a story that makes front-page news! Provide each student with a sheet of white construction paper. Instruct each student to create the front page of a newspaper based on information from the story they have read. Remind the student to include headlines for each article she writes about, as well as captioned pictures. To extend the lesson, encourage students to include weather reports, sports articles, an advice column, advertisements, or want ads, depending on the content of the story.

The Storybook Post

10¢

SNOWSTORM DELAYS The Jolly Postman

This bicycle is no match for the snowstorm last night! The Jolly Postman waits for it to clear up while sipping tea.

Weather Report
Snow continues to fall...see page 2 for details.

INTERESTING INFERENCES

Use everyday situations to help students infer how story characters might react to a situation or resolve a problem. After reading a book together, discuss how the characters responded to certain events in the story. Then have students use what they know about the characters to decide how each character might react to the situations listed below. Have each student select two or three situations and write paragraphs telling how the character might respond.

What would the character do...

⭐ if he found a lost dog on the highway?

⭐ if his best friend ignored him on the playground?

⭐ if while playing a game he saw another player cheating?

⭐ for fun on a rainy day?

⭐ if he forgot his mother's birthday?

⭐ if he found a wallet full of money?

⭐ if he left his homework on the bus?

⭐ to show he was sorry for something he had done?

Character Cards

Most students have sent or received a greeting card in the mail. Discuss with your students the different types of greeting cards that can be purchased, and if possible, show them several examples. Then have each student infer which type of greeting card would be appropriate to send to a character in a story he has read. Distribute a sheet of white construction paper to each student and instruct him to fold it in half. Ask him to decorate the front with an illustration and a relevant message such as "Get Well," "Happy Birthday," "Congratulations," or "Thank You." On the inside of the card, have the student compose a poem or catchy phrase. Provide time for students to share the completed cards with their classmates.

for Miss Nelson, *Miss Nelson Is Missing* by James Marshall

Bon Voyage!

Have students use their inferencing skills to send a story character on vacation! Ask each student to select a character from a story you have read together or from his independent reading. Remind him to consider the likes and dislikes of the character in determining the vacation spot. Have each student write a paragraph explaining his choice of destination, then jot down an itinerary for the character. Distribute a sheet of drawing paper to each student and instruct him to sketch a suitcase shape. Tell him to fill the suitcase with drawings or magazine cutouts showing items that the character would pack. Finally, have each student draw several snapshots of the character enjoying the vacation. Then set aside a special time for each student to present his vacation package to the class.

SEQUENCED STORY CARDS

Have students sharpen their sequencing skills as they record important events from a story. After reading a story together, place students in groups of two or three. Instruct each group to write and illustrate a sentence detailing an event from the story on a 5" x 8" notecard. Call on each group to share its completed card with the class. After the sentence has been read, have the group place its card on the chalk rail in random order. When each group has shared its work, ask the class to help you arrange the cards in the order that they occurred in the story. Compile the sequenced cards into a booklet that summarizes the story.

Time Travel

How do the time and place of a story affect its events? Have students evaluate the relationship between the setting of the story and the cause-and-effect situations. Select a story to read as a class. After students identify several of the cause-and-effect situations, ask them to select a different setting for the story. Discuss how the new place and time period would alter the events in the story. Then have each student write a new version of the story, using the time period and location of his choice.

Character Swap

Imagine the story of "Little Red Riding Hood" with Winnie-The-Pooh in place of the wolf! Show students that characters can have big effects on a story line. Have students brainstorm a list of familiar stories and characters while you record their responses on the board. Have each student select a story and swap one of its characters with one from another story. Challenge each student to rewrite the story with the change in characters. Notice how the character swap affects the outcome of the original story!

FLIPPING OVER CAUSE AND EFFECT

Students will flip over this activity that provides cause-and-effect practice. Select a story that the class has read together and write four events from the story on the board. Pair students and distribute four sets of the cause-and-effect patterns on page 170 to each pair. Instruct each team to think of a cause-and-effect situation for each event listed on the board. Have the partners write the information in the appropriate spaces on the pattern, then cut out each shape. Fold each shape in half and place a dot of glue on the back of each section. Press the right half of the cause section to the left half of the matching effect section. Then glue each unattached end to a sheet of construction paper as shown. Provide time for students to share their completed projects with the class, having the audience predict the effect before the partners flip the paper to show the answer.

Old Slewfoot killed Pa's last hope for a new heifer.

Old Slewfoot killed Pa's last hope for a new heifer.

Pa spent Christmas hunting and slaying Old Slewfoot.

Comic-Strip Sequencing

Turn to the funny papers for a lesson in sequencing. Cut out several comic strips from the newspaper. White-out the words in the speech bubbles and make a class supply of photocopies. Have students use the pictures of the comic strip as clues in determining the sequence of events. Then have students fill in the speech bubbles with text that shows a sequenced idea.

Special Effects

Have students determine how an unexpected event would affect a story. Gather a class set of index cards. Program each card with a different situation that would affect a story—such as a tornado, a flood, or an eclipse. Select a story the class has read together. Have each student randomly select a card and write a paragraph explaining what effect the event would have on the story line. If desired, have each student illustrate the cause-and-effect situation he described.

Summarized Stories

Your students will enjoy creating a shortened version of a chapter book as they practice summarization skills. Select a chapter book that the students have read together. Create a group for every chapter in the book and place an equal number of students in each group. Instruct each group to reread the designated chapter and write a paragraph summarizing its important events. Challenge students to summarize the chapter in five sentences or less, using the word *and* no more than twice. Tell the group to also create an illustration for the chapter. Compile the resulting pages into a book and ask a student volunteer to design a cover. Arrange for the groups to take turns sharing the book with a younger grade or with other classes who have read the book.

The Boxcar Children

summarized by Grade 3

Fact-And-Opinion Debate

Instigate a class debate to reinforce fact-and-opinion skills. Begin the activity by pairing each student with a partner. Instruct each pair to scan a book the class has read and write down three facts and three opinions from the story. When all partners are ready, collect the fact-and-opinion sheets. Read statements from the papers at random. Have the class respond to each statement by giving the thumbs-up sign for each fact and the thumbs-down sign for each opinion. If the class is split on its decision, have students debate the issue. Allow each student volunteer 20 seconds to defend his answer; then have students give a revised thumbs-up or -down sign before you confirm the correct answer.

Fact Standoff

Use a student-generated supply of statements for an activity in recognizing facts and opinions. After the class has read a story or chapter together, have each student write one fact or opinion about the story on a slip of paper. Collect the papers and place them in a container. Draw out one paper at a time and read the statement to the class. If the statement is a fact, each student stands up by her desk. If it is an opinion, the students sits down. Continue until all the statements have been read aloud.

Show Us The Facts (And Opinions)!

Incorporate a fact-and-opinion lesson with a favorite student event—show-and-tell! As each student takes a turn showing an object to the class, he must tell three facts and one opinion about the item. Ask student volunteers to identify which statement was an opinion. Extend the activity by having classmates offer facts and opinions about each item.

It's from Japan. It's handmade. It's pretty. My dad gave it to me.

Opinions In Advertising

Show your students how persuasive opinions can be. Cut out a collection of advertisements from newspapers and magazines. Place students into small groups and distribute several ads to each group. Instruct students to look at the wording of each advertisement and make note of statements that offer opinions instead of factual information. Point out to students that the pictures in the ads can also convey an attitude or opinion about the product. After students have had time to make observations, provide time for each group to discuss its findings with the class.

Oh-So-White

Buy Oh-So-White

The toothpaste for the big, bright smiles!

Prereading Predictions

Develop vocabulary and story sense as students predict story outcomes. Before reading a selection with your class, create a list of important vocabulary words from the story. Include people, places, events, objects, and descriptions that are important to the story. Display the list and have students use the words as clues to predict possible characters, plots, and settings. Record students' predictions; then read the story together. Afterwards refer to the predictions and compare them to the actual characters and events in the story. Conclude the lesson by having students write a summary paragraph using vocabulary from the list.

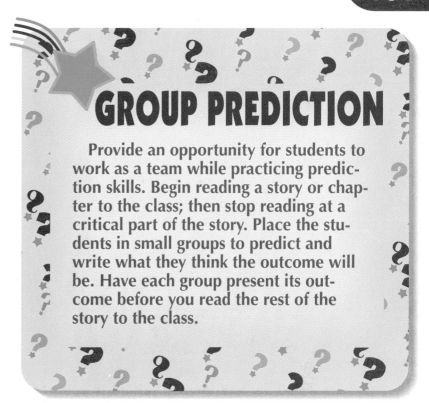

GROUP PREDICTION

Provide an opportunity for students to work as a team while practicing prediction skills. Begin reading a story or chapter to the class; then stop reading at a critical part of the story. Place the students in small groups to predict and write what they think the outcome will be. Have each group present its outcome before you read the rest of the story to the class.

Mystery Item

Put students' predicting skills to the test with a round of mystery items. Ask each student to bring to school a household item placed inside a bag or box. Have students take turns coming to the front of the room with their items. Each student in turn relates five pieces of information about her item—such as what the item is used for, what room it came from, or what color it is. Her classmates offer predictions about the item inside the bag. After a designated number of guesses from the class, the student reveals the item. Students will not only practice making predictions, they will also have the opportunity to reinforce speaking skills.

This item comes in different sizes and colors. It makes your hair look nice.

Is it a hairbrush?

Capitalization Rules

The following items should always be capitalized:

- **the first word in a sentence**
  Examples: **T**he girl went to the store.
  When does the movie begin?
  Shut the door, please.

- **proper nouns**
  — holidays, weekdays, months, special days
  — cities, countries, states, counties
  — names, titles, initials
  — streets, boulevards, buildings, parks

- **the pronoun /**
  Example: Should I bring a sweater?

- **titles and initials**
  Examples: President Lincoln Mrs. Dunlap
  E. B. White Dr. Smith

- **the greeting and closing of a friendly letter**
  Examples: Dear John,
  Your friend,
  Sincerely,

- **titles of books, magazines, newspapers, poems, plays, and songs**
  Examples: The Borrowers
  Ranger Rick®

- **abbreviations**
  Examples: M.D.   Ph.D.

- **acronyms**
  Examples: NAACP
  NASA   YMCA   NFL
  NBC   UN   NIMH

Punctuation Rules

1. **Use a period…**
   - **at the end of *declarative sentences* (statements) and *imperative sentences* (commands)**
     Examples: I like ice cream.
     Bring me a spoon.

   - **after each part of an abbreviation or a person's initials**
     Examples: Mr. Pierson
     C. A. Weaver

2. **Use a question mark at the end of interrogative sentences (questions).**
   Example: Where is the office?

3. **Use an exclamation point to express strong feeling or emotion.**
   Examples: Stop that!
   Watch out!

4. **Use quotation marks...**
   - **to show a direct quote**
     Example: Chris said, "I am going to play golf tomorrow."

   - **to show titles of poems, plays, stories, or songs**
     Examples: "Annie"
     "Row, Row, Row Your Boat"

5. **Use an apostrophe…**
   - **to show omission of letters in contractions**
     Examples: can't
     shouldn't
     didn't

   - **to show possession**
     Example: Crystal's purse is on the table.

6. **Use a comma...**
   - **to separate items in a date or an address**
     Examples: February 17, 1960
     Tampa, Florida

   - **after a greeting or closing of a letter**
     Examples: Dear Mike,
     Sincerely,

   - **to separate words in a series**
     Example: He found rocks, shells, and feathers.

   - **with nouns of direct address**
     Example: Robert, where are you going?

7. **Underline the titles** of books, plays, magazines, movies, television shows, and visual works of art.

Plurals

- The plural of most nouns is formed by adding *s*.
  apple—apples
  cat—cats

- Nouns ending with *ch, sh, s, x,* or *z* are made plural by adding *es* to the singular noun.
  bench—benches
  dish—dishes
  glass—glasses
  fox—foxes
  buzz—buzzes

- Most nouns ending with *o* preceded with a vowel are made plural by adding *s*.
  zoo—zoos
  stereo—stereos

- Most nouns ending with *o* preceded with a consonant are made plural by adding *es*.
  hero—heroes

- Most nouns that end with a consonant followed by *y* are made plural by changing the *y* to *i* and adding *es*.
  fly—flies

- Most nouns that end with a vowel followed by *y* are formed by adding *s*.
  key—keys

- Most nouns ending with *f* or *fe* are made plural by adding *s* if the sound of *f* is still heard in the plural.
  chief—chiefs

- If the *v* sound is heard in the plural, change the *f* to *v* and add *es* to form the plural.
  knife—knives
  wolf—wolves

Contractions

A contraction is a shortened form of a single word or word pair. An apostrophe is used to show where a letter or letters have been omitted to create the shortened form.

words with "am"

I am	I'm

words with "are"

they are	they're
we are	we're
you are	you're

words with "has"

he has	he's
it has	it's
she has	she's
what has	what's
where has	where's
who has	who's

words with "is"

he is	he's
it is	it's
she is	she's
that is	that's
there is	there's
what is	what's
where is	where's
who is	who's

words with "have"

I have	I've
they have	they've
you have	you've
we have	we've

words with "not"

are not	aren't
cannot	can't
could not	couldn't
did not	didn't
do not	don't
does not	doesn't
had not	hadn't
have not	haven't
has not	hasn't
is not	isn't
must not	mustn't
should not	shouldn't
was not	wasn't
were not	weren't
will not	won't
would not	wouldn't

words with "us"

let us	let's

words with "will"

he will	he'll
I will	I'll
she will	she'll
they will	they'll
we will	we'll
you will	you'll

words with "would"

he would	he'd
I would	I'd
she would	she'd
they would	they'd
who would	who'd
you would	you'd

Compound Words

afternoon
airline
airplane
anybody
anyone
anything
anyway
anywhere
armchair
arrowhead
artwork
ballpark
bareback
barnyard
baseball
basketball
bathrobe
bathroom
bathtub
bedroom
bedspread
bedtime
beehive
birdbath
birdhouse
birthday
blackboard
blacksmith
bluebird
boxcar
breakfast
broomstick
buckskin
butterball
buttercup
butterfly
campfire
campground
cannot
cardboard
catbird
catfish
cattail
chalkboard
clothespin
cobweb
copycat
cornbread

corncob
cornmeal
cowboy
cowgirl
cupboard
cupcake
daybreak
daydream
daylight
doghouse
dollhouse
doorbell
doorknob
doormat
doorway
doughnut
downhill
downstairs
downtown
driftwood
driveway
drugstore
drumstick
eardrum
earring
earthquake
eggplant
eggshell
evergreen
everybody
everyone
everything
everywhere
eyeball
eyebrow
eyelash
eyelid
farmland
fingernail
firecracker
fire fighter
firefly
fireman
fireplace
firewood
fireworks
fishbowl
fisherman

flagpole
flashlight
flowerpot
football
footprint
friendship
gentleman
gingerbread
goldfish
grandfather
grandmother
grapefruit
grasshopper
greenhouse
groundhog
hairbrush
haircut
halfway
handshake
headache
headband
headfirst
headlight
headline
headrest
headstand
headstrong
heatstroke
highchair
hillside
homemade
homework
hopscotch
horseback
horsefly
horseshoe
hourglass
houseboat
household
housewife
hubcap
indoor
inside
into
junkyard
keyboard
ladybug
landmark

landowner
lifetime
lighthouse
lookout
lunchroom
mailbox
mailman
mealtime
milkman
milkshake
moonbeam
moonlight
moonscape
motorboat
motorcycle
mousetrap
necklace
necktie
newspaper
nighttime
nightcap
nobody
notebook
nothing
outcome
outdoors
outhouse
outline
outside
overall
overcome
overlook
overtime
paintbrush
pancake
patchwork
peacock
peanut
pillowcase
pincushion
playground
pocketbook
policeman
popcorn
postman
quarterback
railroad
rainbow

raincoat
raindrop
rattlesnake
roadside
rowboat
runway
sailboat
salesman
sandpaper
scarecrow
schoolhouse
schoolyard
scrapbook
seahorse
seashell
seashore
seesaw
shipwreck
shoebox
sidewalk
skateboard
smokestack
snowball
snowflake
snowman
somebody
someday
someone
something
somewhere
spaceship
springtime
stagecoach
stairway
starfish
starlight
steamroller
stopwatch
storeroom
storybook
strawberry
suitcase
summertime
sunburn
Sunday
sundown
sunflower
sunlight

sunrise
sunset
sunshine
sweatband
sweatshirt
sweetheart
swordfish
tablecloth
tablespoon
taillight
teacup
teamwork
teapot
teaspoon
textbook
themselves
thumbtack
toadstool
toothache
toothbrush
treetop
underground
underline
understand
underwear
upright
wallpaper
warehouse
washcloth
watchman
waterfall
watermelon
weekend
whatever
wheelbarrow
whenever
whirlwind
whoever
wildlife
windmill
windshield
wintertime
within
without
woodland
worthwhile
yourself

Prefixes

Prefix	Meaning	Example
ante-	before, in front of	antechamber, anteroom
anti-	against	antifreeze, antislavery
bi-	two, twice	bicycle, biweekly
co-	together	coexist, copilot
counter-	against	counterattack, counterbalance
de-	opposite of, remove from, reduce	decode, dethrone
dis-	not, opposite of	disapprove, disbelief
en-	put on, cover or surround, make	endanger, enlighten
ex-	out of, former	exhale
fore-	in front of	foreground, forefront
hyper-	more than usual	hyperactive, hypersensitive
hypo-	under	hypodermic
im-, in-, ir-	not	impossible, inactive, irresponsible
inter-	together, between	intercontinental
mid-	middle	midway, midterm
mis-	wrong, bad	misjudge, mispronounce, mistreat
mono-	one, single	monotone, monorail
non-	not	nonfiction, nonrefundable
out-	greater, better, outer place	outdo, outlive, outside
over-	beyond, too much	overact, overeat
post-	after	postmodern, postwar
pre-	before, in front of	predawn, preschool
re-	again, back	review, recall, return
sub-	under, part of a whole	subway, substandard
tele-	far away	telephone, teleport
trans-	move from one place to another, across, change	transport, transatlantic, transform
tri-	three	triangle, tricycle
un-	not, opposite of, lack of	untrue, unpack, uneasy

Suffixes

Suffix	Meaning	Example
-able, -ible	able to, capable of	eraseable, reproducible
-al	belonging to, process of action	musical, normal
-ance, -ence, -ancy, -ency	quality, act, or condition	emergency, assistance
-ant	to be in or perform a certain act	attendant, servant
-ar, -er	one who does something	beggar, waiter, driver
-ate	result or act of	refrigerate, ventilate
-dom	area ruled by, condition or state of being	kingdom, freedom
-er,-est	superlative adjective	sweeter, happiest
-ful	full of	joyful, plentiful
-fy	to form into or become	beautify, stupefy
-hood	state of being, membership in a group	childhood, neighborhood
-ic	like, pertaining to	classic, angelic
-ics	study of, act or practice of	athletics, gymnastics
-ion	act, process of	vacation, permission
-ish	nationality, having likeness to	Scottish, childish
-ive	having the quality of, tending to	permissive, instructive
-less	without	homeless, clueless
-let	smallness in size, worn on the body	leaflet, anklet
-like	similar to	lifelike, childlike
-ly	in a certain manner, like, occurring every	slowly, hurriedly, queenly, yearly
-ment	result of, action or process, state or condition	accomplishment, development, amazement
-ness	manner or state of being	happiness, closeness
-or	one who does something, state or act	actor, error
-ship	state of, office, or skill	friendship, internship, horsemanship
-tion, -sion	action, process, or condition	selection, confusion
-ty, -ity	state, quality, or amount	safety, quality
-ward	toward, in the direction of	homeward, westward
-wise	way, direction, in respect to	lengthwise, clockwise
-y, -ey	quality or state of, resembling, place or business, small	stormy, jealousy, bakery, bunny

Homophones

Homophones are words that sound alike but have different spellings and meanings.

ate—eight	do—dew	knead—need	pane—pain	steak—stake
be—bee	eye—I	knew—new—gnu	piece—peace	tail—tale
bear—bare	fair—fare	knight—night	plane—plain	tacks—tax
beet—beat	feat—feet	knot—not	pray—prey	there—their
blew—blue	flour—flower	know—no	principal—principle	through—threw
bored—board	forth—fourth	knows—nose	red—read	to—too—two
break—brake	fur—fir	loan—lone	road—rode	wait—weight
buy—by—bye	great—grate	made—maid	sale—sail	waste—waist
carrot—caret	groan—grown	male—mail	sea—see	wave—waive
cell—sell	hair—hare	meat—meet	sew—so	way—weigh
cents—scents—sense	haul—hall	none—nun	sight—site	week—weak
cereal—serial	hear—here	oh—owe	soar—sore	would—wood
course—coarse	him—hymn	one—won	some—sum	write—right
creak—creek	hole—whole	pail—pale	son—sun	
deer—dear	hour—our	pair—pear	stare—stair	

Synonyms

Synonyms are words that have similar meanings.

above—over	cry—weep	find—discover	intelligent—smart	shout—yell
afraid—scared	damage—destroy	fix—repair	jog—run	skinny—thin
alike—same	different—varied	friend—pal	jump—leap	small—tiny
angry—mad	dirty—filthy	funny—humorous	keep—save	soggy—wet
auto—car	drink—beverage	glad—happy	late—tardy	story—tale
begin—start	drowsy—sleepy	go—leave	look—see	stroll—walk
below—under	easy—simple	grin—smile	loud—noisy	surprised—startled
big—large	end—finish	hard—difficult	many—several	throw—toss
buy—purchase	enemy—foe	healthy—well	neat—tidy	
chilly—cold	false—untrue	home—house	odd—strange	
considerate—kind	fast—quick	hot—warm	rip—tear	
correct—right	fight—quarrel	incorrect—wrong	road—street	

Antonyms

Antonyms are words that have opposite meanings.

above—below	close—open	enemy—friend	hard—soft	poor—rich
add—subtract	cold—hot	false—true	healthy—sick	right—wrong
alike—different	come—go	fancy—plain	left—right	rough—smooth
asleep—awake	crooked—straight	fast—slow	loose—tight	save—spend
backward—forward	cry—laugh	fat—thin	lose—win	short—tall
bad—good	dangerous—safe	few—many	mean—nice	sour—sweet
beautiful—ugly	day—night	float—sink	narrow—wide	tame—wild
begin—finish	deep—shallow	forget—remember	noisy—quiet	terrible—wonderful
believe—doubt	destroy—repair	found—lost	old—new	whisper—yell
big—small	difficult—easy	frown—smile	over—under	
buy—sell	down—up	generous—selfish	play—work	
catch—throw	dry—wet	give—take	peace—war	
clean—dirty	early—late	happy—sad	polite—rude	

Pattern
Use with "Punctuation Signal" on page 149.

Patterns
Use with "Word Trains" on page 152.

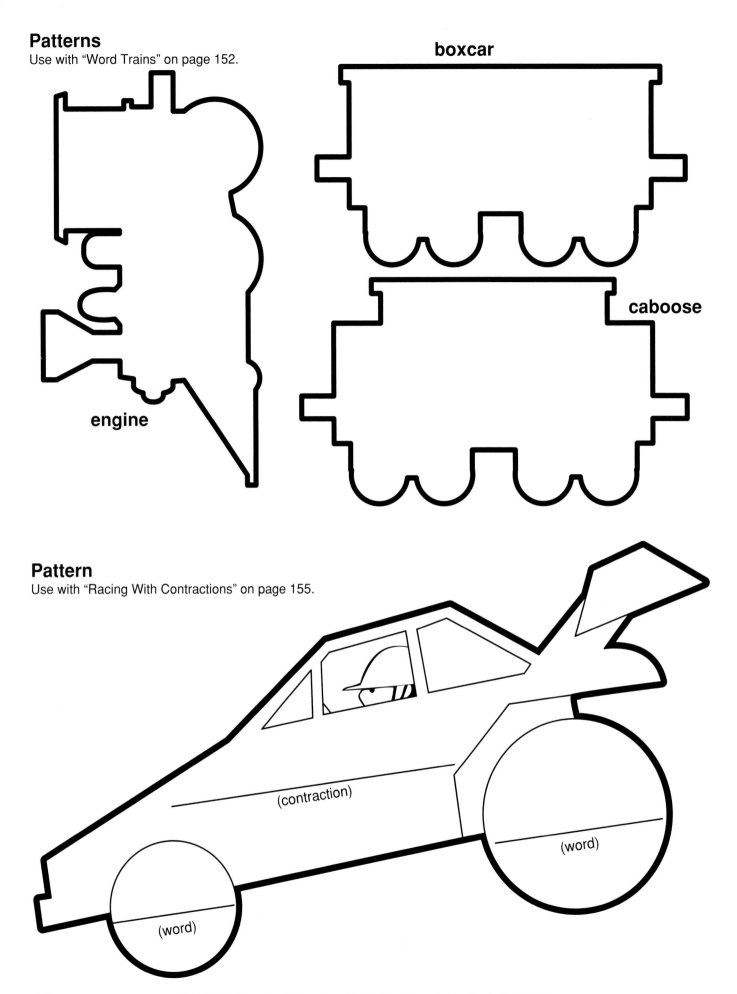

boxcar

caboose

engine

Pattern
Use with "Racing With Contractions" on page 155.

(contraction)

(word)

(word)

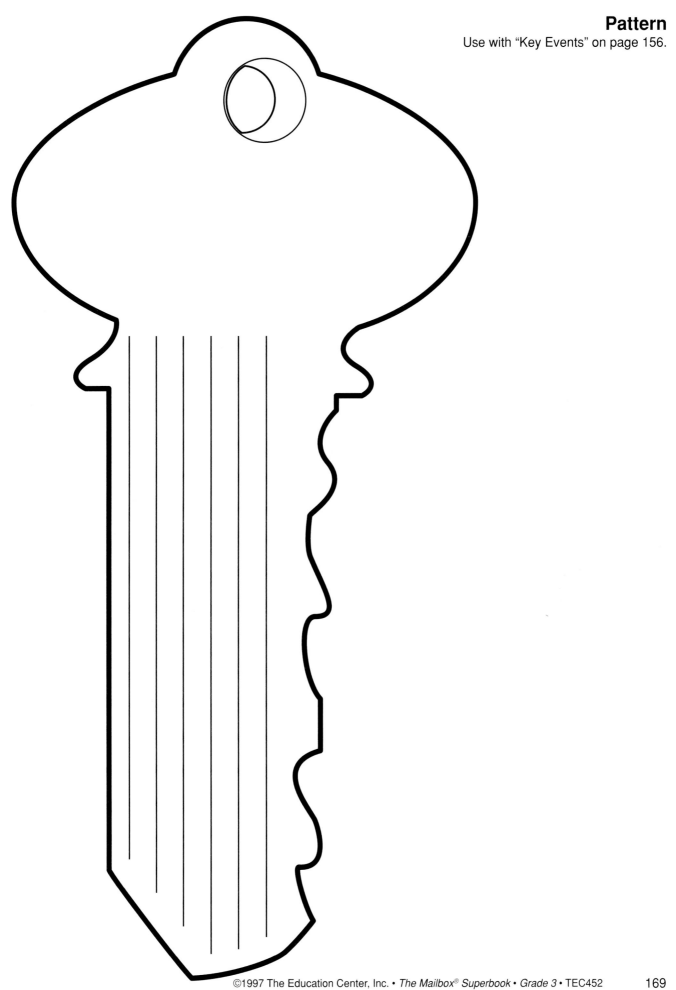

Patterns

Use with "Flipping Over Cause And Effect" on page 158.

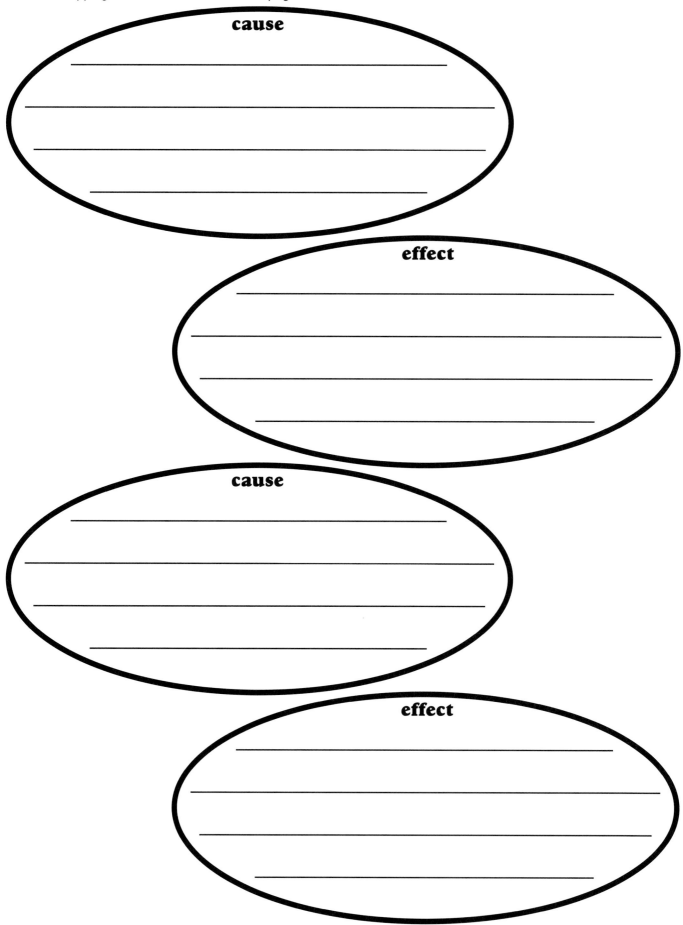

Writing

Writing Conferences

An important part of the writing experience is a conference between the young author and her teacher. Determine how many conferences you can comfortably schedule during your writing period each day. (Most conferences will last between five and ten minutes.) Then schedule a time to meet with each student during the week. If desired, schedule several "open" time slots for students who need to meet for additional help or revisions. The weekly conference schedule will ensure that you meet with each student on an individual basis, and will also provide more one-on-one time for students who need additional instruction.

Rough Draft
Guidelines

Prohibit the use of erasers on rough drafts! Instead, have students cross out unwanted portions of text with a single line or edit their text using the proofreading marks listed on page 183. This will prevent smudges and tears on the paper, and will allow each student to have a visual record of the progress on his written work. He may also want to refer to his original text to retrieve an idea or turn of phrase that would be lost with erasing. Additionally, the student learns that the rough draft is not intended to look like a finished piece of work, but rather a work in progress.

Selecting A Topic

Students occasionally have difficulty deciding on a topic for a story or paragraph. The following methods make choosing a topic easy and fun:

- **Go Fish**
  Program a supply of fish-shaped cutouts with topics or story starters. Place the cutouts in a fish bowl. A student can "fish" for an idea by selecting a cutout from the bowl.

- **Story Spinner**
  Number a spinner as shown, and post a list of topics to correspond with the numbers. A student spins to determine a topic for her story. Post a new topic list periodically to supply students with fresh ideas.

Topics
1. Lost in the woods
2. Shipwrecked
3. Found $1,000
4. Plan a
5. Late
6. Stu
7. Ap
8. Fou

- **Think Thematic**
  At the beginning of a unit or theme-based study, have students brainstorm a list of related topics. Record the responses on chart paper. Keep the list on display for students to refer to when selecting a writing topic.

Ocean
squid
coral
whales
shark
beach
shells

- **Class-Created Topics**
  Keep a file box and a supply of index cards handy for students to jot down interesting topic ideas. After a student records an idea on an index card, have her file it alphabetically or by subject. Allow students to refer to the box when selecting a topic.

Topic Box

Tell about a trip to the grocery store with your mom.

Paragraph Modeling

Students often need a model or formula to help them organize their thoughts into paragraph form. Provide students with the following "recipe" for writing a descriptive paragraph:

Descriptive Paragraph Recipe
1 topic sentence that includes important information about the subject
2 sentences that describe the way the subject looks, sounds, smells, tastes, or feels
2 sentences that tell what the subject does or how it is used
1 sentence that tells your opinion about the subject

yield: one well-written paragraph

Main Idea Map

Use a semantic map and critical-thinking skills to reinforce the concept of the main idea of a paragraph. Announce a topic the class has been studying and have students brainstorm ideas relating to the topic. Record the responses on the chalkboard. When a list has been generated, ask students to find ideas that belong together. Have students think of category titles for the ideas and write the titles as subgroups around the main topic (see example). Inform students that each subgroup title represents a main idea about the topic. Have students help you reorganize the list to determine which items belong in each subgroup. Explain that these items represent supporting details for each main idea. To extend the lesson, assign a subgroup to each student, and have him write a paragraph using the map as a reference. Then compile the completed paragraphs into a class book about the topic of study.

Inviting Writing Centers

Entice students to use writing centers during their free time by making them student-friendly. When a writing center is visually appealing to the students, they will be motivated to participate in the activities. Try the following ideas for setting up writing centers in your classroom:

- Use creative containers—such as sand pails, cookie jars, and jewelry boxes—to hold story starters. Write each story starter on a die-cut shape that matches the theme of the container.

- Have a special brainstorming box that includes task cards. Challenge students to list ten flavors of ice cream, several ways to be a good friend, or different things to do with a cardboard tube.

- Place a class journal in the center. Encourage students to write about a designated weekly topic, such as "Your Favorite Vacation" or "Which animal makes the best pet?"

- Provide a supply of writing paper in a variety of colors or with seasonal borders for students to use as they put their writing skills to work.

OUR CLASS JOURNAL

Young Authors Station

Set up a Young Authors Station with all the materials students need to complete a story from start to finish. Provide lined newsprint for rough drafts, pencils, pens, markers, good quality paper (both lined and unlined) for final copies of text and illustrations, manila folders, and a stapler. Remind students to leave a wide left margin on the final copies so that the binding will not interfere with the text. When a student completes a story, she staples it into a manila-folder cover. She decorates the cover with the title, author's name, and an illustration. For a finishing touch, she composes a paragraph titled "About The Author" for the back cover of her book.

Primary Books

Encourage students to produce their best efforts with a writing assignment designed to be shared with younger audiences. Have your students produce texts such as ABC booklets, counting books, or simple stories. For an extended project, the students could compose question-and-answer booklets. Have a younger class provide questions such as "How do fish breathe underwater?' or "Why does it lightning?" Then your students can use research skills to find the answers to these questions for their booklets.

Why does it lightning?

How do fish breathe underwater?

Say It With Synonyms

Said
declared
stated
yelled
shouted
demanded
whispered
announced
exclaimed

Encourage students to avoid the overuse of words such as big, good, said, and went. Post a list of synonyms for words commonly used in your students' writings. (See the reference on page 184.)

Remind students to refer to the list when they make word choices in their compositions and stories.

Research Writing

This ongoing center will produce a class collection of reference books. Post a desired topic in the center and supply appropriate reference materials. Instruct each student to visit the center and use the materials to write a paragraph relating to the topic. After each child proofreads and edits his work, have him copy the paragraph in his best handwriting and add an illustration to the page. Have students help you organize the completed pages and create a table of contents. Compile the pages into a class reference book. Some curriculum-related topics for the center include:

- the life cycle of different animals
- ways to conserve natural resources
- planet information
- weather conditions and storms
- types of insects
- first-aid procedures for home and school
- types of habitats
- goods and services in the community
- types of careers
- gifts to make for family and friends
- holidays and celebrations
- ocean life

WINTERGREEN CHILLER GUM

FOOD FOR THOUGHT

Make journal writing a special occasion by giving students a treat to reinforce the topic. While gum chewing is usually not allowed at school, let students chew on a piece of sugarless gum while they write about the sticky subject. Instruct students to write a descriptive paragraph about gum, list different ways to use chewing gum, or give directions for blowing a bubble. Set aside one day a week to give your students a treat as a springboard for creative-writing ideas. There's no telling what LifeSavers®, a pretzel stick, or an apple slice might inspire!

Personal Journals

Keep the lines of communication open between you and your students with journal writing. Ask each student to acquire a special notebook to use as his personal journal. Provide time near the end of each day for students to reflect on the school day and jot down a few sentences. Students may also write about any special news, problems, or questions they would like you to address. If a student would like for you to read and respond to his entry, he leaves his journal out on his desk. You are able to establish a private sharing time while reinforcing students' writing skills.

Travel Logs

Provide students with special journals to record information about class field trips. Give each student a sheet of colored construction paper to fold in half. This will serve as the cover of his journal. After each class trip, write a few leading questions on the board to prompt students to write about the trip, or duplicate the "Field-Trip Travel Log" form on page 186. Remind students to include information about the date and time of each trip, the destination, the method of travel, and highlights of the event. Students may wish to add illustrations to their entries. Have each child store the completed papers inside the construction-paper covers. At the end of the year, the entries can be stapled inside the cover, making a nice keepsake of the school year.

FIELD-TRIP TRAVEL LOG

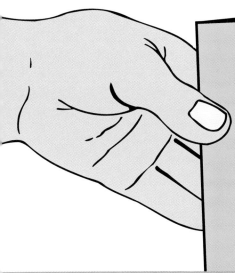

Journal Buddies

For a change-of-pace journal activity, pair students with a journal buddy for the week. After each student has completed a journal entry, have him trade journals with his journal buddy. On the following day, the buddies respond to the entries written the day before, then return the journals to the original owners. Repeat the routine for the remainder of the week. Challenge the buddies to learn at least three new things about each other during the course of their dialogue.

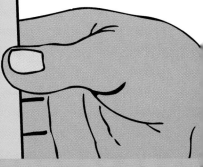

Special-Interest Journals

Revitalize the process of journal writing with special-interest journals. Allow each student to choose a subject or special interest, such as a sports figure, an animal, or a hobby. Each day, have students record information about the subjects in their journals. Encourage each child to write about the subject for a designated length of time, such as a two-week period, before switching to a new topic. This requires the student to investigate a topic with some thoroughness.

Terrific Travel Journals

The Terrific Travel Journal is a wonderful way to build students' writing skills while strengthening parent communication. Supply each student with a pocket folder with brads and several sheets of notebook paper. On a designated day of the week, each student writes a letter to her parents telling them about school happenings. The student places the completed letter in the folder's brads. Before the folder "travels" home, you can place special notes, memos, or handouts in the pockets. Encourage parents to write a note back to their child and place it (as well as any necessary correspondence to you) in the folder before the student brings it back to school. Then provide a time for student volunteers to share the messages their parents have written with the class.

Dear Mom and Dad,
We are studying the layers of the earth. We live on a layer called the crust, just like the crust on a piece of bread!

people

crust

not bread

Brown-Bag Descriptions

Students will put forth their best efforts for descriptive writing when there's a surprise in store! Place a small item—such as a pencil, puzzle, or bookmark—inside brown paper lunch sacks. Distribute a sack to every student. Instruct each student to peek at the item inside his bag. Challenge the student to write a description of the item without mentioning it by name. Provide time for each student to read his description to the class; then have him call on three classmates to try to identify the object. If the item is identified, the student who wrote the paragraph may keep the item as a reward for composing an accurate description.

Noteworthy News

Set the stage for a creative-writing assignment with a handful of headlines! Cut out a class supply of interesting headlines from a newspaper. (Or to save time, cut out several different headlines and make copies of each one to create one per student.) Place the headlines in a container. Pass the container around the room and have each student remove one headline. Instruct each student to write a story and draw an illustration to match his headline. Then have the student glue the headline, story, and picture to a sheet of construction paper. Display the completed projects on a bulletin board for students to enjoy.

City To Put Leash Law Into Effect

25th Annual County Fair Opens

Fire Damage Closes Mall

Grab-Bag Stories

Provide the elements for some very creative writing with a bagful of story ideas. Program a slip of paper for every student with the name or description of a different character. Place the slips of paper into a bag marked "Characters." Repeat the procedure to program slips of paper for settings and plots, making a separate bag for each one. Have each student draw one paper out of each bag. Each student must combine the three elements to create a story. Place the students in small groups to share their completed works.

The handsome prince

a tropical island

tries to run away from home

Mysterious Story Starters

Intrigue your students with the illustrations in *The Mysteries Of Harris Burdick* by Chris Van Allsburg (Houghton Mifflin Company, 1984). The book is actually a collection of mysterious pictures, captions, and titles. Show a picture to the class and read aloud the title and caption. Have each student write a story about the mysterious picture, incorporating the title and caption into the story line. Ask student volunteers to share their mysterious tales with their classmates.

The U.S. Capitol

32¢

Special Deliveries

Practice letter-writing skills while building positive attitudes and self-esteem. Review the parts of a friendly letter with your students. (A reference is provided on page 183.) Then write each student's name on an individual slip of paper. Place the names in a decorated container; then have each student select one. Instruct each student to write a letter to the classmate named on the paper. The letter should include positive remarks and encouraging statements directed to the student. Collect the completed letters; then present each letter to its recipient. If desired, repeat the activity throughout the year to promote a positive classroom environment.

Character Letters

Provide a link between reading and writing by instructing students to write from a literary character's point of view. Use a story that the class has been reading as a springboard for the assignment. Have each student write a letter as one of the characters in the story, using details from the story as a purpose for writing. The character Fern in *Charlotte's Web* could write a letter to her father convincing him to spare Wilbur's life. A student from The Magic School Bus series could write a letter to a friend describing one of her unusual field trips. Provide time for students to share their letters with their classmates, or bind the letters into a class booklet.

Thank-You Notes

Take advantage of special opportunities during the school year to have students practice writing thank-you notes. There will be occasions throughout the year when students are invited to see a play, attend a field trip, hear a guest speaker, or receive a gift. Set aside time after an event for each student to write a note expressing his appreciation. (If desired, use the thank-you-note patterns on page 187.) Students will keep their letter-writing skills sharp, as well as practice good etiquette.

Dear Mrs. Keeling,
Thank you for telling our class about your trip to Africa. I enjoyed hearing about the dancers.
Sincerely,
Lindsey

Writing Poetry

Writing poetry provides an opportunity for students to use creative expression and expand oral and written vocabulary. Most children think of poetry as a rhyming form of literature. Expand your students' awareness of the devices used in poetry by introducing the terminology found on page 185. Then have each student try her hand at writing several different types of poems with the following activities.

soft
furry
purr
climb
chase
jump
sleep

Kittens
by Lindsey
Kittens purr.
They have soft fur.
They chase their tails
And climb in pails.
They like to leap
And then they sleep.

Catalog Poems

Students begin writing a catalog poem with a brainstorming session. After selecting a topic, each student generates a list of words and phrases that relate to the topic. After the list is complete, the student arranges the items into a rhythmic pattern. Rhyming words are not essential, but can add to the fun and challenge.

Sunny days
Purple flowers
Rainbows galore
Insects buzzing
Nests in trees
Gardens blooming

Seasonal Acrostic Poems

Let the changing of the seasons inspire sensory words and images. At the beginning of a season, have each student write the name of the season on his paper vertically. Each letter in the word becomes the initial letter in a line of the poem.

Syllable Cinquains

Challenge students to think of poetry syllable by syllable. In a syllable cinquain, the student creates a five-line poem in which there are a certain number of syllables in each line. Model the format of a syllable cinquain as follows:

Line 1: Title
Line 2: Description of title   2 syllables
Line 3: Action about the title   4 syllables
Line 4: Feeling about the title   6 syllables
Line 5: Synonym for the title   8 syllables
                                       2 syllables

Tadpoles
Amphibians
From egg to fish to frog.
I like to watch them change
     their looks.
Froggies.

CONCRETE POEMS The leaf drifted down to the ground.

Even the most reluctant poets will find success with concrete poetry. In a concrete poem, the shape or design helps express the meaning or feeling of the poem. The words may define, describe, or analyze the subject. Provide unlined paper, stencils, and an assortment of writing instruments for students to use when composing a concrete poem.

Haiku

Introduce your students to haiku, a traditional Japanese form of poetry. These poems are very simple, but rich in imagery; students may wish to illustrate their completed works. The poem consists of three unrhyming lines with a syllable pattern as follows:

Line 1: 5 syllables
Line 2: 7 syllables
Line 3: 5 syllables

The tiny, gray bird
Sits quietly in the tree
As the daylight fades.

Diamante Poems

Students will have to use their knowledge of the parts of speech to write this seven-line, diamond-shaped poem. The student selects a topic, then completes the poem by relating the following information to the topic.

Line 1: topic (noun)
Line 2: two adjectives
Line 3: three action words
Line 4: a four-word phrase
Line 5: three action words
Line 6: two adjectives
Line 7: rename the topic

Football
Fast, exciting
Run, catch, throw
What a great game!
Tackle, block, kick
Rough, tough
Pigskin

Clerihew Verses

Once students become familiar with rhyming couplets, challenge them to write a clerihew. This four-lined verse consists of two couplets and tells about a person. The first line of the poem should end in the person's name.

My name is Matt Carter,
And I like to barter.
I'll trade you this pickle
For only a nickle.

Limericks

Tickle your students' funny bones with a look at limericks. These humorous poems contain five lines. The first, second, and fifth lines rhyme, as do lines three and four. Get your students started with the phrase "There once was a..."

There once was a stubborn old mule
Who refused to study in school.
He said he wouldn't need
To know how to read,
And now we pity the fool.

Delightful Descriptions

Spark creative writing by challenging students to use a variety of literary techniques to describe an object. After selecting a topic, each student must describe it by using a simile, an example of personification and hyperbole, and a metaphor. Extend the activity by having each student paint or draw a picture to accompany the description. Display the finished projects for students to enjoy.

Imagery Exercises

Provide students with the opportunity to practice writing with literary devices. Use the reproducible exercises on pages 188–190 to generate students' creativity with similes, metaphors, personification, and onomatopoeia. Have students store the completed reproducibles in their journals to refer to in other writing assignments.

TWINKLE TIME
TOOTHPASTE

TWINKLE TIME
TOOTHPASTE

Use Twinkle Time and your smile will be brighter than the sun!

Advertising With Hyperbole

Creativity will soar to new heights with the introduction of hyperbole. Explain to students that *hyperbole* is an extreme form of exaggeration. Then let students practice using the technique to write advertisements. Have each student select a product—real or invented—that he would like to advertise. Provide a sheet of drawing paper for the student to illustrate his product. The student also includes persuasive text to promote the product. Remind students that with hyperbole, the sky is the limit in describing the benefits of their products! After the advertisements are completed, provide time for students to share their handiwork with the class.

Personal Word Banks

Have each student compile personal word lists to refer to when working on a writing assignment. Instruct each student to designate several pages in her journal for word banks. Post a suggested list of word bank topics, such as emotion words, shape words, weather words, ways to move, ways to speak, and ways to describe time. Then provide time for students to brainstorm words for each category. Remind students to add to the lists whenever a new term comes to mind.

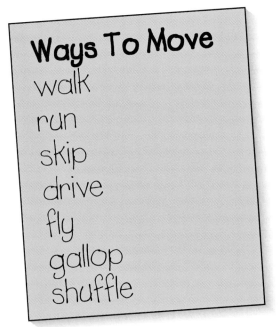

Ways To Move
walk
run
skip
drive
fly
gallop
shuffle

Proofreading Marks

Proofreading Marks

Instruction	Mark In Margin	Mark In Text	Corrected Text
delete	ℓ	the ~~bad~~ dog	the dog
make capital	cap	the dog	The dog
make lowercase	lc	the D̸og	the dog
spell out	sp	②dogs	two dogs
insert comma	⋀	dogs⋀dogs⋀dogs	dogs, dogs, dogs
insert period	⊙	See the dogs⊙	See the dogs.
start paragraph	¶	"Do you see the dog?"¶"I don't see it."	"Do you see the dog?" "I don't see it."

Parts Of A Friendly Letter

• The **heading** includes your address and the date. It is written in the upper right-hand corner.

• The **greeting** usually begins with the word *Dear* followed by the name of the person who will receive the letter. A comma is placed after the name. The greeting is written in the left-hand side, two lines below the heading.

• The **body** contains the message of the letter. It begins on the second line under the greeting.

• The **closing** brings an end to the letter. It belongs two lines below the body of the letter. Closings for a friendly letter often include words or phrases such as *Sincerely* and *Your friend*. Only the first word of the closing is capitalized. The closing is followed by a comma.

• The **signature** tells who the letter is from. It belongs under the closing.

Synonyms For Commonly Used Words

Bad—despicable, disagreeable, evil, harmful, horrible, nasty, rotten, spoiled, unpleasant, wicked, wrong

Beautiful—attractive, elegant, glorious, gorgeous, lovely, magnificent, pretty, splendid, stunning

Big—colossal, enormous, gigantic, great, huge, large, mammoth, tall, tremendous

Cold—chilly, cool, frosty, icy, wintry

Come—approach, arrive, reach

Funny—amusing, comical, humorous, silly

Get—collect, earn, fetch, find, gather

Good—excellent, fine, friendly, kind, marvelous, splendid, well-behaved, wonderful

Happy—cheerful, delighted, glad, joyful, pleased, satisfied

Interesting—challenging, entertaining, exciting, fascinating, intriguing, spellbinding

Like—appreciate, enjoy, relish, savor

Little—dinky, puny, shrimp, slight, small, tiny

Look—discover, examine, gaze, glance, glimpse, notice, observe, peek, see, spy, study, view, watch

Make—build, construct, create, design, develop, invent, produce

Run—dash, flee, hurry, race, rush, sprint

Say—advise, announce, command, declare, discuss, explain, instruct, mumble, mutter, notify, order, roar, sigh, speak, state, tell, vow, whine, whisper, yell

Scared—afraid, alarmed, disturbed, frightened, terrified, troubled, worried

Take—catch, choose, grasp, hold, select, steal

Think—believe, consider, judge

Unhappy—discouraged, gloomy, heartbroken, miserable, sad, sorrowful

General Glossary Of Writing Terminology

Acrostic Poem—a poem in which each letter of the title is used as the initial letter in a line of poetry

Alliteration—the repetition of a beginning consonant. (*Summer slips by silently.*)

Alphabet Poem—each line of the poem begins with a letter of the alphabet in sequential order

Cinquain—a five-line verse with a certain number of syllables or words for each line. A syllable cinquain has a syllable pattern of 2–4–6–8–2. A word cinquain has a word pattern of 1–2–3–4–1.

Clerihew—a four-lined verse about a person. The verse consists of two rhyming couplets; the first line of the first couplet ends with the person's name.

Concrete Poem—a poem in which the shape or design of the words helps convey meaning in the poem

Couplet—a two-lined verse that usually rhymes and expresses one thought

Dialogue—a conversation between two or more characters

Edit—to make changes to improve a work; to get ready for publication

Essay—a short, personal composition in which the writer states her views

Free Verse—poetry that does not include a specific rhyme or rhythm

Haiku—a three-lined Japanese poem about nature. The poem has a syllable pattern of 5–7–5.

Hyperbole—an extreme exaggeration. (*It was hot enough to melt the tires on my car.*)

Imagery—figures of speech or vivid descriptions to create a mental image

Limerick—a funny, five-lined verse. The rhyme pattern is usually AABBA.

Metaphor—a comparison without using *like* or *as*. (*She is a lovely rose.*)

Narrative—a short story or description

Onomatopoeia—when words sound like the action being described. (*The grease hissed in the skillet.*)

Personification—using human qualities to describe an object. (*Raindrops danced across the windowpane.*)

Plot—a series of events that make up a literary work

Prewrite—to get ready for writing by selecting a topic, collecting, or generating information about the topic, and planning what to include in the writing

Proofread—to carefully check a written work for errors

Quatrain—a four-lined stanza. Common rhyming patterns are AABB or ABAB.

Report—an account of facts and information

Revise—to make improvements to a rough draft

Rough Draft—a first-written form of a literary work

Simile—a comparison of two things using the words *like* or *as*. (*She is as lovely as a rose.*)

Tanka—a Japanese, five-lined verse. The poem has a syllable pattern of 5–7–5–7–7.

FIELD-TRIP TRAVEL LOG

Date Of Trip: _____

Place(s) Visited: _____

_____

Vocabulary And Trip-Related Words:

_____   _____

_____   _____

_____   _____

Something I Saw:

(student drawing)

A Summary Of The Trip: _____

_____

_____

_____

_____

_____

_____

_____

_____

_____

_____

_____

_____

_____

_____

_____

_____

_____

_____

About My Drawing: _____

_____

_____

_____

_____

©1997 The Education Center, Inc. • *The Mailbox® Superbook* • *Grade 3* • TEC452

Note To The Teacher: Use with "Travel Logs" on page 176.

©1997 The Education Center, Inc.

©1997 The Education Center, Inc.

Fast As Lightning

A *simile* compares two objects using the words *like* or *as*. Complete the following similes. Then keep this page as a reference to help you with other writing assignments.

Happy as _____

Mad as _____

Quiet as _____

Scared as _____

Tall as _____

Short as _____

Fat as _____

Thin as _____

Strong as _____

Slow as _____

Dark as _____

Bright as _____

The earth is like _____

The moon rose like _____

The rain fell like _____

The ocean is like _____

The wind blows like _____

The sun shines like _____

The candy tastes like _____

The boy ran like _____

The alarm sounded like _____

The snow looked like _____

The flower smelled like _____

The kitten felt like _____

A *metaphor* does not use *like* or *as*. Rewrite six of the above phrases as metaphors.

Example: The earth is a big, blue ball.

1. _____

2. _____

3. _____

4. _____

5. _____

6. _____

Name _____

 # Whispering Wind

Personification is a way to describe something as though it were human. List three human actions for each item. Then keep this page as a reference to help you with other writing assignments.

Example: **wind** <u>whisper, howl, race</u>

1. **rain** _____

2. **clouds** _____

3. **river** _____

4. **waterfall** _____

5. **shadow** _____

6. **tears** _____

7. **winter** _____

8. **sunlight** _____

Use personification to write a sentence for each item.

Example: The wind whispered through the tree branches.

1. **rain** _____

2. **clouds** _____

3. **river** _____

4. **waterfall** _____

5. **shadow** _____

6. **tears** _____

7. **winter** _____

8. **sunlight** _____

Note To The Teacher: Use with "Imagery Exercises" on page 182.

Buzz, *Hiss,* **And Squeak**

Some words imitate a sound. These words are examples of *onomatopoeia.* Use onomatopoeia to list some sounds these objects make. Then keep this page as a reference to help you with other writing assignments.

Example: **bell** <u>clang</u>

1. a balloon bursting _____
2. a rusty hinge _____
3. a horse walking _____
4. a firecracker _____
5. ocean waves _____
6. falling rain _____
7. a telephone _____
8. a candy wrapper _____
9. stepping in mud _____
10. a banjo string _____
11. a happy cat _____
12. a noisy dog _____

What other examples of onomatopoeia can you think of? List the words below.

_____   _____   _____

_____   _____   _____

_____   _____   _____

_____   _____   _____

LITERATURE

LITERATURE

Better Book Reports

Looking for a different way for students to present book reports? Story maps, story wheels, and story outlines serve their purposes, but sometimes a new twist can turn book reporting into an exciting activity. Listed below are several ways for students to have fun while reporting on literature.

Story Sandwiches

Here's a tasty way for students to make a literature presentation—a story sandwich! To complete the report, each student will need a copy of the following fixin's made from the patterns on page 206: two light-brown slices of bread, one green piece of lettuce, one yellow slice of cheese (punch with a few holes if desired), and a pink, tan, or brown slice of meat. Assemble each sandwich in the correct order (with one slice of bread at either end) and fasten the pieces together at the top of the sandwich with a brad. Then instruct each student to compose his book report using this format:

- **top slice of bread:** the title, author, and illustrator of the book
- **lettuce:** a list of characters
- **cheese:** a sentence about the setting of the story
- **meat:** a sentence about the plot of the story
- **bottom slice of bread:** the student's reaction to the story

Mr. Galloway,

Muggie Maggie by Beverly Cleary

Story Collage

Challenge students to formulate a book report by creating a collection of pictures, words, and objects about a story. Instruct each student to tell about the setting, characters, theme, and important events from the book in the form of a collage. Have the student cut out pictures from magazines, glue on small objects, and add his own original drawings to the collage. Have him print the title, author, and illustrator of the book on an index card and add it to the arrangement. Provide time for each student to share his collage with the class. The completed projects make an interesting assembly when mounted on a bulletin board or displayed in the hallway.

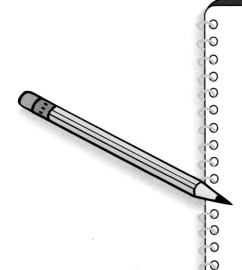

Character Journals

To help students understand the development of character, ask each student to pretend that he is the main character from a book. Have the student create three journal entries that the main character may have written during the course of the story. Remind students to select moments in the story that have important effects on the character. Then place students in small groups to share their entries and compare the events selected by each student.

Story Timelines

To help students gain an understanding of the story line, have them fashion a timeline showing the important events of a book. Give each student or group of students a length of butcher paper. Have students determine the overall structure of the book. Is it more logical to break it down into increments of time, or by story events? Did the story take place over the span of a year, or in a single day? Instruct students to determine the most appropriate way to outline the story, then mark chronological increments on the butcher paper. Label each increment with a sentence, a phrase, or an illustration of a story event and the time it took place. Have students compare the completed timelines to observe the similarities and differences in their classmates' interpretations.

Books That Make The Grade

Make literature-sharing a favorite classroom event as students create report cards for their independent reading selections. After a student has read a book, have her fill out a copy of the report-card form on page 205. Provide 10 to 15 minutes each day for a book-sharing time. Have student volunteers use the report-card forms as guides for telling about their books. At the end of each oral report, the student gives her book a grade and explains why it received that mark. Also instruct each student to write the grade inside the ribbon in the upper right-hand corner of her book report-card form. If time allows, have students in the audience ask questions about the book. Then post the report cards on a reading display or bulletin board titled "These Books Made The Grade!" Encourage students to peruse the display for independent-reading suggestions.

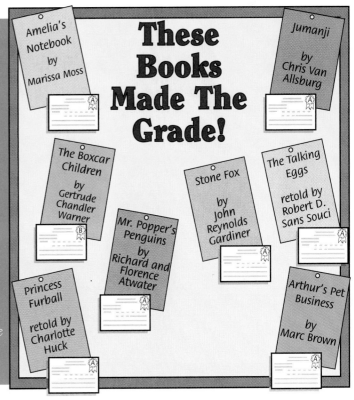

These Books Made The Grade!

- Amelia's Notebook by Marissa Moss
- Jumanji by Chris Van Allsburg
- The Boxcar Children by Gertrude Chandler Warner
- Stone Fox by John Reynolds Gardiner
- The Talking Eggs retold by Robert D. Sans Souci
- Mr. Popper's Penguins by Richard and Florence Atwater
- Princess Furball retold by Charlotte Huck
- Arthur's Pet Business by Marc Brown

Story Vests

Invite students to "wear" a book report by creating a story vest! Each student fashions a vest from a brown paper grocery sack as shown. Provide a supply of drawing paper, markers, construction paper, scissors, and glue. The student decorates the vest with the title and author of the book, pictures relevant to the story, important phrases, and character names. Provide time for a fashion show, where each student in turn displays her handiwork and explains the decorations on her vest. If desired create a display of the vests in a corner of the school library so that other classes can enjoy them as well.

Biography Book Reports

Students will enjoy sharing a biography book report by dressing for the part. Explain to each student that he will play the role of the subject in the biography he has read. Direct students to create a costume to help bring the subject to life. Costumes can be designed from paper bags, butcher paper, or articles of clothing from home. To present the report, the student wears the costume and answers questions from his classmates. Students can brainstorm a list of suitable questions prior to the presentation, or you can post a copy of the questions listed below.

▷ In what time period did you live?

▷ What important things happened in the early years of your life?

▷ What were your influences or inspirations?

▷ For what activities, events, or achievements are you best remembered?

▷ How did your work affect the world today?

▷ What accomplishments brought you the most pleasure and satisfaction?

▷ What three words would you use to describe yourself?

Puppet Presentations

Add a touch of dramatics to book sharing by having each student create a character puppet for the presentation. Supply your students with materials to create puppets from socks, tagboard and craft sticks, or paper bags. The student lets his puppet do the talking during the report, and details are presented from the character's point of view. Give students the option of making two puppets and presenting the report as a dialogue between the characters.

A Dozen Ways To Share A Book

Book reports and literature sharing can be accomplished in a variety of ways. Encourage students to try some of the activities listed below.

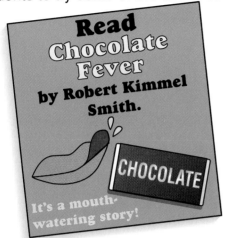

Read
Chocolate Fever
by Robert Kimmel Smith.

CHOCOLATE

It's a mouth-watering story!

○ Make a poster or an advertisement about a book. Use words and illustrations that will persuade others to read the book.

My cat Seal and I travelled a long way to meet Anna, Caleb, and their Papa.

○ Dress as a character from the book, and tell the class about an event from the story as if you really experienced it.

○ Invent a game that correlates with the plot of the book. Design a gameboard, write a list of instructions for playing the game, and add game pieces that relate to the story line.

○ Make a map showing the setting of the story. Include a legend or map key to identify places on the map.

○ Develop a crossword puzzle or word search with character names, setting descriptions, and important story vocabulary.

○ Construct a diorama showing an important scene from the book.

The Talking Eggs

○ Design a book jacket with an illustration that summarizes the story. Include a brief description of the plot on the inside of the jacket.

The Boggart is about a magical being trapped inside a boy's computer. The boy and his sister have a great adventure trying to get the boggart back to his homeland—a castle in Scotland.

○ Tape-record yourself reading aloud your favorite passage of the story.

○ Make a glossary with important words used in the story.

○ Find another book by the same author or a book with a similar subject and compare the two stories.

○ Write a poem, a song, or several riddles about the characters or events in the book.

○ Create a character mobile from a wire hanger, string, and construction paper.

Why Mosquitos Buzz In People's Ears

Literature Links

Incorporate a variety of reading skills into high-interest literature projects. Students may use books from their independent reading, or you may wish to assign a project to follow up a story the class has read together. The following activities will help you integrate basic skills with your choice of children's literature.

Chapter-Book Summaries

Create a class scrapbook with details from a chapter book. Purchase a blank scrapbook or construct one by securing newsprint pages between a poster-board cover. Assign each student or group of students a chapter from the book and designate a page in the scrapbook for each chapter. Instruct the student or group to brainstorm important details from the chapter, then select items to represent the details on the list. Allow students to draw pictures or find actual items to glue on the designated pages of the scrapbook. To complete the page, the student writes a few sentences summarizing the chapter. Provide time for each student (or group) to present his scrapbook page to the class.

Chapter One
Wilbur was the runt of the litter. Fern convinced her father to spare Wilbur's life.

I'll miss our cabin in the Big Woods.

Pa will build us a nice home on the prairie.

Story Sequels

Put an emphasis on making predictions with story sequels. Have each student select a story she has read. Instruct the student to write a paragraph explaining the circumstances in which the characters find themselves at the end of the book. Direct her to pick up from that point and write about what will happen next. Remind students to include several of the story characters in the sequel, as well as to describe any changes in the setting. Encourage the children to illustrate their sequels. If desired bind the stories for your classroom bookshelf so students can enjoy reading their classmates' creations.

Character Conversations

Encourage students to make character inferences by writing a dialogue between two story characters. Place students in pairs to represent two story characters; then challenge them to imagine what each character might say in a specific situation. What would Mary and Laura Ingalls discuss as they rode across the prairie in a covered wagon? How would Encyclopedia Brown confront a suspect in a case? Have students script the conversation, rehearse it, and then model the dialogue for the class. By the end of the assignment, the students will have reviewed several areas of the language-arts curriculum!

Story-Sequencing Chains

A story chain is a hands-on activity for reviewing sequencing skills. For this project students can use a story from their independent reading or a book they have read together as a class. Distribute a copy of the link patterns on page 207 to each student. Instruct the student to write a key event from the story on each link pattern. Then direct each student to cut out each link. To assemble the chain, have the student arrange the events in the correct order of occurrence. Then have him thread the end tab from each link through the opening in the adjacent link and glue it in place. While the glue is drying, give each student one large sheet of construction paper. Instruct the student to fold his paper in half and sketch a shape relevant to the story. Have him cut out the shape so that two are created. Instruct him to write the title of the book on the first cutout and the name of the author on the second cutout. Complete the project by gluing a cutout to each end of the chain. Hang the completed chains around the room for an eye-catching display.

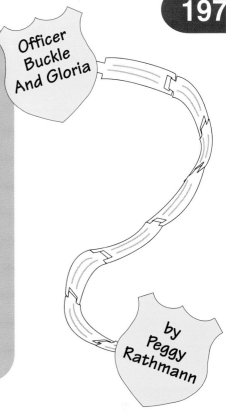

Officer Buckle And Gloria

by Peggy Rathmann

Story Islands

Set sail for a tropical island in a review of story elements. Have each student select a story to use in the activity. Supply the student with scissors, crayons, glue, a sheet of brown and blue construction paper, and a copy of the patterns on page 208. The student uses the materials to create a story island as she follows these directions:

1. Draw the shape of your island on the brown construction paper and cut it out.

2. Draw a border of waves from the blue construction paper and glue it to the bottom of the island.

3. Cut out the shell patterns. Fold each shell in half. Write the title of the book inside one pattern. Write the author of the book inside the second pattern. Color the outside of each shell and glue it to the island.

4. Cut out the palm-tree pieces. Write the name of a character on each leaf. Color the pieces and glue them to the island.

5. Cut out the hut pattern. Write the setting of the story on the roof of the hut. Then color it and glue it to the island.

6. Color and cut out the treasure-chest pattern. Cut the section of dotted lines by the lid. Apply to the back of the shape a thin trail of glue around the outside edge only. Attach the chest to the island.

7. Write the plot of the story on the treasure-map pattern. Fold the paper and slip it in the opening in the treasure chest's lid.

8. Color and cut out the monkey pattern. If you liked the story, draw a smile on the monkey's face. If you did not like the story, draw a frown. Glue the monkey to the island.

Prereading Strategies

Third-grade students take a big step in graduating from story books to chapter books, and the thought of taking on a larger book may intimidate some readers. Provide students with a prereading activity that will pique their interest in a new reading selection and make them feel more at ease with the book. Distribute a copy of the new book to each student and allow time for her to investigate it. Ask student volunteers to point out illustrations, chapter titles, character names, or other items that caught their attention. Then have students dictate a list of questions or predictions about the story while you record them on a list. Refer to the list during the reading of the book. Solicit comments about the predictions and ask for answers to the questions as they are presented in the story. Students will anticipate discovering new information as the story progresses and find that they enjoy reading chapter books!

Literature-Response Journals

Reinforce a variety of language-arts skills by culminating each story with small-group discussions and individual journal entries. With this routine each student will have the opportunity to rehearse responses to the questions prior to writing about them in his journal. As the class begins a new literature selection, post a list of questions that will apply to the story. Leave the list in view for students to refer to for the duration of the book. When the class has finished reading the book, provide time for students to silently reflect on the questions. Then place students into small groups to discuss the questions aloud. Complete the activity by having each student return to his desk and write about each question in his literature-response journal. If time allows, have student volunteers share journal passages with their classmates.

The following questions can be used with any story:

1. Did you like this story? Tell why or why not.

2. How did the story make you feel?

3. What was the most interesting part of the story?

4. If you could be one of the story characters, who would you be? Tell why.

5. Can you relate to any of the events or characters in the story?

6. What were some important words, phrases, or ideas from the story?

7. What will you remember most about this book?

Caldecott Award And Honor Books, 1993–1997

1997 Medal Winner: *Golem* written and illustrated by David Wisniewski (Houghton Mifflin Company, 1996)

Honor Books:

Hush! A Thai Lullaby written by Minfong Ho and illustrated by Holly Meade (Orchard Books, 1996)

The Graphic Alphabet written by David Pelletier (Orchard Books, 1996)

The Paperboy written and illustrated by Dav Pilkey (Orchard Books, 1996)

Starry Messenger written and illustrated by Peter Sis (Frances Foster Books, 1996)

1996 Medal Winner: *Officer Buckle And Gloria* written and illustrated by Peggy Rathmann (G. P. Putman's Sons, 1995)

Honor Books:

Alphabet City written and illustrated by Stephen T. Johnson (Viking Penguin, 1995)

Zin! Zin! Zin! A Violin written by Lloyd Moss and illustrated by Marjorie Priceman (Simon & Schuster Books For Young Readers, 1995)

The Faithful Friend written by Robert D. San Souci and illustrated by Brian Pinkney (Simon & Schuster Books For Young Readers, 1995)

Tops & Bottoms written and illustrated by Janet Stevens (Harcourt Brace & Company, 1995)

1995 Medal Winner: *Smoky Night* written by Eve Bunting and illustrated by David Diaz (Harcourt Brace & Company, 1994)

Honor Books:

John Henry written by Julius Lester and illustrated by Jerry Pinkney (Dial Books For Young Readers, 1994)

Swamp Angel written by Anne Isaacs and illustrated by Paul O. Zelinsky (Dutton Children's Books, 1994)

Time Flies written and illustrated by Eric Rohmann (Crown Books For Young Readers, 1994)

1994 Medal Winner: *Grandfather's Journey* written and illustrated by Allen Say (Houghton Mifflin Company, 1993)

Honor Books:

Peppe The Lamplighter written by Elisa Bartone and illustrated by Ted Lewin (Lothrop, Lee & Shepard Books; 1993)

In The Small, Small Pond written and illustrated by Denise Fleming (Henry Holt And Company, Inc.; 1993)

Raven: A Trickster Tale From The Pacific Northwest written and illustrated by Gerald McDermott (Harcourt Brace & Company, 1993)

Owen written and illustrated by Kevin Henkes (Greenwillow Books, 1993)

Yo! Yes? edited by Richard Jackson and illustrated by Chris Raschka (Orchard Books, 1993)

1993 Medal Winner: *Mirette On The High Wire* written and illustrated by Emily Arnold McCully (G. P. Putnam's Sons, 1992)

Honor Books:

The Stinky Cheese Man And Other Fairly Stupid Tales written by Jon Scieszka and illustrated by Lane Smith (Viking Children's Books, 1992)

Seven Blind Mice written and illustrated by Ed Young (Philomel Books, 1992)

Working Cotton written by Shirley Anne Williams and illustrated by Carole Byard (Harcourt Brace & Company, 1992)

Picture Books And Short Stories

Amelia's Notebook
by Marissa Moss
(Tricycle Press, 1995)

Take a peek inside Amelia's notebook for her insights on moving, friends, teachers, and older sisters.

Cloudy With A Chance Of Meatballs
by Judith Barrett
(Simon & Schuster Books For Young Readers, 1982)

Wacky weather conditions prevail as Grandpa tells a bedtime tale of strange occurrences in the town of Chewandswallow.

Doctor De Soto
by William Steig
(Farrar, Straus & Giroux, Inc.; 1982)

Although he is a mouse, Doctor De Soto is an excellent dentist—and a pretty clever one, too!

Family Pictures: Cuadros De Familia
by Carmen Lomas Garza
(Children's Book Press, 1993)

The childhood memories of a Hispanic artist are told through her illustrations and descriptive text.

Flat Stanley
by Jeff Brown
(HarperCollins Publishers, Inc; 1996)

Stanley wakes up to find that he has been flattened by a bulletin board, and his new shape causes some exciting adventures!

The Garden Of Abdul Gasazi
by Chris Van Allsburg
(Houghton Mifflin Company, 1979)

A lively dog leads a boy through a magician's garden and on the most amazing afternoon of his life!

I'm In Charge Of Celebrations
by Byrd Baylor
(Simon & Schuster Books For Young Readers, 1995)

Inspire students to celebrate the simple joys in life as they read about the author's lyrical account of her own special celebrations.

Lon Po Po: A Red Riding Hood Story From China
translated by Ed Young
(Philomel Books, 1989)

In this Chinese version of Little Red Riding Hood, three clever children outsmart a wolf with supper on his mind.

The Lost Lake
by Allen Say
(Houghton Mifflin Company, 1992)

A boy and his father develop important understandings about each other during their search for a special campsite.

The Magic School Bus® series
by Joanna Cole, illustrated by Bruce Degen
(Scholastic Inc.)

Hop on board the Magic School Bus with Mrs. Frizzle and her students for the ride of your life! From the center of the earth to the far reaches of the solar system, each book takes you on a fact-filled adventure.

Mufaro's Beautiful Daughters
written and illustrated by John Steptoe
(Morrow Junior Books, 1993)

This African Cinderella story follows the journey of two beautiful sisters who encounter unusual creatures as they travel to meet a prince.

My Rotten Redheaded Older Brother
written and illustrated by Patricia Polacco
(Simon & Schuster Books For Young Readers, 1994)

What do you do when you have an annoying older brother who always teases you? This younger sister finds out that having an older brother isn't always such a bad thing.

Nine-In-One Grr! Grr!
by Blia Xiong
(Children's Book Press, 1995)

A tiger travels to ask that her wish for many cubs be granted, but she encounters a tricky bird who changes the outcome of her wish.

The Patchwork Quilt
by Valerie Flournoy, illustrated by Jerry Pinkney
(Dial Books For Young Readers, 1985)

As a young girl and her grandmother piece together a quilt, they help the family remember some very special times.

Roxaboxen
by Alice McLerran, illustrated by Barbara Cooney
(Puffin Books, 1992)

Children find that an empty lot and a wealth of imagination are the perfect ingredients for hours of fun.

The Spinner's Gift
by Gail Radley, illustrated by Paige Miglio
(North-South Books Inc, 1994)

Follow the work of a spinner's thread as it becomes part of a royal gown, a servant's dress, a jeweler's curtains, and a dog's blanket—and then ends up back at the palace.

The Talking Eggs
by Robert D. San Souci, illustrated by Jerry Pinkney
(Dial Books For Young Readers, 1989)

In this magical tale, two sisters with opposite temperaments are faced with unusual tasks—and in the end, each sister gets just what she deserves!

Yeh Shen: A Cinderella Story From China
retold by Ai-Ling Louie, illustrated by Ed Young
(G. P. Putnam's Sons, 1990)

A magical fish helps a young girl win the attentions of a handsome prince in this Chinese fairy tale.

Chapter Books

The Adventures Of Ali Baba Bernstein
by Johanna Hurwitz
(William Morrow And Company, Inc.; 1985)

David Bernstein is tired of his ordinary name and his ordinary life. One day—when he is eight years, five months, and 17 days old—David decides that a new name might be just the thing to make his life more exciting.

Also by Johanna Hurwitz:
Aldo Ice Cream
Class Clown
Class President
The Hot And Cold Summer

Amber Brown Is Not A Crayon
by Paula Danziger
(G. P. Putman's Sons, 1994)

Amber and Justin have been best friends since preschool. They play together, help each other with homework, and even have a system for sharing Oreo® cookies. Now, as third graders, their friendship is tested when Justin's father takes a job in Alabama.

Also by Paula Danziger:
Amber Brown Wants Extra Credit
Everyone Else's Parents Said Yes
You Can't Eat Your Chicken Pox, Amber Brown

Cam Jansen series
by David A. Adler
(Puffin Books)

Cam Jansen is always hot on the trail of a mystery, whether it leads to stolen diamonds, gold coins, or dinosaur bones. In each book in this series, Cam uses her quick wit and photographic memory to connect the clues, solve the mystery, and save the day.

Hank The Cowdog series
by John R. Erickson
(Maverick Books)

Hank and his slow-witted sidekick Drover are the self-appointed Ranch Security team on a Texas spread. The two good-hearted hounds usually stir up more trouble than they keep at bay, but they'll capture the heart and funny bone of any third-grade animal lover.

How To Be Cool In The Third Grade
by Betsy Duffey
(Puffin Books, 1995)

Robbie has a plan for being cool in the third grade—he wants to wear jeans, he wants his mother to quit kissing him at the bus stop, and he wants to have a cool nickname. After the first day of school, Robbie adds one more thing to his list: he wants to keep away from the big bully in his class!

Also by Betsy Duffey:
A Boy In The Doghouse
Hey, New Kid!
The Math Whiz
Virtual Cody

The Hundred Dresses
by Eleanor Estes
(Harcourt Brace & Company, 1974)

Wanda is teased by her classmates because she is different. One day, much to the amusement of the other girls in her class, Wanda announces that she has a hundred dresses in her closet at home. It is only after she moves away that her classmates discover the special meaning behind the dresses.

The Hundred-Penny Box
by Sharon B. Mathis
(Puffin Books, 1986)

The strong relationship between a boy and his great aunt is explored in this story. The importance of family ties, especially with older family members, is shown in a heartwarming way.

Freckle Juice
by Judy Blume
(Simon & Schuster Books For Young Readers, 1984)

How do you get a faceful of freckles? By whipping up a batch of freckle juice! Students will enjoy this I'll-try-anything approach to changing your looks.

Also by Judy Blume:
Otherwise Known As Sheila The Great
The Pain And The Great One

Junie B. Jones series
by Barbara Park
(Random House Books For Young Readers)

The antics of kindergartner Junie B. Jones will delight third-grade readers who are venturing into their first chapter books. The simple, shorter chapters are full of playful language and fast-paced adventure that will have your students laughing out loud.

Little House chapter books
by Laura Ingalls Wilder
(HarperCollins Children's Books)

Selected chapters of the Little House books have been organized into a series of books with easy-to-read chapters featuring specific themes. *The Adventures Of Laura And Jack* contains heartwarming tales of the little girl and her dog, while *Pioneer Sisters* focuses on the special relationship between mannerly, older sister Mary and younger, spirited Laura. Third graders will love these and the other books in the series, just as previous generations have loved the original books.

Marvin Redpost series
by Louis Sachar
(Random House Books For Young Readers)

Third graders will easily identify with the many challenges Marvin faces at home and at school. Each book features real-life situations and a touch of humor—perfect for holding the reader's interest and making Marvin a favorite character of your students.

Mr. Popper's Penguins
by Richard and Florence Atwater
(Little, Brown And Company; 1992)

When Mr. Popper gets a surprise gift of a penguin, his life and house turn upside down! As more penguins arrive, Mr. Popper trains the birds to perform and takes the show on the road.

Mrs. Piggle-Wiggle
by Betty MacDonald
(HarperCollins Children's Books, 1985)

When children become cross, greedy, or forgetful, or refuse to take a bath, their parents turn to Mrs. Piggle-Wiggle. Her delightful cures for every childhood ailment will amuse readers as well as make them consider their own actions.

Also by Betty MacDonald:
Mrs. Piggle-Wiggle's Farm
Mrs. Piggle-Wiggle's Magic

Muggie Maggie
by Beverly Cleary
(Morrow Junior Books, 1990)

Maggie has always considered herself to be "gifted and talented," but when the third grade begins to write in cursive, Maggie refuses to try. In no time at all, she discovers that not only is she unable to write in cursive, she can't read it, either!

Also by Beverly Cleary:
Ramona The Pest
Ellen Tebbits
Emily's Runaway Imagination
Henry Huggins
The Mouse And The Motorcycle
Ribsy

Stone Fox
by John R. Gardiner
(HarperCollins Children's Books, 1983)

Based on a Rocky Mountain legend, this emotional tale of a determined boy and his faithful dog will hold students' interest from beginning to end.

The Stories Julian Tells
by Ann Cameron
(Alfred A. Knopf Books For Young Readers, 1989)

Julian's curiosity sometimes gets him into trouble, but his wild imagination always helps him think of a story for getting back out of it! Julian's stories will delight any reader who has tried to explain his way out of a sticky situation.

Also by Ann Cameron:
More Stories Julian Tells
Julian's Glorious Summer
Julian, Secret Agent

Read-Aloud Favorites

The Best School Year Ever
by Barbara Robinson
(HarperCollins Children's Books, 1994)
The Herdman family, best known for their antics in *The Best Christmas Pageant Ever,* is back and ready for a brand-new school year. Your students will love listening to the notorious adventures of this lovable bunch of misfits.

Bunnicula: A Rabbit Tale Of Mystery
by Deborah and James Howe
(Simon & Schuster Books For Young Readers, 1979)
The Monroe family finds a bunny at a movie theater and brings him home, much to the distress of the family cat, Chester. When Chester notices fang marks in the family's vegetables, he's certain that this bunny is really a vampire!

Caddie Woodlawn
by Carol Ryrie Brink
(Simon & Schuster Books For Young Readers, 1990)
Eleven-year-old Caddie loves being a tomboy on the Wisconsin frontier, but her mother insists that Caddie behave like a lady. With two adventurous brothers always ready for excitement, Caddie would rather run with the boys than stay home and learn to act ladylike.

Charlie And The Chocolate Factory
by Roald Dahl
(Puffin Books, 1988)
Charlie Bucket, who comes from the poorest family in town, finds a dollar on the street one day. He recklessly spends it on a chocolate bar and ends up with a winning ticket to the sweetest contest imaginable!

The Indian In The Cupboard
by Lynne Reid Banks
(Avon Books, 1995)
When Omri receives an old cupboard from his brother, he thinks that it will be a good place to store his special things. But the cupboard does more than just store them—it brings plastic toys to life!

Old Yeller
by Fred Gipson
(HarperCollins Children's Books, 1990)
In this highly emotional story, a stray yellow dog becomes a faithful friend to a frontier family. When the dog becomes exposed to rabies, the family is forced to make a very difficult decision.

Paddinton At Large
by Michael Bond
(Dell Publishing Company, Inc.; 1970)
What could be more outrageous than a small bear riding a runaway lawn mower through town? Just wait—the adventures are only beginning! The wild escapades of Paddington are sure to amuse third-grade listeners.

Sideways Stories From Wayside School
by Louis Sachar
(Random House Books For Young Readers, 1990)
It all started when Wayside School was built; instead of a one-story building with 30 classrooms, it became a 30-story building with one classroom on each floor. Stranger still are the teachers—and the students are not what you'd call an average group, either!

The Sign Of The Beaver
by Elizabeth George Speare
(Dell Publishing Company, Inc.; 1993)
Twelve-year-old Matt must survive on his own until his father returns to their cabin. When his father fails to return after many months, Matt must decide whether or not to move north with the Beaver tribe who has befriended him.

Stuart Little
by E. B. White
(HarperCollins Children's Books, 1974)
Stuart is the smallest member of his family; in fact, he's actually a mouse. But size does not prevent this determined rodent from embarking on new adventures as he sets off to see the world.

Book Report Card

By _____

Title _____

Author _____

This book is: funny   serious   realistic

                      fantasy   fiction   nonfiction

My favorite part of this book is _____

_____

_____

I give this book a grade of _____ because _____

_____

_____

©1997 The Education Center, Inc. • *The Mailbox® Superbook • Grade 3* • TEC452

Book Report Card

By _____

Title _____

Author _____

This book is: funny   serious   realistic

                      fantasy   fiction   nonfiction

My favorite part of this book is _____

_____

_____

I give this book a grade of _____ because _____

_____

_____

©1997 The Education Center, Inc. • *The Mailbox® Superbook • Grade 3* • TEC452

Patterns

Use with "Story Sandwiches" on page 192.

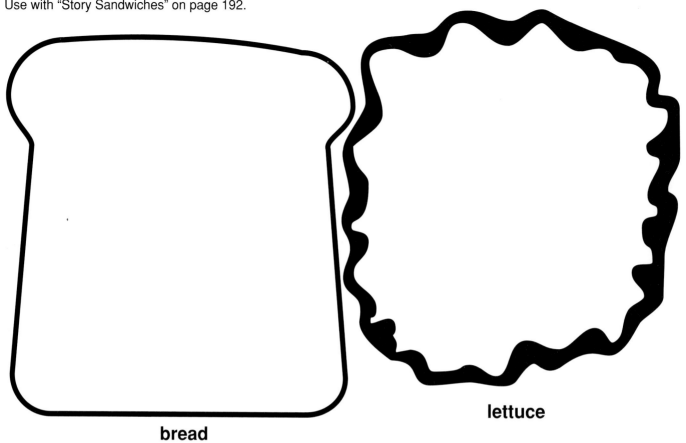

bread

lettuce

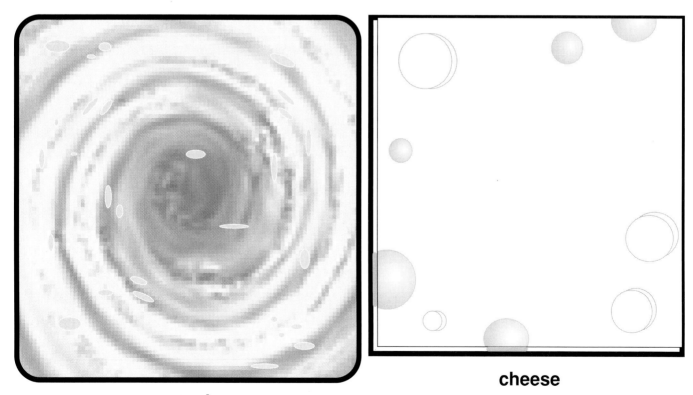

meat

cheese

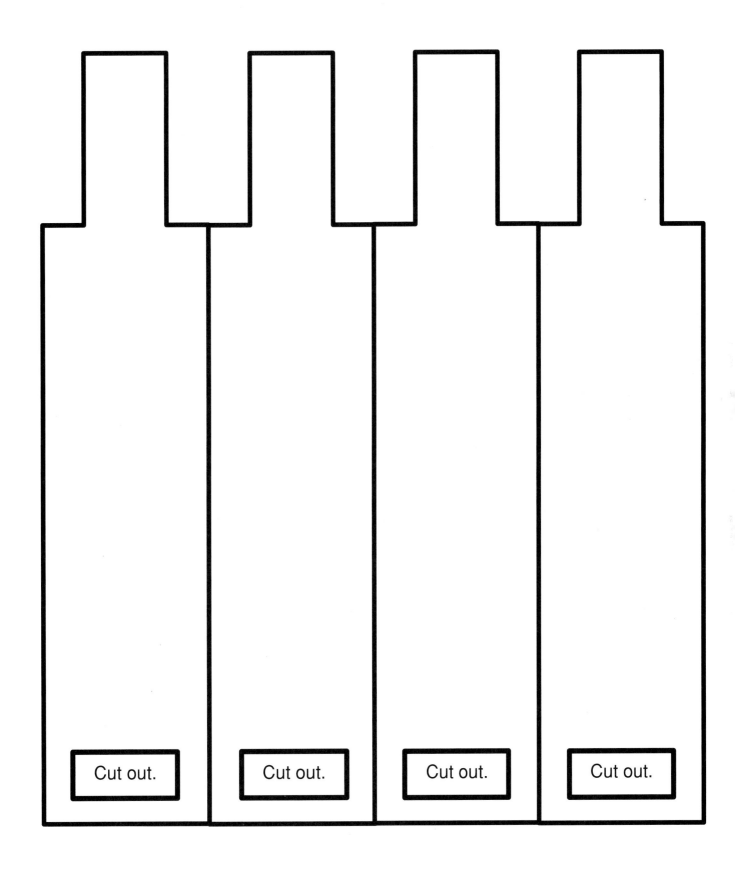

Cut out. Cut out. Cut out. Cut out.

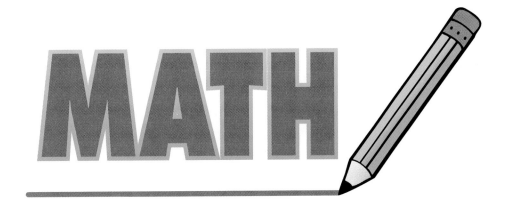

NUMBER CONCEPTS

Number Patterns

Use the hundreds chart on page 224 to encourage students to find patterns while reinforcing number concepts. Provide each student with a copy of the hundreds chart and a crayon. Announce a rule of the day for each student to follow in coloring the chart. Then have students discuss the resulting shape or pattern.

Some rules to coloring the chart are:

● Color all even numerals.

● Color all odd numerals.

● Color all numerals with a five in them.

● Color all prime numbers.

● Color all multiples of three (or four, five, etc.).

● Color all the palindromes (numerals with the same digit in each place—twins).

● Color all numerals that have first digits greater than their second digits.

● Color all numerals that have digits adding up to seven (or eight, nine, etc.).

Daily Math Drill

Incorporate an ongoing number-concept review as part of a daily routine. Cut apart the numerals from the hundreds chart on page 224 and place them in a cup. At the start of each math lesson, pull out six numerals from the cup. Have your students answer the following questions about each numeral:

1. Is the numeral *odd* or *even?*
2. Is the numeral *prime* or *composite?* If the number is composite, name at least two of its factors.
3. Is this numeral a *double* or a *triple?*
4. Is this numeral a *square* or a *cube?*

Then have the students determine which is the least/greatest numeral in the group and have them arrange the numerals from smallest to largest.

NUMBER-LINE REINFORCEMENT

A number line can help review and reinforce basic math concepts. Make an interactive number line on your classroom floor with a strip of masking tape. (Or, if weather permits, draw a number line in chalk on the sidewalk outdoors.) Mark the line in increments that correspond with the difficulty level to be reinforced. Then program a set of task cards with addition or subtraction problems. On the back of each card, draw a number line with a diagram that shows how the problem should be solved (see example). Have each student in turn take a task card and demonstrate how to solve the problem by stepping it through on the number line.

For an additional activity, have students practice skip counting on the number line. Use manipulatives to highlight the desired number pattern. Then have students take turns skipping from one numeral in the pattern to the next while saying the number words aloud.

1
2
3
4
5
6
7
8
9
10
11
12
13
14
$9 + 6 = 15$
15
16
17

On A Roll With Basic Facts

Reinforce addition and subtraction practice with this high-rolling, small-group activity. Place students in groups of three or four. Supply each group with a sheet of paper, a pencil, and a set of three dice. Each student takes a turn rolling the dice and adding the three numbers to the sum of his previous score. The first player to reach 200 points is the winner. The game then operates in reverse, with the players starting from a score of 200 points. When a player rolls the dice, he subtracts the sum of his dice from the previous turn's difference. The first player to reach zero is the winner.

COUPON COMPUTATION

Have students use manufacturers' cents-off coupons to practice computations with money. Collect a supply of coupons, or ask each student to bring several coupons from home. Instruct each student to glue several coupons to a sheet of paper. On the back of the paper, have him add to find the total value of the coupons. Then have each student trade his sheet of paper with another student's. Each student copies the amount of the coupons from the page onto a sheet of notebook paper. After adding the figures, the student checks his work by looking on the back of the coupon page. Repeat the procedure until each student has figured a desired amount of problems.

For practice in subtracting with money, use this variation with the activity. Have each student write a dollar amount on the top of a sheet of paper. The student glues a coupon to the paper, then writes a subtraction problem on the back of the paper using the two amounts. Students repeat the procedure of trading papers, writing and solving the subtraction problems, and checking their work.

MORE COMPUTATION IN STORE

Create a hands-on, real-life activity for computation practice by setting up a classroom store. Collect an assortment of empty cereal and cracker boxes, soda bottles, juice cans, and other clean containers. Mark each item with a price tag for the appropriate skill level. Then create cents-off coupons for several of the items on display.

Instruct student partners to visit the store. One student shops and selects a predetermined amount of items. The second student writes down each price and adds to find the total amount. If the shopper has any matching coupons, those amounts must be subtracted from the total. The partners check the final amount by using a calculator, then each student changes roles.

MULTIPLICATION MANIPULATIVES

Introduce multiplication facts with a special type of manipulative for each set of facts. Students will use the manipulatives to make a visual diagram to help them understand the concept of counting in groups.

When learning the multiplication facts of two, use carnival tick ets as manipulatives. Separate the tickets from a double roll, leaving each ticket pair connected together. Give each student ten sets of tickets. Call out appropriate fact problems and have diagram the problem with the tickets on his desktop, showing that groups of two are counted to arrive at the answer. Then have each student make a set of flash cards for the facts of two.

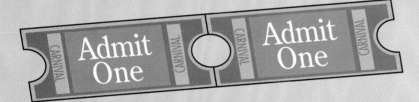

When learning the multiplication facts of three, distribute pattern-block triangles to each student. (Make sure each student has ten triangles.) Students will count the sides of each triangle to help them understand that the facts are solved using groups of three. After using the triangles to determine the facts of three, have each student make a set of flash cards for the facts.

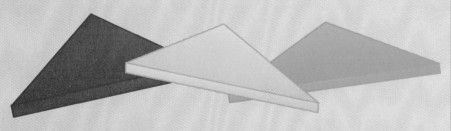

To help students learn the facts of four, distribute ten plastic forks with four tines apiece to each student. Students count the tines on each fork to make one group of four.

The facts of five can be introduced with disposable plastic gloves. The students count the fingers on each glove to make a group of five. After fives have been introduced manipulatives are optional, since students will have a good understanding of the concept of multiples.

Multiplication Readiness

Prior to having students learn their multiplication facts, initiate a daily skip-counting drill. For the first week, have students count by twos to 18 (which will review multiplication facts to nine). Start and end the counting with a different number each day to increase the students' understanding and awareness. The second week, begin skip counting by threes to 27. Advance to the next number every week until you reach skip counting by nines to 81. (Remember to keep reviewing the previous skip-counting patterns periodically.) By the time you introduce multiplication facts, students will already be familiar with the multiples of each number.

3, 6, 9, 12, 15, 18, 21, 24, 27

COUPON COMPUTATION

Encourage students to learn the multiplication facts by enticing them with an ice-cream sundae party. To earn each ingredient for her sundae, each student must learn a set of facts. Test for mastery of each set of facts with a timed test or with individual flash-card reviews. If a student shows mastery of the facts, reward her with a copy of the appropriate sundae pattern(s) on page 225. The patterns are distributed as follows:

As each piece of the pattern is earned, the student colors, cuts out, and glues the piece to her sundae dish. After a designated amount of time has been spent learning the facts, announce the date of the party. Ask parent volunteers to supply the ingredients. Each student uses her assembled paper sundae as a ticket to make a real sundae. What she puts on her sundae is determined by the patterns she earned to make her paper sundae. Your students will love the taste of success!

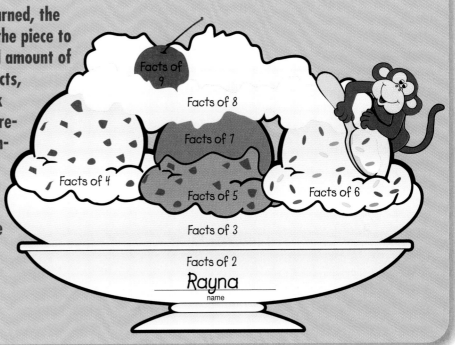

Divisibility Rules

Cash in on this activity for teaching your students some basic divisibility rules. Ask each student to bring in a cash-register receipt that lists about ten items. (If the receipt contains more than ten items, highlight ten of the numbers for use in this activity.) Have students check each amount on the receipt to see if it follows any of these divisibility rules:

- If the numeral ends in an even number or 0, it is divisible by 2.

- If the numeral ends in 0 or 5, it is divisible by 5.

- If the sum of the digits is divisible by 3, then the numeral is also divisible by 3. (For example, $4.38 is tested as follows: $4 + 3 + 8 = 15$. 15 is divisible by 3, so $4.38 is also divisible by 3.)

- If the numeral is divisible by both 2 and 3, it will also be divisible by 6.

- If the sum of the digits equals 9, then the numeral is divisible by 9. (For example, $2.43 is tested as follows: $2 + 4 + 3 = 9$, so $2.43 is divisible by 9.)

- If the numeral ends in 0, it is divisible by 10.

PLACE-VALUE

FREEZE FRAME

This quick-moving game will encourage students to focus on place-value recognition. Prepare for the activity by programming a class supply of 5" x 7" index cards, each with a numeral from zero to nine. Distribute one card to each student. Call on four volunteers to come to the front of the room with their cards. Give them five seconds to arrange themselves and freeze to make the largest numeral possible. Then give the rest of the students a chance to join in. Allow ten seconds for students to arrange themselves in groups of four to make a numeral larger (or smaller) than the one created by the volunteers. Remind students to pay close attention to the place value of each number before they freeze into position. Repeat the activity until each student has had an opportunity to be a volunteer.

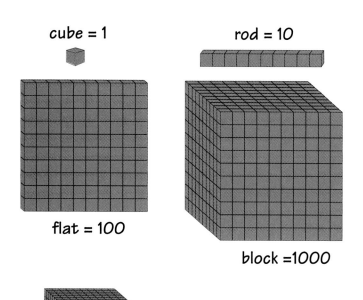

cube = 1

rod = 10

flat = 100

block = 1000

1,123

Place-Value Village

Make use of the base-ten blocks in your room with a place-value building project. By creating towns and buildings of specified numerical values, students will gain an awareness of the visual representations of numbers. If desired, review the value of cubes (1), rods (10), flats (100), and blocks (1,000) before explaining the project.

Place students in small groups. Distribute the base-ten blocks equally among the groups. Assign each group specific values for its village without the other groups knowing its specifications. For example, challenge one group to create a village worth 3,000 cubes and specify that each structure in the village should be worth 500 cubes or less. Challenge another group to build a village worth 3,150 cubes and specify that one building must be worth 900 cubes. Continue assigning specifications for each group. When the villages are complete, provide time for each group to observe the finished projects. Ask students to estimate how much each village is worth!

Place-Value Shuffle

Successful place-value practice is in the cards with this activity! Distribute ten index cards to each student. Instruct each student to program each of his cards with a different numeral from zero to nine. Also give each student a sheet of paper to fold into thirds. Have the student label the sections as *ones, tens,* and *hundreds.* To play the game, each student places his shuffled index cards facedown. As you say, "Flip," each student removes the top card from his stack and places it on a section of his paper. After the card is placed, it cannot be moved. After three cards have been flipped, determine who has made the largest numeral.

For variations on the game, try the following:

* Have each student play as described above, but try to make the lowest numeral possible with three cards.

* Write a numeral on the chalkboard. Have students play as directed above, trying to create a numeral as close to yours as possible.

* Pair students together to play the game as described above. Instruct partners to add their numerals together to try to make the highest or lowest score in the class.

* After students have placed their cards on the paper, announce a place value. The student with the highest (or lowest) numeral in that place earns a point. The first student to earn ten points wins the round.

* Add a fourth section to the paper to include the thousands place. Then play as described above.

PLACE-VALUE BINGO

Reinforce place value with specially designed bingo cards. Create a pattern for the bingo card by marking a sheet of paper into the desired amount of columns and squares (each column will represent a different place value). Distribute a copy of the card pattern to each student. Instruct the student to program each square with a numeral from zero to nine. To play the game, write a numeral on the board. If the student has a matching numeral written in the corresponding place-value column, he may cover it with a bingo chip. Continue playing until a student has a vertical, horizontal, or diagonal line of four covered spaces.

PLACE-VALUE BINGO

1000s thousands	100s hundreds	10s tens	1s ones
4	1	7	3
3	9	5	1
6	7	2	6
8	0	9	8

Measurement CELEBRATION

Designate an Estimation Celebration Day. Include activities throughout the day, such as estimating the number of steps it takes to cross the classroom, the length of a desktop, the height of five math books in a stack, the number of times a student can write her name in one minute, and the number of crackers in a package. Have each student make her estimate, record it on paper, and then find the actual measurement. Compare the estimates to the actual results.

ESTIMATION STATION

Reinforce estimation skills with this simple center idea. Place a box of paper clips and an assortment of items to be measured in the center. As a student visits the center, he writes down his estimation of each object's length in paper clips. Then he hooks the appropriate number of clips together to check his estimation. Each week change the objects to be measured, or replace the paper clips with another nonstandard unit of measurement.

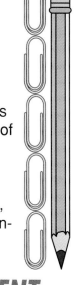

ARTISTIC MEASUREMENT

Make "Metric Masterpieces" using measurement directions for students to follow. Direct students to draw a house eight centimeters tall and six centimeters wide, a door three centimeters tall and two centimeters wide, and other details. Allow students to color their drawings; then have each student trade papers with a classmate to check the measurements.

MEASURING ME

Have each student make a poster titled "Measuring Me." Provide each student with a sheet of construction paper. Instruct the student to visually divide the poster into eight equal sections. Then have the student find the measurements of his hand, thumb, pinkie, index finger, foot, leg from knee to ankle, shoulder to shoulder, and arm from elbow to shoulder. Each student records a measurement in one section of his poster. If desired, have the students label and illustrate each section.

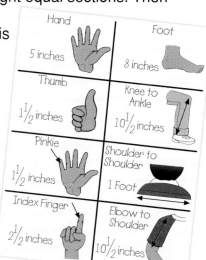

Hand	Foot
5 inches	8 inches
Thumb	Knee to Ankle
$1\frac{1}{2}$ inches	$10\frac{1}{2}$ inches
Pinkie	Shoulder to Shoulder
$1\frac{1}{2}$ inches	1 Foot
Index Finger	Elbow to Shoulder
$2\frac{1}{2}$ inches	$10\frac{1}{2}$ inches

Measurement TREAT

Enlist students' help in cooking up measurement practice. The following easy-to-make recipe requires that each ingredient be measured with a different measuring cup. Place students in groups of four and provide each group with the necessary ingredients and supplies. Have students work together measuring the ingredients to make the treat. Then enjoy the tasty results!

Popcorn Pizzazz

3 cups popped popcorn
3/4 cup dried fruit mix
1/2 cup peanuts

1/3 cup chocolate candies
1/4 cup butterscotch chips
1/8 cup sunflower seeds

* Measure each ingredient and pour it into a large bowl.
* Mix the ingredients together.
* Use a measuring cup to divide the mixture into equal portions.
* Eat and enjoy!

cup cup cup cup cup cup cup cup cup cup cup cup cup cup cup cup

pint pint pint pint pint pint pint pint

quart quart quart quart

half-gallon half-gallon

gallon

Liquid Measurement Equivalences

Use this handy reference chart to show students how liquid measurements compare. To make a chart, each student will need a copy of the patterns on page 226. Instruct each student to color the patterns as follows: gallon—orange, half-gallons—purple, quarts—green, pints—yellow, cups—blue. After coloring each piece, have the student cut out each shape and cut along the dotted lines indicated on the piece. Have each child stack the pieces as shown and staple at the top. Students can readily see the equivalences of each standard measurement by lifting a section of the chart. For example, by lifting a half-gallon section, the student will see that a half-gallon is equal to two quarts, four pints, or eight cups. This pattern can also be adapted to show equivalent fractions.

GRAPHING

Awesome Bar Graphs

 Provide students with graphing practice as they record the number of books that they read each month. Divide the class into four or five groups, and assign each group a color. Post a class-size bar graph programmed with the colors representing each group. When a student finishes reading a book, give him an adhesive dot in his group's color. Instruct him to attach it to the appropriate column on the graph. At the end of the month, compare the results. Then have each student write five questions about the data shown on the graph. Provide time for students to read their questions to the class and call on volunteers to answer.

 Provide each student with a snack-size can of fruit cocktail, a spoon, a paper plate, and a copy of the blank graph on page 227. Instruct each student to program the columns of the graph with the ingredients listed on the can. Have students open the cans and record the number of each type of fruit. As students compare the results, they can enjoy the treat!

Put an assortment of flavored bubble-gum pieces inside a bag and place the bag in front of the class for all to see. Provide each student with a copy of the blank graph on page 227; then instruct each student to program his graph with the different flavors represented in the bag. Invite students one at a time to take a piece of gum from the bag. Tell the class to record the flavor of each piece as it is selected. Then write several questions about the results on the board. Have students use their graphs to answer the questions.

"HOT" LINE GRAPHS

Keep track of your city's high temperatures for one week and use the data to have students construct line graphs. At the end of the week, distribute a copy of the graph on page 227 to each student. Instruct the student to number the left side of the graph paper by ten-degree increments, and to write the dates for the week on the diagonal lines at the bottom of the graph. Show students how to place a dot on the graph above each date to record the temperature.

Extend the activity by recording the high and the low temperatures for a week. Have each student use a different color to record each type of temperature on the graph.

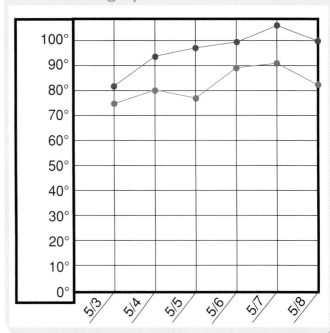

EYE-CATCHING CIRCLE GRAPHS

Introduce the concept of circle graphs with a group activity. Divide the class into groups of eight students. Distribute a copy of the circle graph on page 228 and a supply of crayons to each group. Inform students with like eye color to each color a connecting section of the circle graph with a crayon of the same color. Tell each group to complete the graph's key by placing a color dot for each color represented on the graph and writing the name of the eye color beside it. If desired, compile each group's data on a larger circle graph with a section for each student. Or use the data to show fractional percentages such as 3/8 of the group has blue eyes and 3/8 of the group has brown eyes, 1/8 of the group has green eyes...and 1/8 of the group has gray eyes.

Eye Color

Picture-Perfect Pictographs

Capitalize on student information to create pictographs. Have students choose something to inventory (for example, the pets they own, the numbers of pencils in their desks, or the names of their favorite sports). Distribute a copy of the picture graph on page 228 to each student. Decide on a picture or symbol to represent what was counted. Then assign a value for the picture or symbol (for example, each pencil represents ten objects or each animal picture represents two pets) and fill in the key accordingly. Show students how to program the graph with the necessary information; then have them record the results.

Bottle Graphs

This unusual approach to graphing will reinforce measurement skills. Select several identical empty bottles. Pose a question to the class, such as "What color hair do you have?" Label a bottle for each category mentioned. Have each student input his data by measuring a designated amount of water and pouring it into the correct bottle. After each child has added his data, have the class observe the water level in each bottle to determine which category has the most (and least) water.

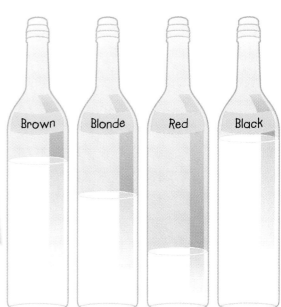

GEOMETRY

GEOMETRY JINGLE

Introduce the names of plane figures with a verse sung to the tune of "Frer Jacques." Include the hand motions to reinforce the properties of each shape.

Quadrilaterals, quadrilaterals,
(hold up four fingers as you say each word)

Triangles, triangles.
(hold up three fingers as you say each word)

Pentagons and hexagons.
(hold up five, then six fingers, respectively)

Pentagons and hexagons.
(repeat)

Polygons, polygons.
(make a closed shape that's not rounded with both hands)

SYMMETRICAL DRAWINGS

Students will demonstrate their understanding of symmetry with this drawing activity. Provide a supply of magazines for students to look through to find a picture of a symmetrical object (such as a face, a sandwich, or a couch). Instruct the student to cut the picture on its line of symmetry, then glue one of the halves to a sheet of drawing paper. Have the student finish the picture by drawing the missing half to create a symmetrical image.

✔ Alphabet Symmetry

Demonstrate the concept of *symmetry* with a set of alphabet stencils. Instruct each student to trace ten different letter stencils on a sheet of paper. Have the student cut out the letters and arrange them in a row on her desk. Ask the student to determine which letters can be cut in half to create two identical shapes. Explain to students that a figure is symmetrical if it has at least one *line of symmetry.* Further explain that a line of symmetry divides the figure into two *congruent parts,* or two parts that are the same size and shape. Tell the student to check her choices by drawing a line of symmetry on each selected letter, and then cutting it in half. If the pieces match up, the line of symmetry was correct.

EAT

Congruent Shapes

Reinforce the concept of *congruent figures* (equal in size and shape) with a set of attribute blocks and a supply of drawing paper. Distribute a sheet of paper to each student and instruct him to fold it to create four sections. The student selects four attribute blocks and traces one block in each section of his paper. After everyone has filled in all four sections, instruct students to compare papers. When a student finds a paper featuring a shape that is congruent to one on his own paper, he has the classmate sign that section of his paper. Remind students that both the shape *and* size of the drawings must match in order for them to be congruent.

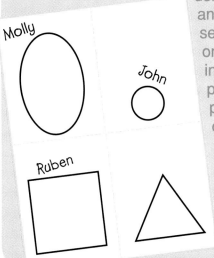

Molly

John

Ruben

SOLID-FIGURE MOBILES

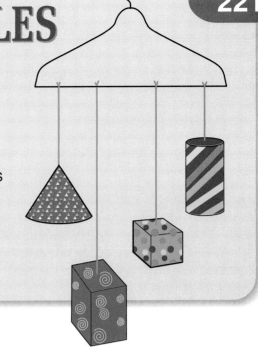

Familiarize students with solid figures by having them construct mobiles. Divide students into groups of four. Provide each group with an enlarged tagboard copy of each pattern on pages 229–230, scissors, glue, markers, thread, and a wire coat hanger. Direct each group to decorate the patterns before assembling them into solid figures. The group attaches a length of thread to each assembled figure, then ties it to a wire coat hanger. For added effect, instruct the group to bend the coat hanger into an interesting shape. Suspend the completed projects from the ceiling for a visual reference to solid shapes.

Area Activity

Students can use the shoebox lid from "Perimeter Project" to explore the concept of area. Provide each student with a supply of one-inch construction-paper squares. Instruct each student to cover as much of the inside of the shoebox lid as possible with the squares. Have him glue each square in place without overlapping or leaving blank spaces. When all squares have been glued in place, have each student measure the length and width of the covered area. Instruct the student to multiply the two numbers together to find the area. Then have each student count the number of squares in his lid. Students will discover that they can find the area by multiplying two numbers or by counting many squares—which way do they prefer?

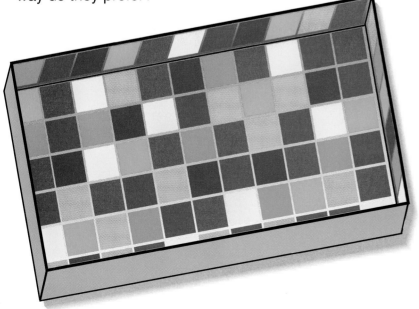

Solid-Figure Show-And-Tell

Present students with a homework challenge that reinforces solid geometric shapes. Ask each student to bring items from home that represent these solid shapes: a pyramid, a cone, a cylinder, a cube, a rectangular prism, and a sphere. Provide time the following day for students to share the objects they brought from home. After sharing the items, have each student place his objects on a table set up for display. Have students group all like figures together to emphasize the name and property of each figure.

☑ Perimeter Project

Initiate a hands-on perimeter lesson with this simple activity. Ask each student to bring a shoebox lid to class. Have her measure one short side (width) and one long side (length) of her lid. Instruct the student to round each number to the nearest inch (or centimeter). Then have her create a column of numbers, writing the width twice and length twice, and adding to find the perimeter. To check her work, the student measures a length of ribbon or lace to equal the perimeter. The student glues the ribbon around her shoebox lid to make sure her numbers added up.

FRACTIONS

Fruity Fraction Introductions

Introduce fractions in a way that will be meaningful to students. Write the fractions *1/2, 1/3,* and *1/6* on the board. Distribute a slip of paper to each student and have her write her name and what she considers the largest of the three fractions on her paper. Collect the papers and then cut pieces of fruit into halves, thirds, and sixths. Call out each name from the slips of paper and give each student the fractional amount written on her paper. Students will quickly recognize that one-half is the largest of the three fractions, especially if they received only one-sixth of a treat!

Lima Bean Manipulatives

Make an inexpensive set of fraction manipulatives with a bag of dried lima beans and a can of spray paint. Working outside, lay the beans in a single layer on a sheet of newspaper. Spray one side of the beans with a coat of spray paint; then allow them to dry. To use the manipulatives, hand each student four beans. Have the student shake the beans in his hand and drop them on his desk. Show each student how to write a fraction by recording the amount of colored sides facing up (the numerator) over the total number of beans (the denominator). Have the student repeat the activity ten times, recording the fractional amount each time. Repeat the activity as needed when introducing other denominators.

FUN FRACTION CARDS

Students can create a poster display to show their understanding of the fraction *one-half.* Supply each student with an index card and have him draw two items on it. Instruct the student to color one of the items and write the fraction *1/2* above the illustrations. Collect the cards and attach them to a piece of chart paper. Display the completed poster in the classroom. Repeat the activity as new fractions are introduced.

TERMINOLOGY TIP

Help students remember which part of the fraction is called the numerator and which is called the denominator. Point out that the **d**enominator is the number **d**own below, and the **n**umerator is the number up **n**orth!

Numerator (Up **N**orth)

Denominator (**D**own South)

Math-Related Literature

Addition:
One Green Island
By Charlotte Hard
Candlewick Press, 1995

Sea Sums
By Joy N. Hulme
Hyperion Books For Children, 1996

Calculator:
Calculator Riddles
By David A. Adler
Holiday House, Inc.; 1995

Division:
Divide And Ride
By Stuart J. Murphy
HarperCollins Children's Books, 1997

The Doorbell Rang
By Pat Hutchins
Greenwillow Books, 1986

Fractions:
Fraction Action
By Loreen Leedy
Holiday House, Inc.; 1994

Give Me Half!
By Stuart J. Murphy
HarperCollins Children's Books, 1996

Geometry:
Grandfather Tang's Story
By Ann Tompert
Crown Books For Young Readers, 1990

The Greedy Triangle
By Marilyn Burns
Scholastic Inc, 1995

Measurement:
Who Sank The Boat?
By Pamela Allen
The Putnam Publishing Group, 1990

Money:
Alexander, Who Used To Be Rich Last Sunday
By Judith Viorst
Simon & Schuster Children's Books, 1987

Pigs Will Be Pigs
By Amy Axelrod
Simon & Schuster Children's Books, 1994

Multiplication:
Each Orange Had Eight Slices: A Counting Book
By Paul Giganti, Jr.
Greenwillow Books, 1992

Sea Squares
By Joy N. Hulme
Hyperion Books For Children, 1993

Six-Dinner Sid
By Inga Moore
Simon & Schuster Children's Books, 1993

Too Many Kangaroo Things To Do!
By Stuart J. Murphy
HarperCollins Children's Books, 1996

Time:
Get Up And Go!
By Stuart J. Murphy
HarperCollins Children's Books, 1996

Nine O'Clock Lullaby
By Marilyn Singer
HarperCollins Children's Books, 1991

Pigs On A Blanket
By Amy Axelrod
Simon & Schuster Children's Books, 1996

Chart
Use with "Daily Math Drill" and "Number Patterns" on page 210.

1	2	3	4	5	6	7	8	9	10
11	12	13	14	15	16	17	18	19	20
21	22	23	24	25	26	27	28	29	30
31	32	33	34	35	36	37	38	39	40
41	42	43	44	45	46	47	48	49	50
51	52	53	54	55	56	57	58	59	60
61	62	63	64	65	66	67	68	69	70
71	72	73	74	75	76	77	78	79	80
81	82	83	84	85	86	87	88	89	90
91	92	93	94	95	96	97	98	99	100

topping

ice-cream
scoop

ice-cream
scoop

cherry

ice-cream scoop

whipped
cream

banana

bowl

name

Patterns

Use with "Liquid Measurement Equivalences" on page 217.

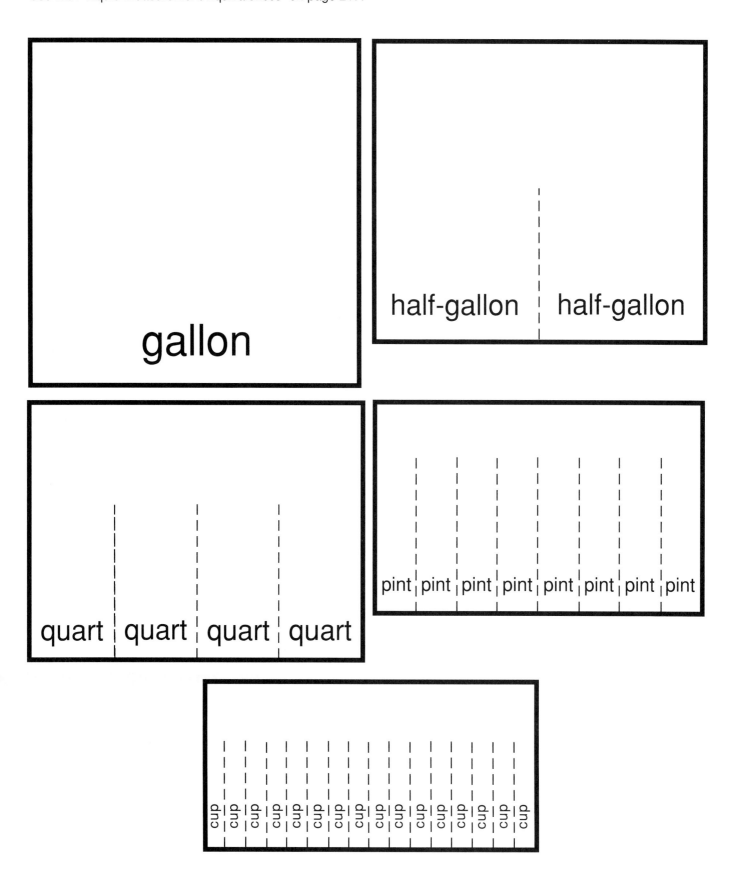

Graph

Use with "Awesome Bar Graphs" and " 'Hot' Line Graphs" on page 218.

Name _____ *Open: bar or line graph*

_____
(title of graph)

Graphs
circle graph
Use with "Eye-Catching Circle Graphs" on page 219.

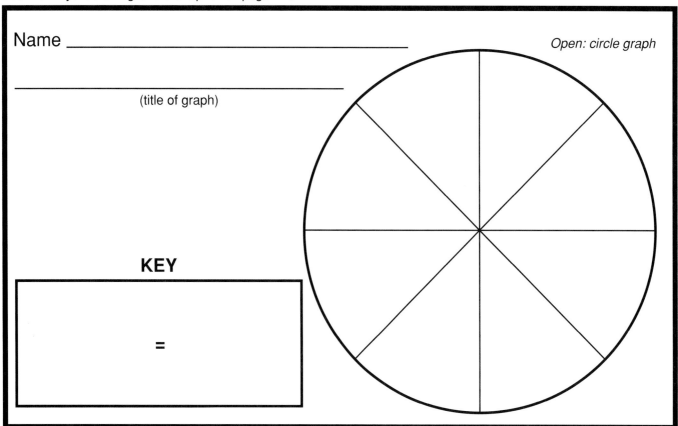

Name _____

Open: circle graph

_____
(title of graph)

KEY

=

picture graph
Use with "Picture-Perfect Pictographs" on page 219.

Name _____

Open: picture graph

_____
(title of graph)

KEY

=

Directions: Carefully cut along the solid lines. Then fold along the dotted lines. Tape together to form a cylinder.

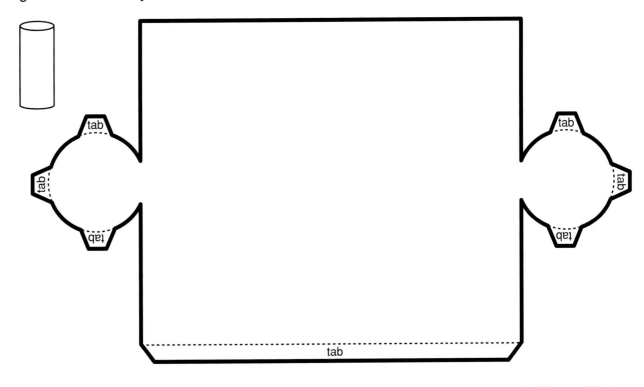

Directions: Carefully cut along the solid lines. Then fold along the dotted lines. Tape together to form a rectangular prism.

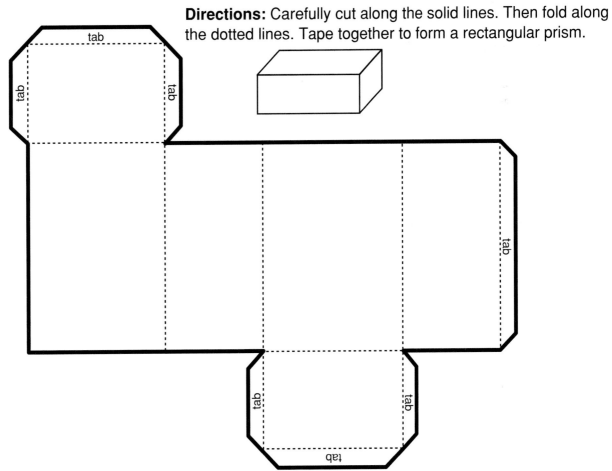

Patterns

Enlarge and use with "Solid-Figure Mobiles" on page 221.

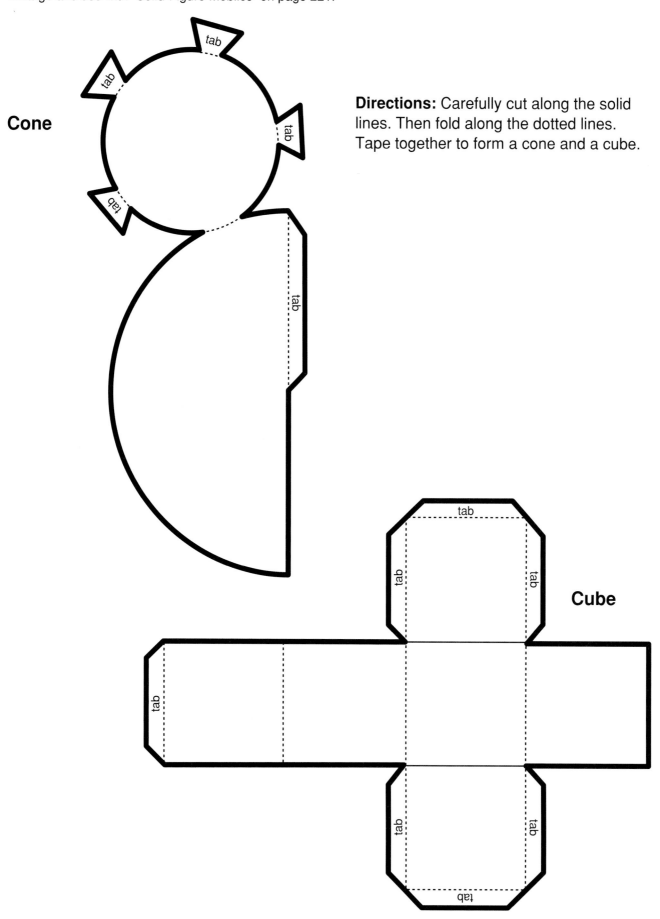

Cone

Directions: Carefully cut along the solid lines. Then fold along the dotted lines. Tape together to form a cone and a cube.

Cube

SOCIAL STUDIES

Hooray For The U.S.A.!

United States Symbols

Introduce the symbols of America by explaining to your students that every nation in the world has images which make people feel pride and respect for their country. The symbols for the United States convey that we are not only strong and brave, but also free and fair. Review the following symbols with your students; then divide the students into groups. Instruct each group to create a poster about one of the symbols listed below.

- **The American Flag**—Sometimes called the "Stars And Stripes." The 13 stripes represent the original 13 colonies, and each star represents a state. The color red stands for courage, the color blue represents justice, and the white stands for purity.

- **The Bald Eagle**—A symbol of strength and victory. The eagle on our dollar bill holds an olive branch to represent peace and arrows to represent strength.

- **The Liberty Bell**—A symbol of American Independence. The bell was first rung on July 8, 1776, to announce that the Declaration of Independence had been adopted.

- **The Statue Of Liberty**—A symbol of democracy. In 1884 the people of France gave the statue to the United States as a gesture of friendship. The statue represents the freedom of people coming to America from many lands.

- **The Washington Monument**—Built to honor George Washington, our first president. The monument is about 555 feet tall and has memorial stones set in its inner walls. People can ride an inside elevator to the top of the monument.

- **The Thomas Jefferson Memorial**—Built to honor Thomas Jefferson, the third president and author of the Declaration of Independence. A 19-foot bronze statue of Jefferson resides inside the monument.

- **The Lincoln Memorial**—Built to honor Abraham Lincoln, our 16th president. Inside the 189-foot-wide memorial is a marble statue of Lincoln sitting in a chair, and tablets showing the Gettysburg address.

Put It To A Vote

Familiarize students with the concept of *democracy*. Explain to your students that in a democracy, the nation is represented by the people who live in it. In the United States, the people help decide on issues by casting their votes. On Election Day, each voter reports to a polling station to cast his vote on a ballot.

The Greeks were the first known voters, holding an election about 2,500 years ago. They voted by dropping a certain colored ball into a pot. (The word ballot comes from the French word *ballotte,* meaning "little ball.") Discuss with your students other ways to vote, such as a show of hands, roll call, voice vote, and secret ballot. Have the class vote on several issues, using a different method of voting each time. Then have students vote on which method they like best!

Famous Places In America

One of the most famous of all American places, the White House, is located at 1600 Pennsylvania Avenue in Washington, D.C. The site for the nation's capitol was selected in 1789, and the city was named in honor of our first president. But it took so long to build the president's house that George Washington was no longer president by the time it was completed!

Have your students research other famous places in America. Post a list of selected places and ask each student to select one place to research. (See the list of suggestions below.) Provide each student with a copy of the report form on page 248 to record information about the famous place. Set aside time for each student to share her completed report with the class.

★ Mount Rushmore
★ Ellis Island
★ The Grand Canyon
★ Mount McKinley
★ Niagara Falls
★ The Everglades
★ The Smithsonian Institution
★ Yellowstone National Park
★ The Alamo
★ The Jamestown Settlement

Patriotic Literature

Arthur Meets The President
by Marc Brown
(Little, Brown And Company; 1991)

Kidding Around Washington, D.C.: A Young Person's Guide
by Anne Pedersen
(John Muir Publications, 1993)

Look Out, Washington, D.C.!
by Patricia Reilly Giff
(A Yearling Book, 1995)

Scholastic Encyclopedia Of The Presidents And Their Times
by David Rubel
(Scholastic Inc., 1994)

The Story Of The White House
by Kate Waters
(Scholastic Inc., 1991)

Wooden Teeth And Jelly Beans: The Tupperman Files
by Ray Nelson, Douglas Kelly, Ben Adams, and Mike McLane
(Beyond Words Publishing, Inc.; 1995)

The First Thirteen

Help your students become familiar with the original 13 colonies with this research project. Have each student work with a partner to create a bag of facts about one of the colonies. To create a bag, give each pair of students a supply of blank index cards and a paper lunch sack with the name of one of the original 13 states written on it. Each pair finds its state on the map and draws a picture of the state on the front of the bag. Then the pair researches the state's capital, tree, bird, motto, and date it became a state. Instruct the pair to write each piece of information on a separate card and store the cards inside the bag. Once all the cards have been completed, have the partners share their research with the class. Then challenge the pairs to display the bags in the order in which they became part of the union.

Native American Cultures

The First Americans

North America has been the homeland of many different groups of people, but the Native Americans were first to call it home. Many scientists believe that the first Native Americans traveled to North America from Asia by walking across the Bering Strait, a land bridge that was not yet covered by water. As herds of animals traveled across the land bridge in search of food, the Native Americans followed. As many years passed, cultures were formed and the people settled into four main areas of North America. Share the following information about each culture with your students; then have them complete the activity described for each regional group of Native Americans.

The Coastal Culture

The Coastal tribes were hunters, gatherers, and fishermen. They lived in the forest region between the Pacific Ocean and the Rocky Mountains. Supplies were plentiful, for the rivers were full of fish and seafood, and the cedar trees provided materials for housing, canoes, and bark clothing. From November to April, the Coastal people lived in longhouses. During the summer they constructed simple huts from cattails and cedar-bark mats. These homes could be easily transported as the people moved around gathering food for the colder months.

The Coastal culture recorded important events on cedar logs called *totem poles*. The poles were carved with animal symbols and painted with mixtures such as berries and crushed salmon eggs. A large totem pole could be over 60 feet tall and could take as long as three years to carve. Have your students make a totem pole for the classroom. Instruct each student to bring a clean, empty oatmeal carton or small box to school. Provide an assortment of construction paper and paints for each student to use to decorate her container. Then assemble the pole by stacking the containers and gluing them in place. Display the finished pole in a corner of your classroom during your study of Native Americans.

Books About The Coastal Culture

Brother Eagle, Sister Sky: A Message From Chief Seattle
illustrated by Susan Jeffers
(Dial Books For Young Readers, 1991)

Coyote And The Fire Stick: A Northwest Coast Indian Legend
retold by Barbara D. Goldin
(Harcourt Brace And Company, 1995)

Old Meshikee And The Shagizenz: An Ojibwe Story
retold by Michael Spooner and Lolita Taylor
(Henry Holt And Company, 1995)

Raven: A Trickster Tale From The Pacific Northwest
by Gerald McDermott
(Harcourt Brace And Company, 1993)

Totem Pole
by Diane Hoyt-Goldsmith
(Holiday House, Inc.; 1990)

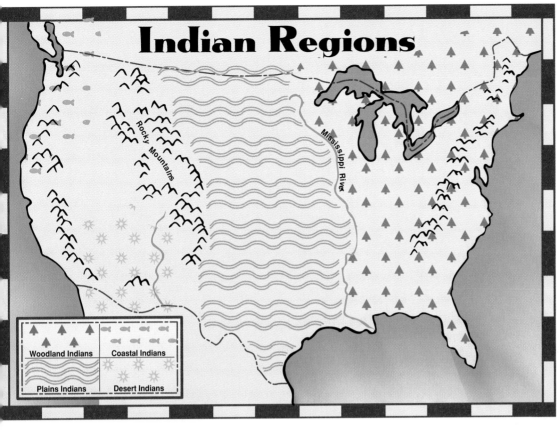

Indian Regions

Woodland Indians
Coastal Indians
Plains Indians
Desert Indians

Rocky Mountains

Mississippi River

The Desert Culture

The Desert people were farmers, fishermen, and nomadic hunters. They lived in the southwest region of the United States, west of the Rio Grande, in a dry, rocky area. They depended mainly on corn for their food source. The people planted their crops at the bottoms of canyons and built irrigation systems to keep the plants watered.

There were two kinds of Desert dwellings: eight-sided log huts called *hogans*, and multifamily *pueblos*, apartment-like structures made from *adobe* (a mixture of stones, clay, straw, and river earth). The Desert people wove clothing from wool they spun into yarn by hand.

Introduce students to the Desert art form of sandpainting. Long ago sandpainting was done by crushing colored rocks to make colored sands. The colored sand was sprinkled from the artist's hand onto a layer of white sand to create a design. Mix some colored sands for your students using powdered tempera paints and salt. Instruct each student to spread a thin layer of glue over a sheet of white paper. Then have each student create a design by sprinkling the colored mixtures over the paper. As they complete their projects, ask students to determine why this art form originated from the Desert people.

Books About The Desert Culture

Annie And The Old One
by Miska Miles
(Little, Brown And Company; 1985)

Antelope Woman: An Apache Folktale
retold by Michael Lacapa
(Northland Publishing Company, 1995)

Arrow To The Sun: A Pueblo Indian Tale
by Gerald McDermott
(Puffin Books, 1977)

Coyote: A Trickster Tale From The American Southwest
by Gerald McDermott
(Harcourt Brace And Company, 1994)

How The Stars Fell Into The Sky
by Jerrie Oughton
(Houghton Mifflin Company, 1992)

The Plains Culture

The Plains tribes were farmers, fishermen, hunters, and gatherers. They settled between the Rocky Mountains and the Mississippi River. They lived in temporary homes called *tipis,* which were made from buffalo hides. Tipis could easily be taken down and carried when the Plains people followed herds of buffalo. The buffalo was very important to the Plains people, for as well as supplying meat, parts of the animal were used to make clothing, shelter, and utensils.

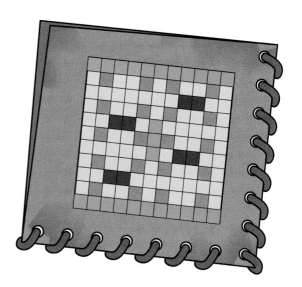

The Plains people carried treasured possessions and dried foods in a special pouch called a *parfleche.* Have your students make a parfleche by simulating the steps of tanning leather, sewing with rawhide, and creating a beadwork design. Give each student an 8 1/2" x 11" piece of brown grocery-sack paper. Instruct the student to carefully crumple the paper over and over until it becomes soft. Show each student how to fold the paper in half and use a hole puncher to create a line of holes along the outside edges as shown. Give each student a length of yarn and have him thread it through the holes to hold the parfleche together. To create a beadwork design, have each student color a pattern using the squares on a piece of centimeter graph paper. Have the student cut out and glue the design to his parfleche. Then have each student select a special item to carry inside his completed project.

Books About The Plains Culture

Buffalo Woman
by Paul Goble
(Simon & Schuster Children's Books, 1987)

Her Seven Brothers
by Paul Goble
(Simon & Schuster Children's Books, 1993)

Iktomi And The Boulder
By Paul Goble
(Orchard Books, 1991)

The Legend Of The Bluebonnet
by Tomie dePaola
(Putnam Publishing Group, 1993)

The Legend Of The Indian Paintbrush
edited by Tomie dePaola
(Putnam Publishing Group, 1991)

The Woodland tribes were farmers, woodsmen, and hunters. They lived in the region between the Mississippi River and the east coast. They had two different types of homes, depending on the kinds of trees in the area. One type of Woodland home was a *wigwam*—a single-family, dome-shaped structure made from a sapling frame covered with sheets of birch bark or cattail mats. The other type of home was a *longhouse*—a multifamily dwelling made by covering a pole framework with slabs of elm bark. The Woodland people used canoes for fishing and transportation. Clothing was made from animal skins and fur.

Woodland children played a game with 6 plum seeds and a pot filled with 100 dried beans. The plum seeds were smoothed and painted white on one side and black on the other. Each child took a turn tossing the seeds into the air. If all seeds landed with the same color showing, the player took 20 beans from the pot and got another turn. If five seeds landed with the same color facing up, the child took two beans and got another turn. If three or four seeds landed with the same color showing, the player did not take any beans and ended his turn. The player with the most beans at the end of the game was the winner. Have your students surmise why the Woodland children used these materials for playing a game. Then have your students play a version of the game using coins instead of plum seeds.

Books About The Woodland Culture

Dreamcatcher
by Audrey Osofsky
(Orchard Books, 1992)

Little Runner Of The Longhouse
by Betty Baker
(HarperCollins Children's Books, 1989)

The Naked Bear: Folktales Of The Iroquois
edited by John Bierhorst
(Morrow Junior Books, 1987)

The Rough-Face Girl
by Rafe Martin
(Putnam Publishing Group, 1992)

Squanto And The First Thanksgiving
by Eric Metaxas
(Simon & Schuster Children's Books 1996)

Exploring The Community

Celebrate the unique features of your community with activities that focus on changes through the years, cultural influences, regional studies, and current events.

Past And Present

Enlist your students' help in creating a display of your community's history. Ask students to collect old photographs showing how your community looked years ago by borrowing pictures from parents, grandparents, and neighbors. (Make sure that all pictures are clearly labeled to ensure a safe return, and are placed in plastic bags when being transported.) Have students identify the different types of businesses shown in the pictures and observe the changes in clothing, automobiles, and common landmarks around the community. Post these photographs on a bulletin board titled "Our Community: The Past."

Extend the project by taking your students on a photo safari of the community. Have parent volunteers bring loaded cameras and assist students in taking pictures of important places in the area. After the photos are developed, display them alongside the others on the bulletin board. Add to the title "…And Present!" Then complete the display by adding past and present restaurant menus, playbills, catalog pages, and other items of interest.

Our Community:
The Past   …And Present!

Kitchens Through The Ages

In The Past	In The Present
pump water (or get it from outside well)	hot and cold water by turning faucet
woodburning stove or kerosene	gas & electric stoves/microwave
icebox	refrigerator/freezer
lanterns/candles	electric lights
boil water/do dishes by hand	dishwasher/disposable dishes
most food prep. by hand	prepackaged food, modern appliances

* Schools
* Farming
* Business
* Fads
* Architecture
* Transportation
* Kitchens
* Recreation And Entertainment
* Communication
* Fashion
* Shopping

Through The Years

Let your students explore the many changes that have taken place in their community through the years with this data-collecting project. Organize students into small groups and assign each group a topic from the list. Have each group gather information about its topic by interviewing community members, researching books from the school or public library, and writing local businesses for information. Once the information is compiled, have each group create a presentation. Encourage each group to incorporate skits, posters, student-made books, and oral reports into its presentation. Invite parents to attend the event, and have a parent volunteer make a video recording of the program to send to community members who helped supply information.

Heritage Banners

Focus on the many different heritages within your community by having students create family banners. Fold a 12" x 18" sheet of construction paper diagonally; then cut along the fold to create two banners. Make a banner for each student in the class. Have each student decorate her banner with a large initial of her family's last name, drawings of flags from her family's country of origin, symbols of favorite family activities, and other important information. Attach the completed banners to a string and display the colorful creations on a classroom wall. If desired, have the class locate each of the countries represented on the banners on a world map.

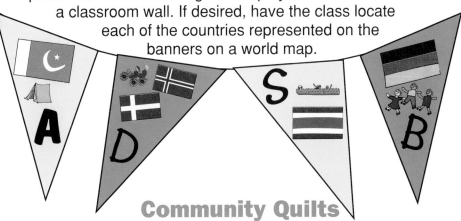

Community Quilts

Share a time-honored tradition with your students by exploring the historical significance of the patchwork quilt. Read either *The Keeping Quilt* by Patricia Polacco (Simon & Schuster Children's Books, 1988) or *The Patchwork Quilt* by Valerie Flournoy (Dial Books For Young Readers, 1985) to your class. Discuss with your students how each piece of the quilt tells about the family's history. Then challenge your students to make a quilt showing your community's history. Help your students research to find important historical events that have taken place in the community. Give each student a square of white construction paper to design a quilt square depicting one of the significant events. Provide a supply of markers, watercolors, or crayons, and encourage students to make their squares bright and colorful. When all the individual squares are complete, attach them to a butcher-paper backing. If desired, have each student use a black marker to add a row of stitch marks around his square. Display the finished quilt in a community center, public library, or courthouse for community members to enjoy.

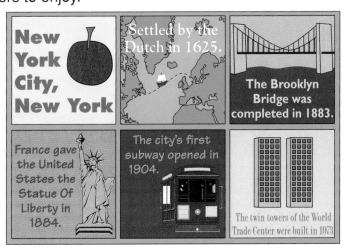

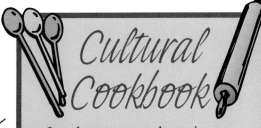

Cultural Cookbook

Involve your students in a project that will encourage family sharing, and will yield some tasty results! Have each student interview family members to find out which foods are important to the family's heritage, or are considered traditional family favorites. Ask each student to use the form on page 249 to write a copy of the recipe and find out why the food is important to the family, where the recipe originated, and when it is traditionally served. Invite parents to send in samples of some of the foods, or assist in preparing one of the recipes with your class. Then help students compile the information they collected into a class cookbook by having each student type or copy the recipe in his best handwriting and compose a sentence or two about its significance to his family. Make a copy of each recipe for every student. Have each student staple the recipes between construction-paper covers. The recipe booklet will be a special and useful keepsake for students and their families.

Community Celebrations

Discuss with your students the holidays and celebrations observed in your community. Have the students brainstorm a list of celebrations. Then place students in groups of four. Distribute 12 index cards to each group. Instruct each group to write the name of a holiday or celebration on each card. Then have the groups use the cards for the following activities:

- Have the group equally divide the cards among the members. Each member reads the name of the celebration on each of his cards, then writes a custom associated with the celebration on the back of the card.

- Have group members write the date or month of the holiday on the back of each card.

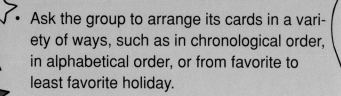

- Ask the group to arrange its cards in a variety of ways, such as in chronological order, in alphabetical order, or from favorite to least favorite holiday.

- Ask the group to sort its cards into local events, national celebrations, or worldwide holidays.

- Have each group make a chart showing the colors and symbols associated with the holiday.

Traveling The Region

Take your students on a trip through your region without ever leaving the classroom. Post a large map of your community and its neighboring areas. Then design a weeklong itinerary that has students traveling to a different location each day. Have each student use a notebook as a travelog. On Monday have students look at the map to determine the mileage from your town to the first location and record it in their notebooks. Have them also make notes of highways, street names, or important landmarks along the way. Then have students continue to keep track of their mileage and travel notes throughout the rest of the week. At the end of the week, have students compare notes and mileage calculations.

To culminate the trip, ask each student to select one of the destinations on his journey for further study. Have each student write to the location's Chamber of Commerce to ask for information. Then have each student make a poster about the location using the information he receives. Display the finished travel posters for students to read as they learn more about the surrounding regions.

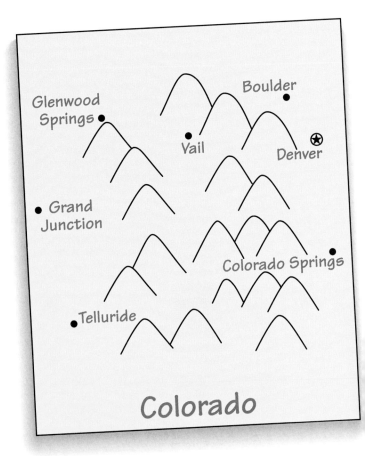

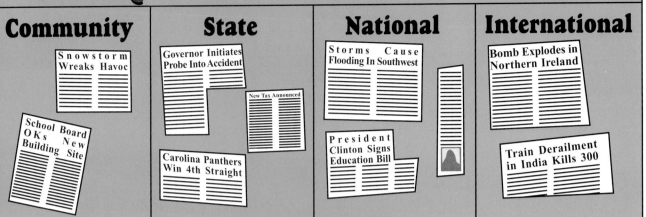

Community	State	National	International
Snowstorm Wreaks Havoc	Governor Initiates Probe Into Accident	Storms Cause Flooding In Southwest	Bomb Explodes in Northern Ireland
School Board OKs New Building Site	New Tax Announced	President Clinton Signs Education Bill	Train Derailment in India Kills 300
	Carolina Panthers Win 4th Straight		

Newsworthy Events

Show students how their community makes its mark in the news as you reinforce geographical terminology. Divide a bulletin board into four sections and label each section as shown. Encourage students to bring to school newspaper or magazine articles that describe current events. (If a student hears a story on the radio or television, she may write down a few sentences to tell about the event.) Provide time during the day for students to share their articles with the class. After a student reads or describes an event, have the class vote to determine where the article should be placed on the bulletin board. Allow students to take the articles home at the end of the week (or use the articles for the activities described below) so that the bulletin board is clear for a new round of articles.

The new post office will open next week.

Rainy skies continue throughout the area.

Caption Match

Keep your students aware of community happenings and reinforce reading skills at the same time. Collect several newspaper photos with captions that show events happening in your community. Glue the photos to a sheet of tagboard for durability; then cut the captions away from the photos. Code the back of the matching pictures and captions for self-checking. Place the pieces in a learning center and challenge students to match each caption with the correct photograph. Students can help update the center by bringing current newspaper photographs from home.

Current Community Events

Use a highlighting marker to encourage students to keep up with current community happenings. Obtain a class supply of highlighters, or ask each student to bring one from home. Then find a current newspaper article about the community. Copy a class supply of the article and distribute one to each student. Read the article together; then have students locate the sentences that answer the five *W* questions (who, what, where, when, and why). Ask each student to highlight the key information. Their efforts will make the news article more understandable to them, and will provide practice in locating important details.

$ $ $ Calling All Consumers $ $ $

Whether your third graders have birthday money to spend, a weekly allowance in their pockets, or a few dollars saved from doing chores, they are part of the economic system. They have wants, needs, and many choices to make. Help your students become clever consumers with activities that reinforce good economic decisions.

Consumer Collages

Reinforce the concept of the three basic consumer needs—food, shelter, and clothing—by having students make a collage of each need. Cut a large shape from bulletin-board paper to represent each need. Instruct each student to draw or find an example of a picture that shows each type of need. Have each student glue his pictures to the corresponding shapes. Then display the completed collages during your study of economics to help students remember the basic needs.

What About Wants?

Although basic needs are of vital importance to every consumer, it's hard to ignore the wants! Have students look at consumer wants through the eyes of an advertiser. Gather a supply of sale catalogs for students to peruse. Have them circle items that are wants rather than needs. Students may be surprised to find that most items are things a consumer wants, but does not necessarily need. Ask students to surmise why advertisers show so many items that people do not have to have in order to survive. Then have each student design an advertisement for a want and a need. Which one is more tempting to the consumer?

Community Goods & Services

When it comes to spending money, consumers have to pay for both goods and services. Help students recognize the difference between the two with this group activity. Review with students that *goods* are things that are made or grown for consumers to buy, such as stereos, fresh fruit, or automobiles. A *service* is a type of work that someone performs for you, such as cutting your hair, cleaning your teeth, or helping you solve a legal problem. The community is full of workers that sell goods and perform services.

Place students in small groups and provide each group with several sheets of construction paper, scissors, glue, and markers. Instruct each group to brainstorm a list of five goods and five services that can be purchased in your community. For each item on the list, the group creates a construction-paper symbol and writes a sentence on it telling about the item. Have each group glue its symbols to a sheet of chart paper for a poster display of goods and services in your area.

Consumers & Careers

Students often dream of becoming professional football players, famous singers, or movie stars. Whatever their career ambitions, part of being a consumer is earning money to purchase wants and needs. Have students focus on the importance of preparing for a career by considering several aspects of the world of work.

Have each student secretly select a career, write its name on a notecard, and seal it in an envelope. On the outside of the envelope, have the student write five clues about the career. Place the sealed envelopes in a container. Select several envelopes to read to the class each day. After the clues have been read, allow students to guess the career. Then open the envelope to reveal the answer.

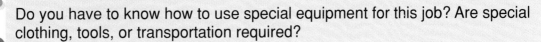

1. I take temperatures and weigh my patients.
2. I clean my patients' teeth, if they need it.
3. I bathe and dip my patients, if they have fleas or a skin problem.
4. I treat my patients when they are sick and help them to feel better.
5. My patients are usually furry or hairy and like to purr or lick you a lot.

Extend the activity by asking students to consider these questions about each career:

Can anyone make this career choice? Is it something you can learn to do, or do you have to have certain natural abilities? (For example, can anyone become an opera singer or a professional basketball player?)

Do you need to have special training for this career? Do you need to go to college, medical school, or law school?

Does this job provide a good or a service? Will the job always be in demand?

Do you have to know how to use special equipment for this job? Are special clothing, tools, or transportation required?

Will you have to change locations for this job? Will you work by yourself, or be around other people?

What are the benefits to this career? What are the drawbacks?

Planning Ahead

After students have had a chance to consider several different types of careers, ask each student to describe the type of job for which she feels best suited. Have each student begin by listing factors to consider when making her choice, such as a need for higher education, a desire to work alone, and a willingness to travel. Then have each student list several careers that match those qualifications. Remind students that with hard work and determination, many things are possible!

Crystal
1. I want to work with a lot of people.
2. I want to live in a big city.
3. I want to go to college.
4. I want to wear pretty clothes to work.
5. I like to do math.

Making The Most Of Maps

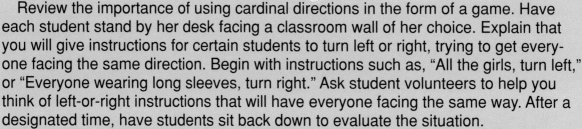

Headed In The Right Direction

Review the importance of using cardinal directions in the form of a game. Have each student stand by her desk facing a classroom wall of her choice. Explain that you will give instructions for certain students to turn left or right, trying to get everyone facing the same direction. Begin with instructions such as, "All the girls, turn left," or "Everyone wearing long sleeves, turn right." Ask student volunteers to help you think of left-or-right instructions that will have everyone facing the same way. After a designated time, have students sit back down to evaluate the situation.

Tell students that there is a way to instruct everyone to face the same direction. Use an index card and a piece of tape to label each classroom wall with the appropriate cardinal direction. Then have everyone stand again, facing different directions. Give the instructions, "All the girls, face north," and "All the boys, face north." As everyone stands facing the same direction, explain to students that in order to understand maps and give directions, we have to have unchanging reference points.

A Bird's-Eye View

Introduce your study of maps by having your students look at the world as mapmakers—from above. Ask students to imagine that they are floating near the ceiling looking down at the classroom. What would the desks look like? What would doors, windows, and chalkboards look like? Distribute a sheet of drawing paper to each student and have him make a map of the classroom from a bird's-eye view. Then have students compare their completed maps with their classmates'. Did everyone see the classroom in the same way?

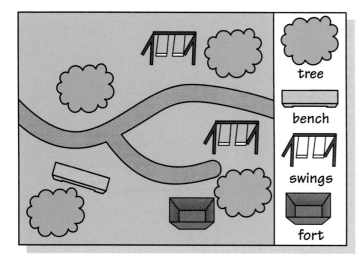

tree
bench
swings
fort

Making A Legend

Use the concept of drawing a bird's-eye view to reinforce map legends. Take your students outdoors and have them draw the school playground as it would look from above. Then have each student create a legend for his map showing objects such as trees, benches, and the different types of playground equipment. Then challenge each student to use his imagination to design a map of a new playground. Remind him to include a legend that explains the objects shown on his map.

Shown To Scale

Using a map scale is more meaningful when students are familiar with the location. Obtain a class supply of county or state maps that clearly show points of interest. Distribute a map and a ruler to each student. After explaining how to use the mileage scale on the map, ask students to determine the number of miles between their city and various locations. Then challenge each student to write a problem relating to distances on the map. Compile the problems into a set of learning-center task cards for students to complete.

Great Grids

Capitalize on students' interests to provide practice with plotting points on a grid. Create an overhead transparency of the grid on page 250. Use a wipe-off marker to draw a symbol in several of the grid boxes. Then show the transparency to students, demonstrating how to identify the location of each symbol using specific coordinates. Then duplicate a class supply of the grid pattern and distribute a copy to each student. Call out a series of coordinates and instructions for plotting a point, such as:

- (5, C)—Write your first initial.
- (8, F)—Color the square using your favorite color.
- (3, E)—Write the number of people in your family.
- (10, B)—Draw a picture of your favorite fruit.
- (2, G)—Write the month of your birthday.

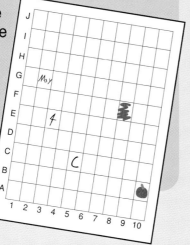

Extend the activity by having students create grids using symbols that relate to their favorite topics. Have each student trade grids with a classmate to determine the coordinates of each symbol. Then have the two students check the answers together.

The Dot Connection

Help your students recognize and locate continents, oceans, major countries, and other places with a package of fluorescent self-sticking dots. When introducing a region on the map, place a colored dot on the area. Also place a dot of the same color to the corresponding area on the globe. Students will be able to see the same area presented in two different ways, helping to reinforce its location.

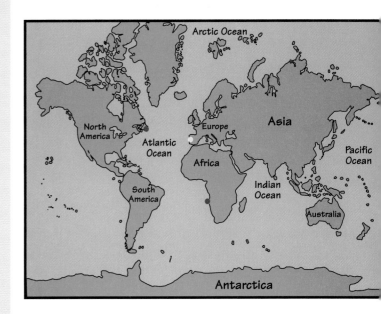

Stating The Facts

Place students in small groups for an activity that highlights different regions of the United States. Assign each group a specific U.S. region. Instruct each member of the group to select a different state within the region to research. Provide the group with reference materials, and each member with a sheet of white construction paper and a supply of markers. Have each student list the name of his chosen state, its motto, its state tree and flower, and its nickname. Also instruct the student to list three interesting facts about the state. Provide time for each group to present its findings to the class.

Exploring The United States

Use the U.S. map on page 251 to promote geography awareness while reinforcing basic skills. Distribute a copy of the map to each student. Have each student label her map by looking at a reference such as a classroom map, a textbook map, or an encyclopedia. Then have students use their maps for one or more of the following activities:

- Color your state blue. Color the states that border it yellow.
- Find a state that is smaller than your state. Color it green.
- Find a state that is larger than your state. Color it purple.
- Write a riddle about a state using cardinal directions as clues. Have a classmate refer to her map to solve the riddle.

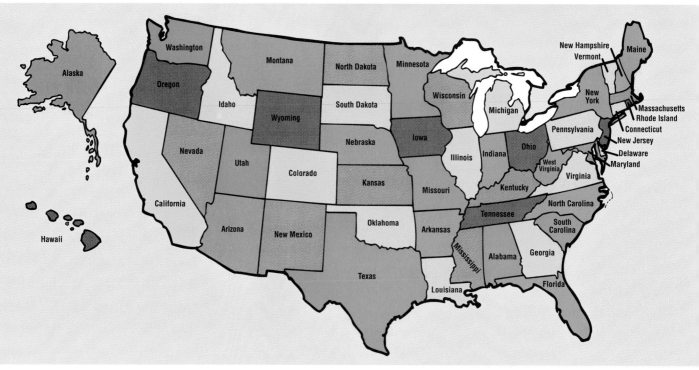

Signed, Sealed, And Delivered

Incorporate mapping skills with a graphing activity. Ask students to bring several postmarked envelopes from home. (Remind students to ask their parents' permission first.) Cut off each postmark and attach it to its matching state on a class-size map (or an enlarged copy of the map on page 251). At the end of a ten-day period, tally the postmarks and discuss the results. Then have students organize the information and post the results on a classroom graph.

Come To Order

Put your students' researching skills to use as they discover the year each state achieved statehood. Assign each student two or three different states to research. Provide access to a set of encyclopedias or other reference books for each student to locate the dates of statehood. Then have each student report his findings to the class, while his classmates record the dates on their U.S. maps. Have the students use this information to answer questions such as, "Which state was first to join?", "Which was last to join?", and "Which year had the most states join?" Then have each student create a question that can be answered with the information on the map. Provide time for each student to ask his question and call on a classmate to answer.

Waters Of The World

Although the continents are very large land masses, most of the earth's surface is covered by water. Have your students label the major oceans and bodies of water on the world map. Then play a game to reinforce to your students how much of the earth is covered by water.

Provide an inflatable globe for students to use in this discovery game. Have your students sit in a circle and take turns tossing the globe to each other. Each time the globe is caught, the student looks at her right thumb to see if it is touching land or water. Make a tally mark on the board to show the result of each catch. After everyone has had a turn to catch the globe, have students observe the results. There should be more tally marks for the water category; since there is more water on the earth's surface, the chances of landing on it are greater.

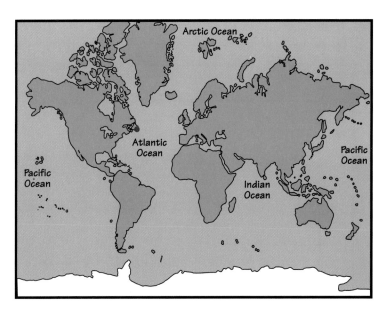

Where In The World?

Students can use the world map on page 252 to investigate a world of information. Distribute a copy of the map to each student and have him label each continent. Then have students use their maps to pinpoint the continents of these unique features:

- The world's largest land gorge is in **North America**. Located in Arizona, the Grand Canyon is one mile in depth.

- The world's highest measured sand dunes are in **Africa**. Dunes of the Saharan sand sea have been measured at a height of 1,525 feet.

- The world's highest waterfall is in **South America**. The Salto Angel (or Angel Falls) in Venezuela has a total drop of 3,212 feet.

- The world's largest exposed *monolith* (a single great stone) is in **Australia**. It rises 1,143 feet above the desert plain of the Northern Territory.

- The world's largest high plateau is in **Asia**. The Tibetan Plateau has an average altitude of 16,000 feet, and has an area of 77,000 square miles.

- The world's smallest independent country is in **Europe**. The State of Vatican City is entirely within the city of Rome, Italy.

- The world's largest body of freshwater is in the form of an ice cap that covers **Antarctica**. The ice cap is up to 15,700 feet deep in certain areas.

Extend the activity by having each student research to find another interesting fact about each continent. Have each student write each fact on a separate slip of paper and attach it to the matching continent on a class-size world map.

Famous Place Report

Draw a picture of the famous place in the box.
Then complete the information about the place.

1. What is the name of this famous place?_____

2. Why is it famous?_____

3. Where is the place located?_____

4. List three interesting facts about this place.

   • _____

   • _____

   • _____

> **Bonus Box:** Would you like to visit this place? Tell why or why not.

What's Cooking?

Recipe for _____

Submitted by_____

Ingredients:

Directions:

1. Why is this food special to your family?

2. Does this recipe originate from a special country?

3. Who first prepared this recipe for your family?

4. Is there a special time or occasion when your family uses this recipe?

Name_____Open grid

	1	2	3	4	5	6	7	8	9	10
J										
I										
H										
G										
F										
E										
D										
C										
B										
A										

Note To The Teacher: Use with "Great Grids" on page 245.

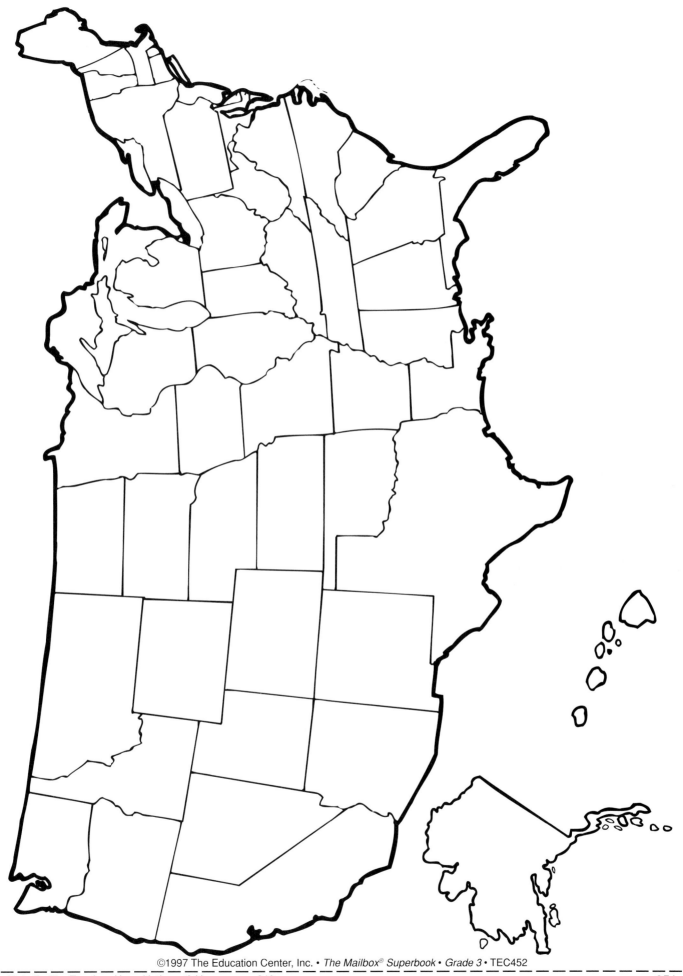

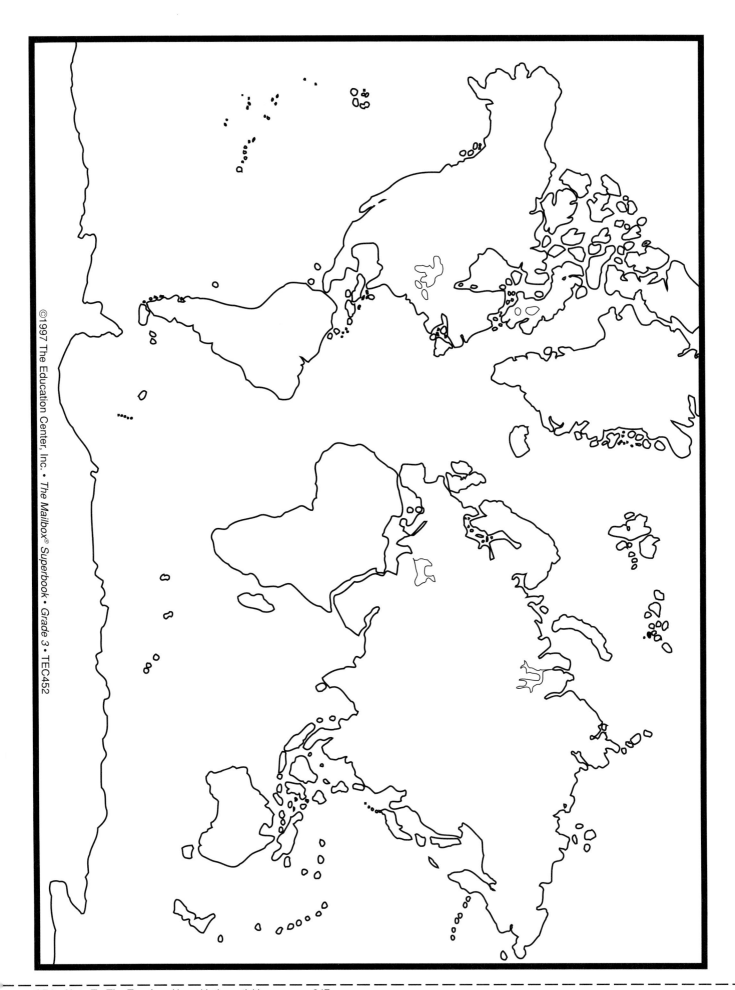

SCIENCE

THE SOLA

Scaling The Solar System

Make your students part of an interactive solar system model with this out-of-doors activity. Select nine student volunteers to represent the planets, one to represent the Sun, one to represent Earth's Moon, three to represent the asteroid belt, and the remainder to represent comets or meteors. Introduce your students to each heavenly body with the information below. Then have each student create a costume or prop that is appropriate for his role in the solar system.

Sun—The Sun is the only star in our solar system. It is only medium-sized, but a million Earths could fit inside it. The Sun is not solid, but is made of burning gases.

Mercury—Mercury is the first planet from the Sun. One side of Mercury always faces the Sun and is very hot. The other side faces away from the Sun and remains cold. Mercury does not have a moon in its orbit.

Venus—Venus, the second planet, is sometimes called the Evening Star because it is visible in the early evening sky during certain times of the year. The thick clouds that surround Venus hold in heat, making it the hottest planet. Venus does not have a moon in its orbit.

Earth—Earth is the third planet from the Sun. It takes one year, or 365 days, to travel around the Sun. The Earth is home to many plants and animals, and is the only planet to have water in a liquid state.

Earth's Moon—The Moon is not a planet. It is a satellite that revolves around the Earth. The Moon has no light of its own and shines only by reflecting the Sun's light.

Mars—Mars is the fourth planet from the Sun. It is sometimes called the *red planet* because of the iron-rich stones and dusty soil that give it a red appearance. It is named after the Roman god of war and has two moons.

Asteroid Belt—The asteroid belt is a ring of rocks that orbits around the Sun. They stay in orbit between Mars and Jupiter, separating the inner and the outer planets.

Jupiter—Jupiter is the fifth and largest planet. It is made up of gas and does not have a solid surface. At least 16 moons orbit around Jupiter.

Saturn—The sixth planet, Saturn, is known for its beautiful rings. The rings are really pieces of ice that circle the planet. More than 20 moons orbit around Saturn.

Uranus—Uranus, the seventh planet, has an unusual orbit—the planet spins on its side! This causes half of the planet to face the Sun for 42 years, while the other side remains in darkness. Uranus has 15 moons.

Neptune—Neptune, the eighth planet, has eight moons. It has a bluish color and is named after the Roman god of the sea.

Pluto—The ninth planet, Pluto, is the smallest and coldest planet. A large moon named Charon orbits Pluto. Scientists think that at one time, Charon and Pluto may have been moons in Neptune's orbit.

Comets—Comets are not planets, but they also move around the Sun. A comet is a clump of ice mixed with dust and frozen gases. As it moves through space, it leaves a trail of dust and gas that resembles a tail.

Meteors—Meteors are often called *shooting stars*. But they are not really stars at all. They are actually pieces of falling rocks that burn up in the atmosphere.

Making A Model

When each student has had a chance to prepare for his role in the solar system, take the class outdoors with a yardstick, a large supply of yarn or string, and a pair of scissors. Have each student representing a planet measure a length of string to show his distance from the Sun. (Refer to the chart below.) Place the student representing the Sun in the center of the area. Then have each planet, in order, hand one end of his string to the Sun and slowly walk away until the string is tight. Position Earth's Moon next to planet Earth. Instruct the students representing the asteroid belt to hold hands and make a line between Mars and Jupiter. Instruct the students representing the meteors and comets to position themselves among the planets.

Planet	Actual Distance From Sun	String Length
Mercury	36 million miles	1 yard
Venus	67 million miles	about 2 yards
Earth	93 million miles	about 2 1/2 yards
Mars	142 million miles	about 4 yards
Jupiter	484 million miles	about 13 1/2 yards
Saturn	885 million miles	about 24 1/2 yards
Uranus	1,780 million miles	about 49 1/2 yards
Neptune	2,790 million miles	about 77 1/2 yards
Pluto	3,660 million miles	about 101 1/2 yards

When everyone is in place, have Earth's Moon slowly walk around Earth. Remind the student to always face Earth. This will demonstrate that as it orbits, one side of the Moon always faces the Earth and the other side always faces away.

Instruct the planets to slowly begin to walk around the Sun, while the Sun stays in its fixed position. (It will be necessary for the student representing the Sun to hold the strings above his head so they will not become tangled.) Remind Earth's Moon to continue in its orbit and the asteroid belt to move as the planets do. To demonstrate rotation, instruct each planet to slowly turn in a circle as it orbits the Sun. Point out that Uranus's orbit would actually resemble a cartwheel, since it would normally orbit on its side! Then have the comets and meteors move through the planets and find a resting place to sit down, as though they had burned up while passing through the planets' atmospheres.

To culminate the activity, call a halt to the solar activity and have each student state a fact about the heavenly body he is portraying. Then return to the classroom and share some of these solar system stories:

— *The Magic School Bus Lost In The Solar System* by Joanna Cole (Scholastic Inc., 1990)
— *The Planets In Our Solar System* by Franklyn M. Branley (HarperCollins Children's Books, 1987)
— *The Far Planets* by Donna Bailey (Raintree Steck-Vaughn Publishers, 1994)
— *The Near Planets* by Donna Bailey (Raintree Steck-Vaughn Publishers, 1993)
— *A Tour Of The Planets* by Melvin Berger (Newbridge Communications, Inc.; 1994)
— *The Planets* by Gail Gibbons (Holiday House, Inc.; 1993)
— *Stars And Planets* by David Lambert (Raintree Steck-Vaughn Publishers, 1994)

PLANET ORDER

Display the phrase
"My Very Educated Mother Just Served Us Nine Pickles."
Show students how the first letter of each word corresponds with the first letter of each planet in the solar system, and how the sentence arranges the letters to show the planets' correct order from the Sun. Challenge students to think of another sentence using those letters to begin the words.

What's In A Name?

As you continue your study of the solar system, the students may be curious about the names of the planets. The planets in our solar system were named after figures in Roman mythology. Share with your students the history behind each planet's name:

PLANET	NAMED FOR
MERCURY	THE SPEEDY MESSENGER OF THE ROMAN GODS
VENUS	THE ROMAN GODDESS OF LOVE AND BEAUTY
EARTH	GAEA (jē-ə), OR MOTHER EARTH; A TITAN WHO MARRIED URANUS
MARS	THE ROMAN GOD OF WAR
JUPITER	KING OF THE ROMAN GODS
SATURN	FATHER OF JUPITER; SON OF EARTH AND URANUS
URANUS	KING OF THE SKY AND FATHER OF SATURN
NEPTUNE	THE ROMAN GOD OF THE SEA
PLUTO	THE ROMAN GOD OF THE UNDERWORLD

Encourage your students to research more about these figures in Roman mythology, and surmise why each planet was named for that figure. Then point out these correlations:

— Mercury has the fastest orbit around the Sun, similar to the speedy messenger of Roman mythology.
— Venus is the brightest planet, named for the goddess with illuminating beauty.
— Earth is home to all living things, named for Gaea or Mother Earth.
— Mars is a red planet, representing the blood-soaked god of war.
— Jupiter is the largest planet, a fitting symbol for the king of the gods.
— Saturn is the second largest planet. In Roman mythology, the god Jupiter was the son of the god Saturn.
— Uranus was the first planet observed since ancient times; therefore, it was named for the sky god.
— Neptune is blue, symbolizing the god of the sea.
— Pluto is the farthest and coldest planet, similar to the cold and distant underworld.

How Do We Know?

With so much distance and so many harsh conditions separating us from the other planets, students may wonder how we gather information about our solar system. Although many astronauts have explored outer space, manned missions have not yet managed to get very far away from Earth. Much of what we know about our solar system is due to information collected by space probes. Probes can survive extreme conditions that an astronaut could not endure.

Most probes are built and launched in a numbered series. There were seven *Surveyor* probes that studied the Moon. In addition, there have been 12 *Mariner* probes, 14 *Pioneer* probes, 2 *Voyager* probes, and many others that have explored the solar system. About twice the size of a car, a probe can stay in space for more than 20 years. It can collect and transmit information and photographs about the planets, the Sun, the Moon, comets, asteroids, and general space conditions. The space probe *Mariner 9* mapped the entire surface of Mars, recorded its surface temperature, and took over 7,000 photographs of the planet. *Pioneer 10* and *11* have passed by Jupiter and Saturn, and are now headed out of our solar system and toward interstellar space.

Have your students research to find out the travels and discoveries made by space probes. Then have them use the information to create a timeline of solar discoveries. As new space probes are launched, have the students update the timeline to show that we are still learning about our fascinating galaxy.

Greetings From Outer Space!

Include interplanetary greetings in your study of the solar system. After your students have learned some basic facts about the planets, have each student select a planet to use in a letter-writing assignment. Give each student an unlined 5" x 7" index card. Instruct the student to illustrate his chosen planet on one side of the card. On the other side of the card, have him write a postcard message to a friend as though the student were visiting the planet. In his message, have the student include four facts about the planet. Then provide time for each student to share his planet postcard with the class for a fact-filled solar review.

Planetary Poetry

Share some out-of-this-world poetry with your students. *Blast Off! Poems About Space*, selected by Lee B. Hopkins (HarperCollins Children's Books, 1995), is a collection of poems about the planets, the astronauts, and the mysteries of space. After reading several poetry selections aloud, encourage each student to compose a poem that celebrates the celestial skies. Remind students to include in their poetry factual information they have learned during their study of the planets. Then provide time for a special poetry-sharing session to culminate your study of the solar system.

The Earth

Getting To The Core Of Things

Begin your study of the Earth with this tasty introduction activity. Provide each student with a peanut M&M's® candy. Have each student carefully bite the candy in half, keeping one-half of it for observation. Ask students to discuss their cross sections of the candy. In the discussion, point out that there are three layers of the candy—an outer candy shell, a middle section of chocolate, and a peanut in the center. Explain to the students that the candy is much like a model of the Earth.

Inform students that if the Earth were cut into a cross section, there would also be three layers to observe. Explain the following information about each section while students observe the candy models:

- The **crust** is a thin outer layer that covers the Earth, much like the shell on the candy. The continents and the oceans are part of the crust, which ranges from 5 to 20 miles in depth.

- The **mantle** is the middle section of the Earth, represented by the chocolate layer of the candy. It is made of solid rock and is about 1,800 miles thick.

- The **core** is in the center of the Earth, just like the peanut in the candy. Scientists actually consider the core to be in two parts. The **outer core** is made of melted metal and is about 1,400 miles thick. The **inner core**, at the very center, is made of a hot but solid ball of metal. It is about 1,600 miles thick.

Journey To The Center

Take your students on a journey through the layers of the Earth with the help of Ms. Frizzle and her magic school bus. As you read *The Magic School Bus Inside The Earth* by Joanna Cole (Scholastic Inc., 1987), your class joins Ms. Frizzle's students as they travel through the crust, mantle, outer core, and inner core—and come out through a volcano on the other side! Along the way, your students will learn about fossils, the three different types of rocks, and changes to the Earth.

Other Earth-wise books to share with your students include:
— *How To Dig A Hole To The Other Side Of The World* by Faith McNulty (Live Oak Media, 1991)
— *Planet Earth, Inside Out* by Gail Gibbons (Morrow Junior Books, 1995)
— *Our Patchwork Planet* by Helen R. Sattler (Lothrop, Lee & Shepard Books; 1995)

space
thermosphere
mesophere
stratosphere
troposphere

Digging Up Dirt

After explaining to students about the Earth's three layers, send them on a soil safari to discover the many materials in the Earth's crust. To prepare for the dig, gather a class supply of plastic cups, small sifters or colanders, magnifying glasses, and old newspapers to spread out on the floor. Then distribute a cup to each student and lead the class outdoors. Instruct each student to scoop up a cup of soil. (If possible, have groups of students collect soil from slightly different locations, such as from under a tree, by the parking lot, near the sandbox, or from the playground.)

Take the students back to the classroom to observe their findings. Spread layers of newspaper on the floor; then provide each student or group of students with a sifter and a magnifying glass. Instruct each student to take a turn pouring the contents of her cup into the sifter over the newspaper. Then have the student use a magnifying glass to examine the soil that sifted through, as well as the soil remaining in the sifter, for objects such as plant and animal remains or rocks. Have each student make a list of her findings, then compare the list to her classmates' findings.

The Air Up There

Surrounding the Earth is a blanket of air called our *atmosphere*. The atmosphere extends hundreds of miles above the Earth. The air in the atmosphere is composed of about 78% nitrogen, 21% oxygen, several other gases, and water droplets and ice crystals in the form of clouds.

The atmosphere protects the Earth by blocking out the strongest heat from the Sun while holding in enough heat to warm the planet. Nearly all weather occurs in the lowest layer of the Earth's atmosphere, or *troposphere*. The troposphere begins at the Earth's surface and extends six to ten miles up. The farther away from the Earth, the thinner the air becomes. At about 1,000 miles above the Earth, the atmosphere gradually becomes space.

The atmosphere also contains the air that people, plants, and animals need to live and breathe. Increase your students' awareness of the need to take care of the air in the Earth's atmosphere. Have students observe an air filter from a heating or cooling system at your school. Explain to students that the system pulls air in, heats or cools the air, and filters the dirt from the air before blowing it back out. Remind students that the dust and dirt accumulated on the filter were actually in the air. Ask students to consider that since the air outdoors cannot be filtered before we breathe it, what can be done to keep the air as clean as possible?

The Changing Earth

The Earth's crust is in a constant state of change due to *weathering,* the wearing away of soil or rock. Sometimes the changes occur so slowly that they are hard to detect. Other changes happen quickly and are easily apparent. Use the following activities to show your students the types of weathering that affect the surface of the Earth.

Water Erosion: Water moving across the Earth's surface can cause changes to the crust. As water from rivers and streams moves, the soil around it is affected. Sometimes water carries with it pieces of rock that hit against the soil as they travel. Heavy rain can also change the lay of the soil. Have your students demonstrate the effects of water erosion with a dirt-filled pan and a spray bottle with an adjustable nozzle. Fill the bottle with water, and have students experiment spraying the soil with various pressures. Have students discuss their findings.

Plants: Although plant roots help keep soil in place to prevent wind and water erosion, they can also cause changes to the Earth's surface. Roots push through the soil, widen cracks in rocks, and sometimes push through man-made structures. Tell students to be on the lookout for sidewalks or driveways that are being changed by plant growth. If possible, arrange for pictures to be taken of such examples so that they can be shared with the class.

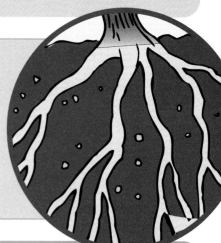

Wind Erosion: As strong winds move across the land, loose soil is picked up and carried away to new places. (The roots of plants help hold soil in place.) Show students the effects of wind erosion with the help of a blow-dryer, a large cardboard box, and a tray of sand. Place the tray inside the cardboard box. Hold the blow-dryer several feet away and turn it on its lowest setting. Ask students to observe any changes to the sand in the tray. Then continue to experiment with different settings and distances, making sure that students are not in danger of getting sand in their eyes. Have students discuss their observations.

Temperature: As temperatures change on the Earth, so does the Earth's surface. Hot temperatures can cause the soil to crack, rocks to expand and break, and water to dry up. Cold temperatures can cause the water that has seeped inside rocks to freeze and expand, creating a force strong enough to break the rocks apart. Demonstrate this occurrence by filling a plastic bottle to the top with water and securing the lid tightly. Place the bottle in the freezer overnight; then show the students the results. Ask students how this relates to problems with water pipes during the winter.

Volcanoes: Volcanoes can cause quick and drastic changes to the Earth. Most volcanoes are located along seacoasts, where the Earth's crust is weak. Deep in the Earth's mantle, hot molten rocks and hot gases escape through the weakened crust, causing the volcano to erupt. These areas are called *hot spots*. Molten lava and ash pour from the volcano, covering the crust with a new layer of material. Demonstrate the action of a volcano with a hot plate, a spoon, a raw egg, and a pan of boiling water. Tell students that the egg, like the Earth, has three main layers. Gently make a few cracks in the egg's shell to simulate weakened areas of the Earth's crust. Then have students gather around the pan as you use the spoon to lower the egg into the boiling water. Explain that as the egg heats up, it will act much like the heated materials inside the Earth's mantle. The liquid in the egg will escape through the weakened places in the shell, just as magma pushes through the weak places in the Earth's crust.

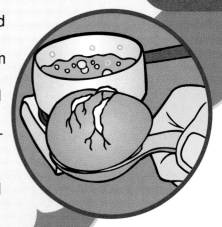

Earthquakes: Another quick change to the Earth's surface can result from an earthquake. An earthquake occurs when underground rocks slide, grind, and scrape against each other. Earthquakes can cause the crust to form ridges or cracks in places where the rocks have shifted. Show students the effects of an earthquake with a tasty demonstration. Supply each student with three slices of bread, a tablespoon of peanut butter, a tablespoon of jelly, a paper plate, and a plastic knife. Instruct each student to spread a layer of peanut butter on one slice of bread, place another slice on top of that, spread a layer of jelly, and then top with the remaining slice. Explain that this model represents the many sediment layers of the Earth's crust. Then have each student use his plastic knife to cut the sandwich into two pieces. Have each student look at the cross section of the layers, then try to put the halves back together. What changes do students notice to the layers and to their broken models? How does this show the changes that happen to the Earth's crust after an earthquake?

Man: As we build homes, shopping centers, parking lots, and roadways, the Earth's surface experiences many changes. We also change the Earth as we cut down trees, dam up streams, and mine for minerals. Supply each student with a napkin, a chocolate-chip cookie, and a toothpick for a look at the changes man can cause. Tell each student to imagine that the cookie is the Earth's surface and the chocolate chips are minerals that can be mined for profit. Have each student use his toothpick to "excavate" the chips from the cookie. Ask students to describe their cookies' surfaces after they have been mined. Then tell students that they probably excavated only the chips that were on the surface. Encourage the students to try to remove other chips in the cookies as well. Discuss the results of the intense mining—is that the way the cookie crumbles?

It's A Fact!

Remind students that although the Earth has been around for millions of years, we must take great care of our planet's air, land, water, and natural resources. Share the following facts with your students and ask them to consider each statement as they answer the accompanying questions.

Fact! Each person throws out about four pounds of garbage a day. How many pounds a day is that for the entire class?

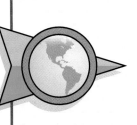

Fact! More than 500,000 trees are cut down to make the Sunday papers in America. How many trees would be cut down for a month's worth of Sunday papers?

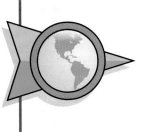

Fact! In one year, each family receives enough junk mail to equal 1 1/2 trees. How many trees would be cut down for a family in a four-year period?

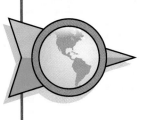

Fact! Approximately 80 acres of rain forest are cut down every minute. How many acres are cut every five minutes?

Fact! Americans throw away enough trash each year to fill a line of garbage trucks that is 40 trucks wide and extends from New York to Louisiana. Look on a map to see how long those lines would be!

The Three Rs

Inform students that when it comes to conservation, the three *R*s are *reduce, reuse,* and *recycle.* Each term describes a very important concept in taking care of the Earth.

Reduce the amount of nonbiodegradable products such as Styrofoam® and aerosol cans you and your family use. Also purchase products that use little or no packaging.

Reuse items. Do not discard after only one use. Reuse the product for the same or another function. Grocery sacks are often re-used. After unloading your groceries, you can use the sacks as wastebasket liners or overnight bags, or you can take them with you on your next trip to the grocery store and use them again.

Recycle items instead of throwing them away. Aluminum cans, glass jars and bottles, plastic, newspapers and magazines, as well as other items can be recycled into the same product or made into a new product.

To demonstrate each of these concepts, set up three boxes in your classroom. Label each box with *Reduce, Reuse,* or *Recycle.* Encourage students to bring in examples of items to put in each box. Invite students to take objects from the Reuse box if they can put them to good use. Arrange for the items in the Recycle box to be taken to a recycling center. Then have your students find the best way to discard of the items in the Reduce box, and remind them to be careful of purchasing those items again in the future.

Let's Do Lunch!

Invite students to use their lunch period as a learning experience. Have students bring their lunchboxes and trays to the classroom for a conservation discussion over lunch. As students begin to eat, write the words *reusable, recyclable,* and *refuse* on the board. Ask the students to consider how the items in their lunches fit into the categories. After everyone has finished eating, ask students to study the items remaining from their lunches. Have each student list his remaining items and tell which categories they belong in. Record the responses on the board. After all items have been recorded, have the students discuss the results. Have them offer suggestions for minimizing the refuse category.

Renoirs Of Recycling

Now that your students are aware of the three *R*s of conservation, have them use their knowledge to create artistic displays. Ask each student to bring in a collection of clean, unwanted items (such as empty cereal boxes, cardboard tubes, egg cartons, and catalogs) from home. Provide each student with a sheet of 12" x 18" tagboard. Instruct each student to use items from the collection to create a conservation collage. Each collage can contain a message about taking care of the Earth, show different items to recycle, or simply display an abstract design. Post the completed projects on a bulletin board with the title "The Renoirs Of Recycling."

Friends Of The Earth

Take your class on a walk around the school grounds or to a nearby park in an effort to reduce litter. Provide gloves and a trash bag for each student, discuss safety measures regarding broken glass and rusty cans, and then lead the class on a cleanup mission. If possible, weigh each bag after the trash pickup is completed. Students will be amazed by the amount of litter that accumulates and take pride in their efforts to reduce litter.

Get into recycling or you'll be into garbage right up to your neck.

Recycle A Good Story

Share some stories of environmental awareness with these Earth-friendly books:

— *Just A Dream* by Chris Van Allsburg (Houghton Mifflin Company, 1990)
— *The Giving Tree* by Shel Silverstein (HarperCollins Children's Books, 1964)
— *The Paper Bag Prince* by Colin Thompson (Knopf Books For Young Readers, 1992)
— *The Lorax* by Dr. Seuss (Random House Books For Young Readers, 1971)

ROCKS ALL AROUND

After students have had a chance to observe the contents of the Earth's crust as described in "Digging Up Dirt" on page 259, they will notice that a great deal of the crust is composed of rock. Share with students that there are three kinds of rocks, and describe the characteristics of each:

- **Sedimentary rocks** are formed as soil, rocks, and plants are buried and pressed together over long periods of time. The pressure causes the materials to stick together and form into rocks.

- **Igneous rocks** are formed as fiery molten material explodes from volcanoes. The resulting rocks will vary depending on how quickly the material cooled, the amount of gas in the material, and the type of minerals the material contained.

- **Metamorphic rocks** are formed when sedimentary and igneous rocks become buried deep within the Earth. The pressure of the heavy sediment combined with the great heat from deep within the Earth cause the sedimentary and igneous rocks to change, or *metamorphose,* into different appearances or mineral compositions.

ROCK HOUNDS AT WORK

After describing the three kinds of rocks listed on the left, inform students that rocks are also classified by certain characteristics. Introduce these characteristics by asking each student to collect six rock samples from her neighborhood and bring them to school. Have each student sort her rocks and describe the characteristics she used to do so. Reinforce that rocks can be sorted by color, shape, hardness, and mineral content. Your students probably used color and shape to sort their rocks. Have students try some of the following tests to discover characteristics regarding the hardness and mineral content.

ROCK HARDNESS:
Each student will use her fingernail, a penny, a table knife, and a small glass mirror to determine the hardness rating of her rock.

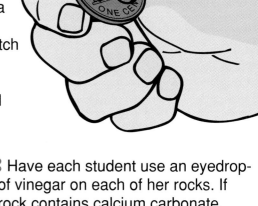

Very Soft—The rock can be scratched by a fingernail.
Soft—The rock can be scratched by a penny, but not by a fingernail.
Medium—The rock can scratch a penny, but not a table knife.
Hard—The rock will scratch a table knife, but not the glass.
Very Hard—The rock will scratch the glass.

CALCIUM CONTENT:
Have each student use an eyedropper to place a few drops of vinegar on each of her rocks. If the vinegar bubbles, the rock contains calcium carbonate.

STREAK TEST:
Have each student scratch her rocks against an unglazed porcelain tile. The color of the streaks will show certain minerals. Have her compare the results to see if any rocks leave the same color of streak.

Sedimentary Storytellers

Much of the Earth's history can be learned from studying *fossils*. A fossil is the remains or evidence of a plant or animal that is no longer alive. After a plant or animal dies, it can become trapped between layers of sediment. After many years, the outline of the plant or animal is pressed into the hardened sediment. The result is a fossil that can tell us about the types of living things that have been on the Earth.

Have your students create "fossils" from plaster of paris. Instruct each student to find a small object such as a shell or a leaf. Have the student lightly coat the outside of the object with petroleum jelly. Mix the plaster of paris according to package directions. Pour a small amount into a plastic cup for each student. Tell each student to gently place his object on top of the plaster mixture, then allow the plaster to dry. Have each student carefully remove the object from the dry plaster to reveal a "fossil" of the object.

Rock Research

Culminate your study of rocks with a research project and classroom display. Provide several well-illustrated rock books for students to peruse. Have each student select a type of rock to research. Distribute an index card to each student, and have him list five facts about the rock. Then supply each student with a small amount of air-drying salt dough. Have each student form the dough into the shape of his rock. After the dough has dried, have students use paints, glitter, and sandpaper to put the finishing touches on their models. Display each model with its accompanying fact card to create a classroom rock collection.

Rocks At Work

Remind students that rocks can be used for many different purposes. Have students brainstorm uses for rocks, such as jewelry, magnets, building materials, and landscaping. Students may be surprised to learn that two important classroom tools come from rocks: chalk is soft, white limestone, and pencil lead is a soft mineral called graphite. Then have students follow the steps below to make a form of sidewalk chalk, imitating a product of natural limestone. Then take the students outside to try out their colorful rock-related tools.

Materials For Each Student: 1 cardboard tube, 1 square of plastic wrap, 1 rubber band, petroleum jelly.

Directions:

1. Coat the inside of your cardboard tube with a thin layer of petroleum jelly.

2. Use the rubber band to secure the plastic wrap around one end of your tube.

3. Fill the tube with a well-stirred mixture of 5 tablespoons plaster, 3 tablespoons water, and 1 tablespoon liquid tempera paint.

4. Allow the mixture to dry; then peel away the cardboard to reveal a stick of colored sidewalk chalk.

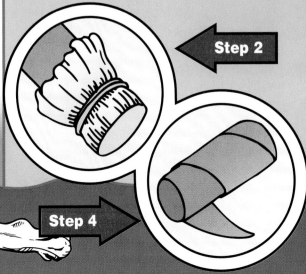

Step 2

Step 4

Earth's Moon

Beyond the Earth's atmosphere lies its Moon, a satellite over 240,000 miles away. Although it is difficult to determine the size of an object so far away, you can show students how the Moon compares in size to the Earth by displaying a basketball to represent the Earth and a baseball to represent the Moon. After they have an idea of the Moon's size, share these facts with your students:

• The Moon revolves around the Earth, much like the Earth revolves around the Sun. The Moon rotates once in the same amount of time it takes to orbit the Earth once, so the same side of the moon always faces Earth.

• Our investigations of the Moon reveal that it does not support life. It is also without air, water, clouds, or weather of any kind.

• Although the Moon is one of the brightest objects in the night sky, it does not produce any light of its own. The Moon merely reflects light from the Sun.

• The moon circles the Earth once every 27.3 days. The word *month* is derived from an Old English word meaning "moon"; it takes approximately one month for the Moon to complete its orbit.

Phases Of The Moon

Students will be aware that the Moon changes its appearance in the night sky, but may not understand the reason why. Remind students that the Moon is a dark object that reflects the Sun's light. The Sun can shine only on one-half of the Moon at a time (just as it can shine only on one-half of the Earth at a time, creating night and day). In addition, the Moon is constantly changing its position in relation to the Earth and the Sun as it revolves in its orbit.

When the Moon is between the Earth and the Sun, the side that is reflecting light is facing away from the Earth. The side that we see during that time is completely dark. That phase is called a *new moon*.

Each day after the new moon, as the Moon continues its orbit, we can see a little bit more of the lighted half of the Moon. As the lighted part appears larger, we say that the Moon is *waxing*.

About two weeks after the new moon, the entire lighted side of the Moon is facing the Earth. We are able to see a full circle of light, or a *full moon*.

For the next two weeks, the lighted part of the Moon will appear less and less. We say that the Moon is *waning*. It will continue to wane until it reaches the new moon phase; then the cycle repeats itself.

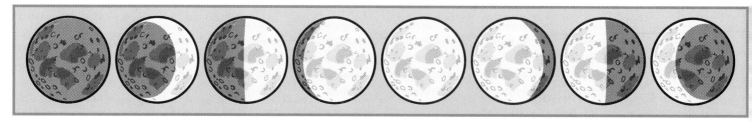

Waxing And Waning

Demonstrate the different phases of the Moon with a Styrofoam® ball, a flashlight, and a pencil. Use a black marker or tempera paint to color one-half of the ball. Poke the sharpened end of the pencil into the ball. Darken the room, and then have a student volunteer shine the flashlight on you. Sit about four feet away from the flashlight. Invite the students to sit behind you to observe the phases.

Hold the pencil in front of you, just above your head, with the white side of the ball facing you. Point out that the side of the Moon facing you is receiving no light. This represents a new moon.

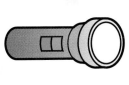

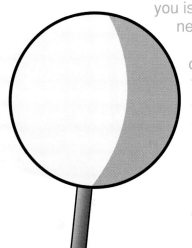

Slowly turn in a counterclockwise circle, always keeping the white side of the ball facing you. As you turn, direct students' attention to the increasing amount of light shining on the ball, representing the waxing phase. Pause briefly at the full moon stage before showing the Moon beginning to wane.

Conclude the activity by asking students to observe the Moon during the next few nights. Then discuss the different phases your students observe.

Measuring On The Moon

Students may be surprised to learn that the Moon's gravity is only one-sixth of that on Earth. That means that if they were on the Moon, your students could jump six times higher and farther than they do now. Have students calculate their athletic abilities on the Moon with a jumping activity. Take students and a measuring tape outdoors or to the gym. Mark a starting point for the jumpers. Have each student make two horizontal jumps. Measure the distance of each jump, and instruct each student to use his farthest measurement to determine how far he would have jumped on the Moon. As students marvel at their distances, point out that there once was a cow that jumped *over* the moon—now, did the difference in gravity have anything to do with that?

Turning The Tides

When it comes to the ocean, the Moon holds a great attraction! The Moon's gravitational pull on the Earth's waters causes them to rise and fall, creating the tides. Show students this effect by having each of them create a model of the moon's gravitational pull. Distribute a tagboard copy of the patterns on page 273 to each student. Instruct each student to color the Earth and Moon pictures; then have students cut on the heavy lines around the circles and on the dotted section under the Moon illustration. Give each student a square of blue cellophane to tape behind the cut-out section. Tell each student to place the Moon circle atop the Earth circle and secure with a brad as shown. As students spin the top circle, they will see how the movement of the moon pulls on the waters of the Earth, causing the changing tides.

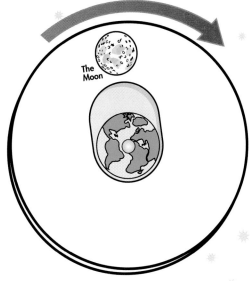

The Moon

Weather Watch
Weather Words

Familiarize your students with weather terminology by providing hands-on learning activities. For each weather word listed below, have students complete the activity described. With firsthand experience of weather conditions, the forecast for success is clear and bright!

Clouds—a collection of water vapor changed into floating water droplets as warm air rises and cools
Try This: Give each pair of students two small clear plastic cups. Fill one cup 1/3 full of hot water. Instruct the student pair to place the empty cup upside down on top of the first cup, making sure the rims meet to form a seal. Observe as a cloud forms, as the hot air rises from the water and meets with the cooler air in the second cup. (For added effect, darken the room and have students observe their cups with flashlights.)

Fog—a cloud of tiny water droplets close to the ground
Try This: Pour hot (but not steaming) water into a clear container. Wet a cloth with ice water and drape it over the mouth of the container so that the tip of the cloth rests just above the water line. Have students observe the fog forming around the cloth as the warm air begins to cool.

Evaporate—to change from a liquid state into a gas, such as water vapor
Try This: Provide each student with a small paintbrush and a container of water. Instruct each student to paint the word *evaporation* on the chalkboard with water. Have students observe how the letters disappear as the water evaporates.

Lightning—a giant spark of electricity flashing through the sky
Try This: Choose a cool, dry day to have students rub their feet across a wool or nylon carpet. Turn out the lights. Have each student touch one of his classmates and watch (and feel!) as an electrical spark is created.

Rain—combined water droplets too heavy to be supported by the air
Try This: Fill a glass jar with ice cubes. Have students observe as drops of water form on the outside of the jar. Have your students wipe away the moisture and watch as it forms again. Explain that the water vapor in the air around the jar condenses into a liquid form as it cools. When moisture in clouds cools, it forms drops that fall as rain.

Snow—water in the air frozen into tiny crystals that fall to the Earth
Try This: Have the student pour 3 tablespoons of boric acid crystals (available at a drugstore) into a jar. Fill the jar to the top with water. Place the lid on the jar and screw it on tightly. Mix the crystals and the water by shaking the jar vigorously. Then place the jar on a flat surface. A few of the crystals will dissolve but most will float around like a snowstorm.

Thunder—an explosion given off by the expansion of air heated by lightning
Try This: Demonstrate the relationship between thunder and lightning by having students role-play. Position one student (in the role of the lightning) by the light switch. Ask the other students (the thunder) to place their hands on their desks with their fingers laced together. Have the student at the light switch darken the room, then flip the lights on and off quickly to simulate a flash of lightning. After the flash of light, the students at their desks unclasp their hands and clap in unison. Why the pause between the light and the sound? Explain to students that light travels faster than sound, causing a slight delay in the time they see the lightning and hear the thunder.

Wind—the movement of air caused by warm air rising around the Equator and cooler air moving in to replace the heated air.
Try This: Have each student cut a spiral from a paper circle. Tell the students to each tie a thread to one end of their spirals and take turns suspending them over a hot lightbulb. Have students observe as the heated air above the bulb rises, causing the spirals to move.

Tornado—a storm in which the wind moves upward in a narrow, circular funnel
Try This: Have student partners fill a one-liter soda bottle three-quarters full of water. Instruct them to add a few drops of food coloring and a large squirt of liquid dishwashing detergent to the water. Give each pair a six-inch strip of plastic ribbon to place in the bottle. Tell the partners to secure the lid tightly, turn the bottle upside down, and swirl the contents to create a tornado effect.

Water Cycle—the process by which water collects on the Earth, evaporates into the air, condenses into clouds, and then falls back to the Earth as precipitation
Try This: Have students fill small glass jars with a quarter-inch of water. Instruct them to place the lids on the jars, then store the jars near a sunny window. Have students observe the jars throughout the day. Point out that as the water in a jar is heated, it turns to vapor and evaporates. The vapor collects at the top of the jar. When the vapor begins to cool (this may occur overnight), it will condense and fall in drops back to the bottom of the jar.

Wonderful Weather Reading

Share a whirlwind of weather books with your students.
— *It's Raining Cats And Dogs: All Kinds Of Weather And Why We Have It* by Franklyn M. Branley (Houghton Mifflin Company, 1987)
— *Weather Words And What They Mean* by Gail Gibbons (Holiday House, Inc.; 1990)
— *What A Beautiful Day!* by Tilde Michels (The Lerner Group, 1992)
— *Cloudy With A Chance Of Meatballs* by Judi Barrett (Simon & Schuster Children's Books, 1978)
— *Return To Chewandswallow: A Sequel To Cloudy With A Chance Of Meatballs* by Judi Barrett (Simon & Schuster Children's Books, 1997)
— *The Cloudy Day* by Jane Stroschin (Henry Quill Press, 1989)

Welcome To The World Of
Plants

Begin your unit on plants with a brainstorming session. Ask your students to think of all the products we get from plants. Record the responses on the board. Then have students demonstrate their understanding with a group activity. Provide a supply of old magazines for students to use to cut out examples of plant products. Place students in small groups to sort their pictures into different categories, such as food, building materials, paper products, clothing, and decoration. Distribute a piece of chart paper, glue, and a marker to each group. Instruct each group to list the categories and glue the pictures under the appropriate headings. Display the completed posters during your study of plants.

Seed Sort

Put classification skills to work as students sort and classify seeds. Ask students to bring examples of seeds to class. Remind them to look for seeds in fruit, from plants in their yards, in seed packages, and on trees. If desired, bring in a few seeds that students may have not considered, such as a coconut, an avocado pit, poppy seeds, a raw peanut, and kernels of popcorn. Place the seeds in a central location for students to observe. Then ask groups of students to visit the center and determine ways to group the seeds. Provide a time for students to discuss their conclusions with the class. Then use the seeds for the following activity.

It Starts With A Seed

Most students know that many plants start out as small seeds—now you can show them how the transformation takes place! Ask each student to bring in a clear glass jar from home. Instruct each student to line the inside of the jar with two folded, wet paper towels. (To keep the towels in place, crumple a third towel and stuff it in the center of the jar.) Give each student several bean seeds, and have her place them in between the paper towels and the side of her jar. Find a warm, dark place to store the jars. Have students check their jars daily to keep the towels moist and observe the changes from seeds to plants.

How Does Your Garden Grow?

After students have observed the seeds in the sorting activity above, have them further their investigations by studying the different types of seeds as they grow. Send notes home with students requesting that parents send their empty Styrofoam® egg cartons to school. Fill the cups of the egg cartons with potting soil. Have students plant seeds in each cup, making sure to label which type of seed is in each cup. Then place the "gardens" in a sunny location, and have students take note as the seeds begin to grow. Have students record observations about which seeds sprout first, which produce leaves the fastest, which grow tallest, and the differences in leaves and stems. If possible, transplant the seedlings to an outdoor location for further study.

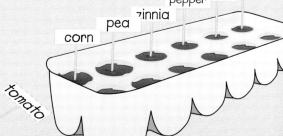
squash
bean
pepper
zinnia
pea
corn
tomato

The Parts Of A Plant

Students will agree that flowers are known for their beauty and fragrance. But students may not know that flowers provide a way for many plants to *reproduce*, or make new plants. Familiarize your students with the parts of a flowering plant:

1. leaf—the part of a plant that uses sunlight to create food for the plant

2. petal—the brightly colored part of a plant that attracts insects with its sweet nectar and color; insects help transfer pollen from one flower to another

3. pollen—a powder produced in the flower of a plant; the pollen helps the plant develop seeds, which create new plants

4. roots—the part of a plant that absorbs water and minerals from the soil

5. seed—the small *embryo* (or young plant) produced by a plant

6. stem—the main stalk of a plant that connects the roots, leaves, and flowers

Eat Your Vegetables!

Now that students are familiar with the different parts of a plant, challenge them to bring edible plant parts for show-and-tell. Challenge your students to find edible roots (such as turnips, carrots, and radishes), leaves (such as spinach, lettuce, and cabbage), seeds (such as peas, corn, and kidney beans), stems (such as celery and asparagus), and flower clusters (such as cauliflower and broccoli). After each student shares his plants and identifies their parts, assist students in washing the vegetables. Then hold a plant-tasting party!

Portrait Of A Plant

Reinforce the parts of a plant by having your students create colorful diagrams. Each student will need a 9" x 12" sheet of white construction paper, a copy of the patterns on page 274, a green pipe cleaner, a piece of string, glitter, crayons, scissors, and glue. Instruct each student to make the model as follows:

1. Use a brown crayon to draw a horizontal line about two inches up from the bottom of the paper. Color the bottom portion of the paper brown to represent the soil.

2. Glue the green pipe cleaner perpendicular to the soil to represent the stem.

3. Color and cut out the petal and leaf patterns. Glue them in the appropriate places on the stem.

4. Apply a small amount of glue in the center of the petal pattern. Sprinkle with glitter to represent the pollen.

5. Unravel the string. Glue it under the stem to represent the root system.

6. Label each part of the plant as shown.

Display the completed diagrams on a bulletin board titled "Plant Portraits."

Getting In Touch With Plants

Provide a truly hands-on experience with this plant-related art project. Give each student two sheets of drawing paper and brown and green crayons; then take the class outside to create rubbings of tree bark and leaves. Demonstrate how to place a sheet of paper over the bark and lightly rub a brown crayon over the paper. Repeat the activity to create leaf rubbings using the other sheet of paper and the green crayon. Provide time for each student to make rubbings. Back in the classroom, have each student create a tree by cutting a trunk and branches from his bark rubbing and leaves from the leaf rubbings. Instruct the students to each assemble and glue the pieces on a sheet of construction paper. If desired, have students add additional details to their projects before displaying them in the hallway or other prominent place.

More Plant Pizzazz

Incorporate the following activities into your study of plants:

- Visit a plant nursery or tree farm to learn about different types of trees. Then try to identify the trees on the school grounds.

- Have each student grow an edible sprout garden. Instruct the students to each wet a paper towel and place it in a shallow tray. Sprinkle each paper towel with mustard, celery, radish, wheat, cress, and alfalfa seeds. After the seeds sprout, allow the students to taste the sprouts. Discuss the different flavor of each type of sprout.

- Have students bring in a collection of leaves from home. (Remind students to have an adult identify any unfamiliar leaves, as some plants are poisonous to the touch.) Place the leaves and a magnifying glass in a learning center. During free time have students observe the leaves using the magnifying glass.

- Have students research plants from different habitats. Assign groups of students to find out about desert, forest, polar, jungle, ocean, or rain forest plants. Provide time for each group to share its findings with the class.

Growing With Literature

Plant these green-thumb books in your classroom:
— *The Tiny Seed* by Eric Carle (Simon & Schuster Children's Books, 1991)
— *The Reason For A Flower* by Ruth Heller (Putnam Publishing Group, 1983)
— *A Seed Is A Promise* by Claire Merrill (Scholastic Inc., 1990)
— *The Tremendous Tree Book* by Barbara Brenner and May Garelick (Boyds Mills Press, Inc.; 1992)
— *Red Leaf, Yellow Leaf* by Lois Ehlert (Harcourt Brace & Company, 1991)
— *A Tree In A Forest* by Jan Thornhill (Simon & Schuster Children's Books, 1992)
— *Mighty Tree* by Dick Gackenbach (Harcourt Brace & Company, 1996)
— *From Seed To Plant* by Gail Gibbons (Holiday House, Inc.; 1991)
— *Plants Do Amazing Things* by Hedda Nussbaum (Random House Books For Young Readers, 1977)

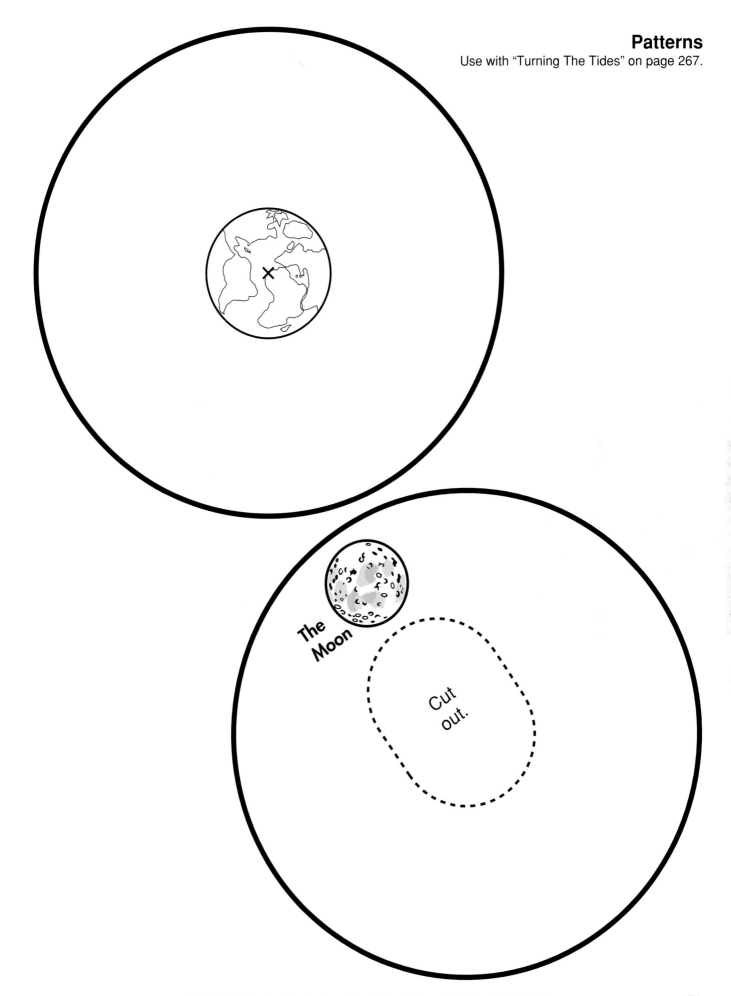

The Moon

Cut out.

Patterns
Use with "Portrait Of A Plant" on page 271.

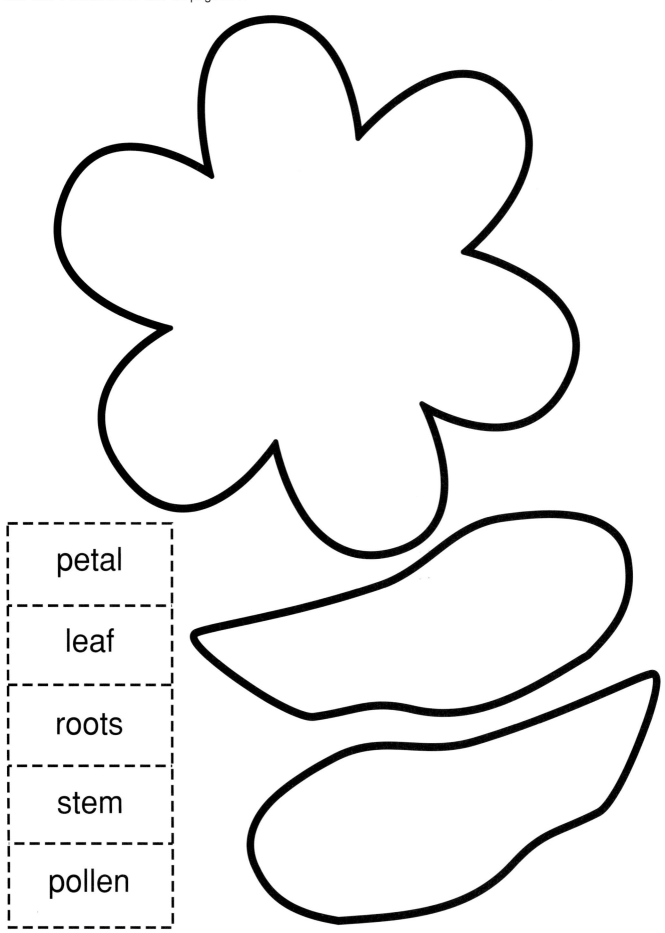

petal

leaf

roots

stem

pollen

HEALTH & SAFETY

NUTRITION

SENSIBLE SNACKING

Try this activity to help students understand the variety of healthful snacks that are available to them. To do this, first divide the students into a desired number of groups. Challenge each group to create a list of as many snacks as possible. Ask students to share their lists as you record their responses on the chalkboard. Discuss the results with your students; then have students help you arrange the list into two columns. If desired, duplicate copies of the list for students to take home and share with their parents. Then reward students' hard work with a healthful snack of raisins, carrot sticks, or apple slices.

PYRAMID POWER

What is shaped like a triangle and packed with fabulous food facts? The Food Guide Pyramid, of course! Explain to your students that the U.S. Department of Agriculture (USDA) and the Department of Health and Human Services (DHHS) have developed a set of guidelines for good eating habits. These guidelines are arranged in a pyramid to show the proportions of a healthful diet. Familiarize your students with the Food Guide Pyramid by having them create a model to display in the classroom. Draw a large triangle on a piece of bulletin-board paper and use a marker to visually divide it into sections as shown below. Program each section with its name and recommended servings. Divide the class into six groups and assign each group a section of the pyramid. Instruct each group to find or draw pic-tures of food that belong in its section. Have the students glue their pictures in the appropriate places on the pyramid. Then post the completed pyramid in a prominent place for students to refer to during their study of nutrition.

Fats, Oils, and Sugars Group
(use sparingly)

Milk, Yogurt, and Cheese Group
(2-3 servings)

Meat, Poultry, Fish, Dried Beans, Eggs, and Nuts Group
(2-3 servings)

Fruit Group (2-4 servings)

Vegetable Group (3-5 servings)

Bread, Cereal, Rice, and Pasta Group (6-11 servings)

FAT IS NOT WHERE IT'S AT!

Now that students are familiar with nutrition labels, have them check for fat content. Explain that besides being high in calories, foods that are high in fat can cause health problems such as heart disease, obesity, and cancer. Make an overhead transparency of a nutrition label and show students where to look for information regarding fat content. Then have students compare labels from candy, chips, cookies, and crackers to see which are highest in fat. (Students may notice that some candies are actually low in fat. That's because sugar, although high in calories, contains no fat.) Then have students use their findings to write a paragraph comparing a low-fat snack to one with a higher fat content. Ask student volunteers to share their paragraphs with the class.

RAIDING THE REFRIGERATOR

Provide practice for your students in creating well-balanced meals. To do this, draw pictures of cupboard shelves and the inside of a refrigerator on a length of bulletin-board paper. Supply students with magazines and instruct them to cut out pictures of healthful foods to glue to the cupboard shelves and the refrigerator. Display the well-stocked shelves in a corner of the classroom. Have student pairs visit the center to create a meal menu using the items displayed on the shelves. If desired, have resources available so that students can determine the fat grams or calories in their meals. What's for dinner? Just check the menu!

A TASTY READING LIST

Share these mouthwatering books with your students.
— *Gregory, The Terrible Eater* by Mitchell Sharmat (Scholastic Inc., 1984)
— *What Food Is This?* by Rosmarie Hausherr (Scholastic Inc., 1994)
— *The Hungry Thing* by Jan Slepian and Ann Siedler (Scholastic Inc., 1988)
— *The Hungry Thing Returns* by Jan Slepian (Scholastic Inc., 1993)
— *The Hungry Thing Goes To A Restaurant* by Jan Slepian (Scholastic Inc., 1993)
— *The Edible Pyramid* by Loreen Leedy (Holiday House, Inc.; 1994)
— *D. W., The Picky Eater* by Marc Brown (Little, Brown And Company; 1995)

LET'S GET COOKIN'!

Enlist the help of parents and students in compiling a cookbook that's full of healthful recipes. In advance send a note home to parents asking them to assist their child in locating a healthful recipe to bring to school. Have each student copy his recipe onto a sheet of paper. Afterward have students help you arrange the recipes into categories such as snacks, main dishes, salads, and desserts. Then, as a class, compose a list that details the dietary guidelines as suggested by the USDA and the DHHS. Bind the dietary guidelines, the completed recipes, and a few blank pages between construction-paper covers. If desired, have student volunteers color a picture of the food pyramid to place on the cover. Then let a different student take the resulting cookbook home each night. Encourage each family to try one of the recipes from the cookbook, and invite them to write a comment about the recipe on the blank pages. This book will win rave reviews from students and parents alike!

SUGAR, SUGAR, EVERYWHERE

Surprise students with a sugar-filled fact: each year the average American eats 125 pounds of sugar! Show students a five-pound bag of sugar and explain that it would take 25 bags of that size to equal 125 pounds. Students may also be surprised to learn that sugar is added to many common foods and labeled as glucose, fructose, maltose, lactose, or corn syrup. Supply students with copies of food labels you have duplicated from cereal, bread, cracker, and chip packages. Have students look at the ingredients list of each label to see if the product contains sugar. Inform students that the ingredients are listed in order from the greatest amount to the least amount. Ask, "Where does sugar appear on each list?" Then encourage students to look for labels at home that show low sugar contents. Have them bring the labels in to share with the class. Then post the labels on a bulletin board titled "Here's To Healthy Eating!"

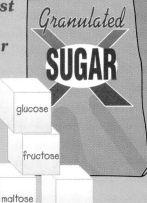

DENTAL HEALTH

MILLION-DOLLAR SMILES

Get your study of dental health off to a smiling start! Give each student a green construction-paper copy of the million-dollar-bill pattern on page 286. Instruct each student to cut the oval shape from the center as indicated on the pattern. Then have each student tape a school photo of himself behind the oval cutout so that his face can be seen through the opening. Mount the bills on a bulletin board titled "Our Million-Dollar Smiles."

BANK ON DENTAL HEALTH!

If desired, extend the "Million-Dollar Smiles" activity by giving each student a pink construction-paper copy of the piggy-bank pattern on page 286. Instruct each student to complete the sentence "A dental-health tip you can bank on is…" at the top of his cutout. Mount the banks amid the million-dollar-bill patterns on a classroom bulletin board.

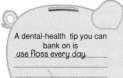

A dental-health tip you can bank on is
use floss every day.

BRUSH UP ON TECHNIQUE

Use this activity to ensure that your students know the proper tooth-brushing technique. Begin by asking a dental hygienist or dentist to visit your classroom to demonstrate for students the correct way to brush one's teeth. (If a dental-health worker is not available to visit your classroom, demonstrate the steps outlined below for your students.) Afterward challenge each student to list the steps involved in the proper brushing technique. Then, once the student demonstrates his tooth-brushing proficiency to you, pair him with a younger student. Encourage the student to teach his younger partner the finer details of keeping teeth clean and shiny.

PROPER BRUSHING TECHNIQUE

Hold your toothbrush at a 45-degree angle against the gum line. Move the brush back and forth with short strokes that are about half a tooth wide.

Brush the outer surface of each upper and lower tooth.

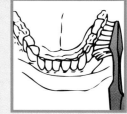

Brush the inner surface of each upper and lower tooth.

Hold the brush flat to brush the chewing surfaces of your teeth. Gently brush your tongue.

DENTAL-HEALTH DATA

Get to the root of dental-health data by sharing this information about teeth with your students.

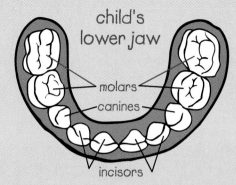

child's lower jaw

molars
canines
incisors

* *Children have 20 teeth, called deciduous or baby teeth. Baby teeth begin to fall out when a child is about six years old.*

* *An adult's mouth is larger and has 32 teeth. These are called permanent teeth.*

* *Teeth are held in the jaw by roots.*

* *The teeth in the front of the mouth are thin and sharp for biting and tearing food. These teeth are called incisors.*

* *The teeth in the back of the mouth are flat for grinding and crushing food. These teeth are called molars.*

* *The sharp, pointed teeth between the incisors and molars are used to help bite food. These teeth are called canines or cuspids.*

* *Teeth are covered witha a loyer of enamel. Enamel is harder than bone, so teeth are very strong.*

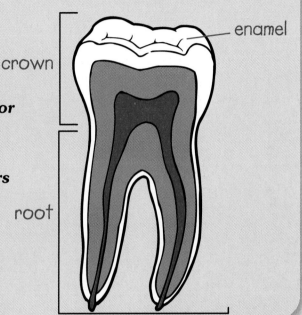

crown
enamel
root

THE ABCS OF DENTAL HEALTH

Challenge your students to create an alphabet book of dental-health tips. Begin by assigning each student a letter of the alphabet. (If you have fewer than 26 students, ask several student volunteers to take a second letter.) Next brainstorm dental-health-related words for each letter of the alphabet and list students' responses on the board. Challenge each student to think of a dental-health statement that corresponds to his assigned letter, using the student-generated list for assistance if necessary. Then, on a sheet of construction paper, have each student write and illustrate his dental-health tip. Bind the completed projects into a book titled *Dental Health From A–Z.*

A
A is for ache.
Brush your teeth to help prevent toothaches.

F
F is for fluoride.
Fluoride helps protect our teeth.

BOOKS YOU CAN SINK YOUR TEETH INTO!

Share these terrific tooth tales with your students.

— *How Many Teeth?* by Paul Showers (HarperCollins Children's Books, 1994)

— *The Berenstain Bears Visit The Dentist* by Stan and Jan Berenstain (Random House Books For Young Readers, 1981)

— *Arthur's Tooth* by Marc Brown (Little, Brown And Company; 1986)

— *Doctor De Soto* by William Steig (Farrar, Straus & Giroux, Inc.; 1990)

— *The Missing Tooth* by Joanna Cole (Random House Books For Young Readers, 1988)

FIRE SAFETY

THE FACTS OF FIRE SAFETY

Help your students become fire-safety smart by sharing these important tips:

1 Every family should discuss a fire-drill procedure for their home. Discuss several ways to exit the house. Have a designated meeting place outside so that all family members can be accounted for.

2 If a door is hot to the touch, don't open it. There could be a fire on the other side.

3 You should walk, not run, during a fire. Running causes more oxygen to reach the fire, causing the flames to grow.

4 If a room is filled with smoke, crawl under the smoke rather than walk through it. The air near the ground will be cooler and less smoky.

5 If your clothes catch on fire, remember to stop, drop, and roll.

6 Once you are safely outside the house, call 911 from a neighbor's phone.

7 Cool a burn with cool water for about 20 minutes. Do not apply butter or ointment to a fresh burn; they hold in heat.

HELPFUL OR HARMFUL?

Try this activity to get students thinking about the good and bad qualities of fire. Have each student fold a sheet of white construction paper in half. Tell him to label the two halves with the headings "Fire is good because…" and "Fire is bad because…." Ask each student to complete the sentences and illustrate his thoughts. Conclude the lesson by asking student volunteers to present their resulting posters to the class.

"PAWS" FOR FIRE SAFETY

Invite your students to make these delightful Dalmatians that double as fire-safety reminders. To make a Dalmatian, have each student use a black crayon to draw facial features on a nine-inch paper plate as shown. Next have her cut random circular shapes from black construction-paper scraps, then glue the shapes to her paper plate. Have each student glue her resulting Dalmatian behind a sheet of construction paper that bears a fire-safety message. Then instruct each student to cut two paw shapes from white construction paper. Have her glue the paws atop her sheet of construction paper as shown. Staple the completed projects to a bulletin board titled " 'Paws' For Fire Safety."

FIRE-SAFETY SCAVENGER HUNT

Encourage your youngsters to become fire-safety inspectors for a day or two! Give each student a copy of the reproducible on page 287. Have him take the sheet home and look for the named items. Present each child who returns his completed list to you with a fire-safety inspector badge similar to the one shown. Or, if desired, give a copy of the certificate on page 287 to each student who has a predetermined number of checked items.

Official Inspector

Ruben

ON A "ROLE" FOR FIRE SAFETY

Prepare your students to react in case of a fire-related emergency. Program a set of index cards with different situations, such as "The smoke-detector alarm goes off" or "When you reach for the doorknob, it's hot to the touch." Place students in small groups and distribute a programmed index card to each group. Provide time for each group to privately discuss the situation on its card; then have each group perform a short skit to show the proper way to react to the situation. Afterward lead the class in a discussion of the procedures that were demonstrated to review basic fire-safety know-how.

DOs AND DON'Ts DISPLAYs

Have your students make dioramas that show safe and unsafe household rooms. Begin by asking students to name potential fire hazards that can occur in the home—such as frayed electrical cords, unattended room heaters, and smoking in bed. List the responses on the board. Then ask students to name practices that would decrease the likelihood of having a fire, such as having a working smoke detector and keeping a fire extinguisher in the kitchen. Supply each student with a shoebox and a variety of materials such as markers, fabric scraps, construction paper, yarn, glue, and scissors. Have students work in pairs as they use the materials to create a likeness of a safe and an unsafe room. Display the resulting dioramas in a prominent classroom location.

RED-HOT READING

Use this red-hot reading list to enhance your fire-safety studies.

— *Fire Trucks* by Peter Brady (Capstone Press, 1996)
— *Fire! Fire!* by Gail Gibbons (HarperCollins Children's Books, 1984)
— *Fire Fighters A To Z* by Jean Johnson (Walker Publishing Company, Inc.; 1985)
— *The Fire Station* by Robert Munsch (Annick Press Ltd., 1991)
— *Fire Fighters* by Ray Broekel (Children's Press®, 1981)

STAYING SAFE

HOME ALONE

Certain circumstances may find a student at home by himself for a period of time. Remind students that when it comes to staying safe in this situation, it may be wise *not* to tell a stranger that there is not an adult around. Have your students brainstorm phrases to tell strangers who call or come to the door while they are at home by themselves. (Also reinforce that a child should not open a door to a stranger, and in most cases should ignore the doorbell or knocking instead of trying to relay a message through a closed door.) Then have each student practice a mock telephone conversation in which you assume the role of a stranger asking to speak to an adult. Encourage students to use phrases such as, "My mother is taking a nap right now," or "My dad is in the shower." Students will be prepared for safety if the home-alone situation should ever arise!

WHAT WOULD YOU DO?

Have your students demonstrate decision-making skills that may keep them safe in risky situations. Program a set of index cards, each with a different safety-related situation (see the examples below). Have student pairs randomly select a card and act out the situation for the class. After each role-play, discuss the students' actions. Ask the class to decide whether the students made safe decisions. For each situation, encourage students to discuss alternative actions and the resulting consequences. Then conclude the activity with a big round of applause for the student performers.

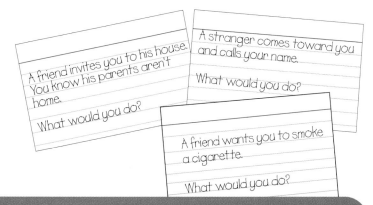

A friend invites you to his house. You know his parents aren't home.

What would you do?

A stranger comes toward you and calls your name.

What would you do?

A friend wants you to smoke a cigarette.

What would you do?

FAIRY-TALE FUN

Begin a unit on identifying safety risks with this nifty idea! Divide your students into a desired number of groups. Give each group a copy of a different fairy tale—such as Snow White, Goldilocks And The Three Bears, or Little Red Riding Hood—to read. Provide each group with a sheet of chart paper and a marker; then challenge each group to identify the personal-safety risks that occurred in its fairy tale. Encourage each group to discuss the possible consequences of each risk. Afterward provide time for each group to share its findings with the class.

Snow White

She took food from a stranger.

Goldilocks And The Three Bears

Goldilocks went inot a stranger's house.

Little Red Riding Hood

She talked to a stranger.

SAFETY SMARTS

Post a chart of safety-smart ideas for students to read. Encourage students to think of additional tips to add to the list. Get your chart started with these safety ideas:

- Always inform an adult of where you are going and when you plan to return.

- Call home if possible when you know that you are going to be late or you have a change in plans.

- Never get into a car with someone you don't know.

- Beware of strangers who say that they know your parents. Discuss a family password that your parents would share with someone if they wanted him or her to be in contact with you.

- Beware of strangers who say they need help finding directions, or need your help in some other way.

- Never accept candy, money, or a gift from a stranger.

- Never let a stranger get close enough to touch or grab you.

- Always tell an adult if you suspect that someone was putting you at risk.

SAFE-AND-SOUND LITERATURE LIST

Encourage safety habits with this collection of literature.

— *Dinosaurs, Beware! A Safety Guide* by Marc Brown and Stephen Krensky (Little, Brown And Company; 1984)
— *The Berenstain Bears Learn About Strangers* by Stan and Jan Berenstain (Random House Books For Young Readers, 1985)
— *Flossie And The Fox* by Patricia C. McKissack (Dial Books For Young Readers, 1986)

IT'S A LIFESAVER!

Emphasize personal-safety tips by having each student complete this writing activity. Begin by having students name ways to ensure personal safety. (If desired, refer to the ideas listed in "Safety Smarts.") Then give each student a colored construction-paper copy of the pattern on page 288. Encourage him to write a personal-safety message on the pattern; then have him cut along the heavy solid line and the dotted line as indicated. Mount the completed projects on a bulletin board titled "It's A Lifesaver!"

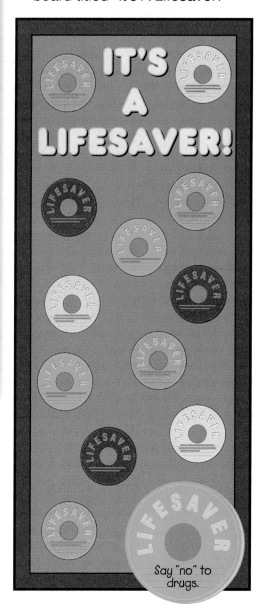

Say "no" to drugs.

Character EDUCATION

THE POWER OF POSITIVE THINKING

Make positive thinking an ongoing effort in your classroom by reminding students to use words that encourage instead of discourage. Enlist your students' help in creating a list of words and phrases that encourage a positive atmosphere. Post the resulting list in a prominent classroom location. When a student incorporates language from the chart into classroom discussion, verbally reward him by saying, "I like the way you said that!" or "What a good way to state your thoughts!" If a student forgets to state something in a positive manner, gently remind him to speak more positively by saying, "Can you use a word from the chart to say that in a different way?" Before long the power of positive thinking will come naturally!

What do you think?

I have a different opinion.

Let's talk about that answer.

Interesting idea!

Good job!

Can you explain that idea?

SEASONAL ESTEEM BUILDING

Begin each new season with an esteem-building activity that doubles as a decorative display. Program a class supply of seasonal cutouts, each with a different student's name. Randomly distribute a cutout to each student, making sure that no one gets his own name. Instruct each student to write a positive comment about the person named on his cutout. Collect the completed shapes and mount them on a bulletin board for a seasonal display filled with compliments about each classmate.

ACCENTUATE THE POSITIVE

End each day on a positive note by having students recall good things that happened during the day. As students are preparing to go home, take a few minutes to encourage them to share statements such as "I made a good grade on my math paper," or "I tried my best on the spelling test." If a student can't think of a positive comment, offer a suggestion such as, "I noticed that you used good manners in the cafeteria," or "I saw you being supportive of your team at recess. Way to go!" Your students will leave with a good feeling about themselves and their day at school.

GOOD-DEED SPOTTERS

Encourage your students to look for the best in their classmates by recruiting good-deed spotters. Display a box or other container labeled "Good Deeds" in your classroom. Tell your students to be on the lookout for classmates who perform kind and helpful acts during the week. Invite students who observe such an action to write it down on a piece of paper and slip it into the "Good Deeds" box. At the end of the week, open the box and read aloud all the entries. Students will be reminded that their good deeds do not go unnoticed, and your class will focus on positive behaviors!

Molly helped me with a math problem.

Joe held the door for me.

GOOD DEEDS

WORDS WITH CHARACTER

Reinforce character-building qualities with this vocabulary-enhancing activity. Program a set of index cards with character traits—such as *honesty, helpfulness, responsibility, courtesy,* and *compassion.* Place the cards in a container. At the beginning of each week, draw one card from the container and write it on the board. Have students explain what they think the word means; then have a student volunteer share the dictionary definition with the class. Throughout the week have students look for examples of the chosen character trait in the classroom, in literature, and at home. Provide several opportunities during the week for students to report their observations with the class. If desired, post the card used each week in a building-block-style display in a prominent classroom location. Remind students that the featured words are building blocks for developing a positive character!

responsibility

sincerity

modesty   trustworthiness

helpfulness   honesty

A MONTH OF MANNERS

Dedicate a month to practicing manners! Have your students brainstorm a list of common courtesies, such as opening the door for others, saying "please" and "thank you," and using good listening skills. Then select one of the behaviors for the class to focus on each day. If the list doesn't include enough behaviors for the entire month, repeat some of the manners, or have a combination day, in which several manners are practiced.

Please hand me that pencil.

POSITIVE REDIRECTION

Set the stage for supportive behavior by using a positive-response technique. When students answer questions aloud in class, refrain from acknowledging that an answer is incorrect. Instead restate the student's response to make a correct statement. For example, if you ask a student to name an example of a liquid and the student replies, "a rock," respond as follows: "A rock is a good example of a solid. An example of a liquid is water." In this manner you have preserved the student's dignity by minimizing the feeling that he was wrong. You have also reinforced the correct answer, which benefits the entire class!

THE CHARACTER CONNECTION

Look to these books for lessons on character and self-esteem.

—*The Rag Coat* by Lauren Mills (Little, Brown And Company; 1991)

—*Brave As A Mountain Lion* by Ann H. Scott (Clarion Books, 1996)

—*The Terrible Thing That Happened At Our House* by Marge Blaine (Scholastic Inc., 1991)

—*The Talking Eggs* by Robert D. San Souci (Dial Books For Young Readers, 1989)

—*The President Builds A House: The Work Of Habitat For Humanity* by Tom Shachtman (Simon And Schuster

Pattern
Use with "Million-Dollar Smiles" on page 278.

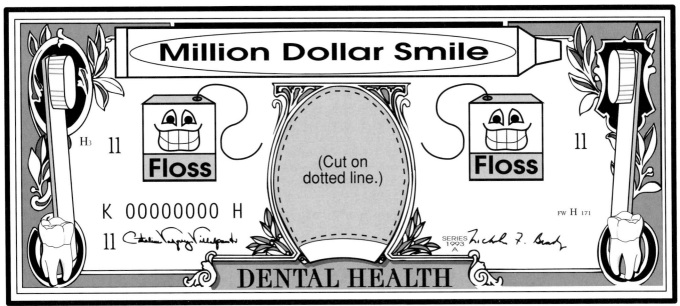

Pattern
Use with "Bank On Dental Health!" on page 278.

A dental-health tip you can bank on is

_____

_____

_____

Name_____

Be A Fire-Safety Inspector

Read the list below.
Look around your house for the items and conditions on the list.
Put a check by each item that you find as described.

_____ The electrical cords are in good shape and are not frayed.
_____ There is a working smoke detector on each level of my house.
_____ All flammable materials are properly stored away from open flames or extreme heat.
_____ The electrical outlets are not overloaded.
_____ All matches and lighters are stored safely away from small children and extreme heat.
_____ There is at least one fire extinguisher in my house.
_____ There is a list of emergency numbers by the telephone.

If an item isn't checked, what can be done to fix the problem?
Ask an adult to help you find a solution.

Fire-Safety Certificate
This certifies that

_____
(student)

has completed a fire-safety inspection of
his/her house and is on the lookout
for fire prevention.

Signed _____
(teacher)

Date _____

Fire-Safety Certificate
This certifies that

_____
(student)

has completed a fire-safety inspection of
his/her house and is on the lookout
for fire prevention.

Signed _____
(teacher)

Date _____

Pattern

Use with "It's A Lifesaver!" on page 283.

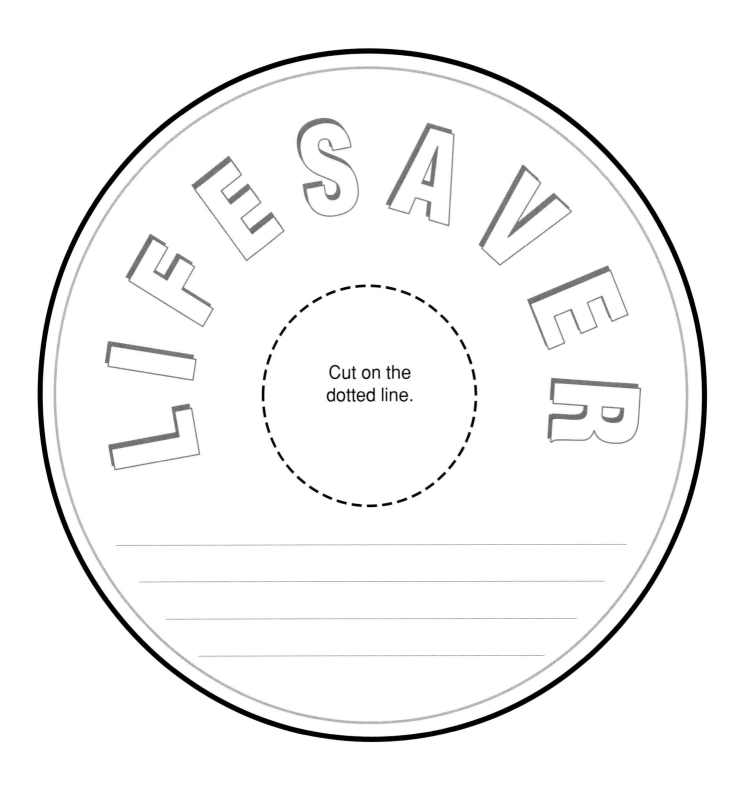

Cut on the dotted line.

HOLIDAY & SEASONAL

Johnny Appleseed's Birthday
(September 26)

Introduce your students to a character known for his love of apples—Johnny Appleseed. Share the adventurous tall tale *Johnny Appleseed* by Steven Kellogg (Morrow Junior Books, 1995) with your students. Then challenge your class to travel along Johnny's route by recording his journey on a map of the United States. Provide each student with a map and a red crayon. Read the story a second time, having students draw an apple on a state each time it is mentioned. After reading the story, have the students draw lines to connect the apples. Extend the activity by having students research to find which states are currently major apple producers. Instruct them to color those states on their maps with a green crayon.

National Clock Month
(October)

This monthly observance provides the perfect opportunity to reinforce clock-related skills. Try the following "time-ly" projects with your students:

- Invite students to bring a variety of time-telling devices to school, from watches to alarm clocks to oven timers. Have them categorize the timepieces by different attributes.

- Discuss the difference between face clocks and digital clocks. Ask students to explain the advantages of each type of clock.

- Instruct each student to create an outline of his school day and compare it to his weekend schedule. Then have him create a word problem relating to the two schedules.

- Finally, share some up-to-the minute literature such as *Clocks And More Clocks* by Pat Hutchins (Simon & Schuster Books For Young Readers, 1994) and *The Grouchy Ladybug* by Eric Carle (HarperCollins Children's Books, 1996).

National Popcorn Poppin' Month
(October)

Celebrate National Popcorn Poppin' Month with a collection of taste-tempting literature. Make a batch of popcorn for your students to enjoy as you share poppin' good titles such as *The Popcorn Dragon* by Jane Thayer (Morrow Junior Books, 1989) and *Popcorn* by Frank Asch (Parents Magazine Press, 1979).

World Poetry Day
(October 15)

Heighten your students' appreciation of poetry with a day of verse, rhyme, and poet studies. Introduce your students to the wild and wacky rhymes of Shel Silverstein, the kid-pleasing verses of Jack Prelutsky, and the flowing language of Eloise Greenfield. Then have each student try her hand at writing couplets, haiku, or a cinquain. Or use the following structure as a model for writing Pyramid Poetry:

Line 1: Name of a person
Line 2: Two adjectives describing the person
Line 3: Three "ing" words that tell about activities the person likes
Line 4: A four-word sentence that begins with "He (She) is ____."

Gina
smart pretty
reading thinking correcting
She is a really good copy editor.

National Author's Day
(November 1)

Who are the most popular authors among third-grade readers? Find out by having students create a display of their favorite authors' works. Ask each student to look in the library for books written by a favorite author. Have her select several books and create a poster showing the covers and characters from the stories. Display the posters in the hallway, cafeteria, or library. For added fun encourage each student to dress as a character from one of the stories featured on her poster. Have her tell about the story from the character's point of view.

Game And Puzzle Week
(annually, the last week in November)

Welcome Game And Puzzle Week into your classroom by setting up a game center in a corner of the room. Encourage students to bring favorite games and puzzles from home. Ask students to surmise which problem-solving skills they use as they play each game. Stress the importance of playing fair, taking turns, and enjoying the game as opposed to focusing on winning every time. Extend the activities by having students research different games from around the world. Then take the class to the gym to try out some multicultural recreation.

World Hello Day
(November 21)

Encourage students to help spread cheerful greetings on World Hello Day. Explain to students that the purpose of this day is to promote peace through communication. To participate, each student should extend a greeting to ten or more people during the day. Add a decorative touch to the affair by having students create posters featuring salutations from around the world. Provide your class with poster boards, markers, and this list of world-class greetings:

Buenos dias Spanish
Guten tag German
Hallo Dutch
Morn Norwegian
Ciao Italian
Bonjour French

See pages 298–303 for seasonal reproducibles.

WINTER

St. Nicholas Day

(December 6)

This holiday tradition was brought to America by Dutch settlers. It honors St. Nicholas, a man declared patron saint of children because of the kindness, goodwill, and generosity he bestowed upon them. Share the story *The Baker's Dozen: A St. Nicholas Tale* retold by Aaron Shepard (Simon And Schuster Books For Young Readers, 1995). Your students will enjoy the insight into early colonial life, a lesson about generosity, and the story behind a "baker's dozen." After reading the story, have your class mix up a baker's dozen (or two!) of gingerbread cookies for all to enjoy.

La Posada

(December 16)

The nine days before Christmas are very special in Mexico. On each day children form a procession reenacting Mary and Joseph's search for a *posada*, or lodging. The children travel to a different house each day, where they knock on the door and ask for lodging. At first they are refused, but when they are finally admitted, a feast and a candy-filled pinata await them. Read *Nine Days To Christmas* by Marie H. Ets (Puffin Books, 1991) to your class. Afterward place students in small groups and have each group decorate a paper grocery sack to resemble a pinata. Ask your students to bring treats from home to fill each sack. Then lead them in a procession that concludes in a room suitable for breaking pinatas.

Hanukkah

This eight-day Jewish tradition is held to commemorate a Jewish victory over Syrian rule in the second century B.C. Observers of the holiday light one candle in a special holder called a *menorah* each night for eight nights. This is in memory of a legend that, when the temple was rededicated, a lamp burned for eight nights even though it had only a small amount of oil. Explore other traditions of the holiday by reading *Hershel And The Hanukkah Goblins* by Eric A. Kimmel (Holiday House, Inc; 1989) with your students. After hearing about Hershel's dreidel game, students will be eager to spin a dreidel for themselves.

Kwanzaa
(December 26–31)

This African-American festival is based on the traditional African festival celebrating the harvest of the first crops. The celebration begins on December 26 and lasts for seven days. It centers on seven African practices and ideals of unity, self-determination, collective responsibility, cooperative economics, purpose, creativity, and faith. Each evening the family lights one of seven candles in a special candleholder called a *kinara*. They discuss the principle for the day and often exchange gifts. Near the end of the holiday, the community gathers for a feast called a *karamu*. Your students will enjoy the story of a young girl who discovers the true meaning of this holiday in *Imani's Gift At Kwanzaa* by Denise Burden-Patmon (Simon & Schuster Books For Young Readers, 1993). After reading the story, have your students show their *Kuumba*, or creativity, by making a gift for someone special.

National Children's Dental Health Month
(February)

In observance of National Children's Dental Health Month, invite a local dentist into your classroom. Ask her to share the importance of good dental hygiene along with some tooth-care tips. Afterward ask each student to keep a chart for one week to track the number of times he brushes and flosses his teeth, and eats healthful snacks. At week's end, have students bring their charts to school. Look at each child's chart; then provide praises and suggestions related to his dental-health habits.

(For additional dental-heath activities, see pages 278 and 279.)

Black History Month
(February)

February marks the observance of Black History Month. This month is used to recognize contributions and achievements of African-Americans. Have your students join in this time of special recognition. Early in the new year, create a list of notable African-Americans and their achievements; then have each student research a person on the list. During February have one or two students per day read their findings to the class. If desired, reserve space on a bulletin board to display each report on the day it is read.

See pages 304–311 for seasonal reproducibles.

SPRING

National Nutrition Month
(March)

This monthlong event is held to teach Americans the value of good nutrition. Try this research project to give your students a healthful outlook on eating right. Have your students research a list of healthful foods and the positive effects they have on the human body. Draw an outline of a body on chart paper; then have students record each food on the body outline near the area that is most helped by the food's nutritional value. The end result will show students the impact that healthful foods have on all parts of their bodies. *(See pages 276 and 277 for additional nutrition activities.)*

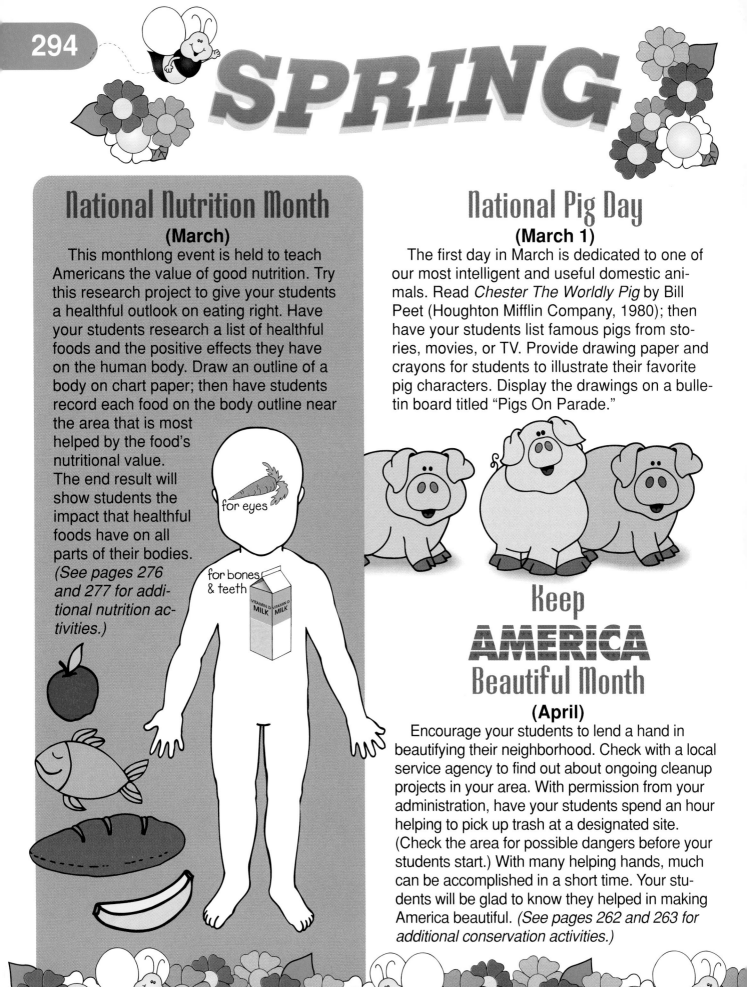

for eyes

for bones & teeth

VITAMIN D MILK VITAMIN D MILK

National Pig Day
(March 1)

The first day in March is dedicated to one of our most intelligent and useful domestic animals. Read *Chester The Worldly Pig* by Bill Peet (Houghton Mifflin Company, 1980); then have your students list famous pigs from stories, movies, or TV. Provide drawing paper and crayons for students to illustrate their favorite pig characters. Display the drawings on a bulletin board titled "Pigs On Parade."

Keep AMERICA Beautiful Month
(April)

Encourage your students to lend a hand in beautifying their neighborhood. Check with a local service agency to find out about ongoing cleanup projects in your area. With permission from your administration, have your students spend an hour helping to pick up trash at a designated site. (Check the area for possible dangers before your students start.) With many helping hands, much can be accomplished in a short time. Your students will be glad to know they helped in making America beautiful. *(See pages 262 and 263 for additional conservation activities.)*

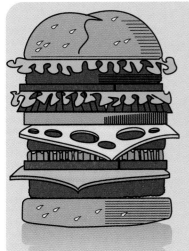

Zoo And Aquarium Month
(April)

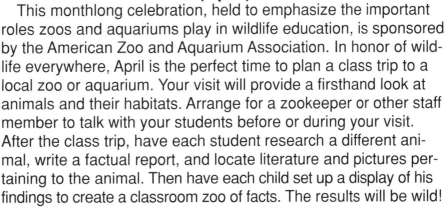

This monthlong celebration, held to emphasize the important roles zoos and aquariums play in wildlife education, is sponsored by the American Zoo and Aquarium Association. In honor of wildlife everywhere, April is the perfect time to plan a class trip to a local zoo or aquarium. Your visit will provide a firsthand look at animals and their habitats. Arrange for a zookeeper or other staff member to talk with your students before or during your visit. After the class trip, have each student research a different animal, write a factual report, and locate literature and pictures pertaining to the animal. Then have each child set up a display of his findings to create a classroom zoo of facts. The results will be wild!

National Bike Month
(May)

This annual celebration promotes the fun and functional aspects of bicycling. National Bike Month is the perfect time for some hands-on bicycle safety instruction. Invite a member of your local police department (or other community agency promoting bike safety) to speak to your class. If possible plan to have a bicycle and a helmet at school the day your guest visits. Have a student volunteer demonstrate each safety tip as it is discussed. End the lesson by giving each student a safe-rider certificate.

Cinco De Mayo
(May 5)

Each year on the fifth of May, Mexicans celebrate a national holiday commemorating a military victory in 1862. Use this celebration as an opportunity to expose your students to the Spanish language. With the help of a Spanish-English dictionary, label some of the items in your classroom with their Spanish names. Challenge students to use this new vocabulary throughout the day.

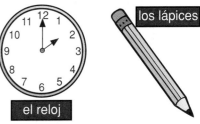

el libro
los lápices
el reloj

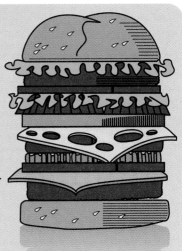

National Hamburger Month
(May)

Hold a Great Hamburger Search in your classroom in honor of National Hamburger Month. Poll your students to determine their favorite fast-food hamburgers; then have a taste-off in your classroom. Have each child cast his vote again to determine the favored hamburger among your students. Then have each child write an order for the ideal hamburger by recording a list of toppings he prefers.

See pages 312–315 for seasonal reproducibles.

SUMMER

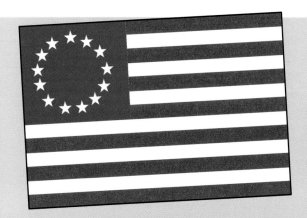

Flag Day
(June 14)

On June 14, 1777, the Second Continental Congress decided that "...the flag of the United States be thirteen stripes, alternate red and white; that the union be thirteen stars, white in a blue field, representing a new constellation." Provisions were made to add a new stripe and new star each time a state came into the union. By 1792 the flag boasted 15 stars and stripes, and it was apparent that it was becoming much too unwieldy. It was decided to add a new star each time a state joined the union, but to limit the number of stripes to the original 13. Challenge each student to design a flag to represent your classroom. Remind them to consider the school colors and mascot, the number of students, and other important information when creating their designs.

Summer Begins
(June 21)

Have your students become authors as they prepare for the summer holiday. Ask each student to make a list of favorite after-school, family, and summertime activities. Then have her write a paragraph explaining each idea. Ask each student to include any important supplies, directions, safety tips, or illustrations needed for each activity. When the class collection is complete, photocopy a set for each child. Have her bind her copy of summer-fun ideas before taking it home. Each child will have an endless supply of summer fun at her fingertips during the long break from school.

Independence Day

Typically celebrated with fireworks and parades, this U.S. holiday has important significance in the history of our country. It was on July 4, 1776, that the Continental Congress approved the Declaration of Independence—which represented the official birthday of the United States. To celebrate in your classroom, host a birthday party in honor of the United States. Invite your students to wear red, white, and blue clothing, or to dress as someone who attended the first July Fourth celebration (such as Benjamin Franklin or Thomas Jefferson). Provide each child with a rectangular sugar cookie; small amounts of red, white, and blue icing; and star-shaped sprinkles. Have each student decorate his cookie to look like the American flag. Serve red punch with these high-flying treats. Wrap up the holiday with a parade around the school to show off your students' patriotic garb.

National Ice Cream Month

(July)

Celebrate ice cream—one of summer's most popular foods—with a sundae party. In advance ask parent volunteers to send ice cream, toppings, and paper goods to school. Make a list of the different ingredients available and have each student draw and label the sundae she will create with them. Challenge each student to name her creation with a catchy title.

Set out the ingredients and have small groups of students build their ice-cream treats. While students are enjoying their sundaes, have each student show her original drawing, tell the name of her treat, and give a taste report on her creation.

See pages 316–318 for seasonal reproducibles.

Space Week

(week including July 20)

What a special day for space history! On July 20, 1969, Neil Armstrong and Buzz Aldrin became the first men to set foot on the moon. In addition, July 20 is also the anniversary of the day NASA tested the first successful rocket engine (1964), and the day the Viking I space probe landed on Mars (1976). Share with your students the story *Floating Home* by David Getz (Henry Holt And Company, 1997) which provides a wealth of astronaut information in a fictional story setting. Then have each student write a story about an imaginary space adventure—with himself in the astronaut seat!

- honest
- trustworthy
- friendly
- caring
- kind
- understanding

Friendship Day

(August 3)

Friendship Day is a day to acknowledge old friends and celebrate new friends. Ask your students to brainstorm a list of qualities that they appreciate in a friend. Then have them use the list of words to inspire friendship poems. Make a copy of each poem to bind as a class collection. Place the original poems on a hallway wall to display your students' appreciation of friendship.

Autumn Addition

Add the numbers on each leaf.
Outline the leaves using the color code.

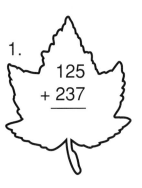
1.
125
+ 237

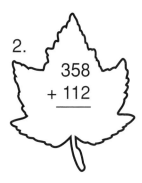
2.
358
+ 112

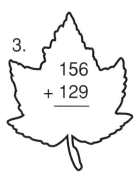
3.
156
+ 129

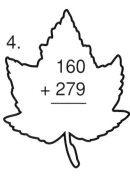
4.
160
+ 279

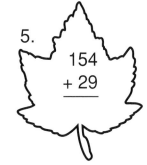
5.
154
+ 29

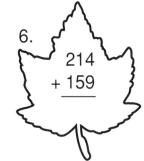
6.
214
+ 159

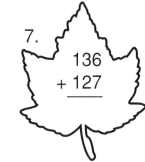
7.
136
+ 127

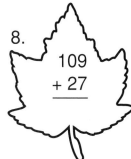
8.
109
+ 27

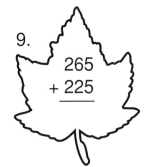
9.
265
+ 225

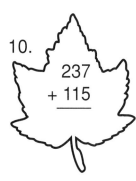
10.
237
+ 115

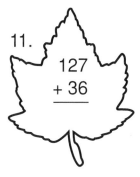
11.
127
+ 36

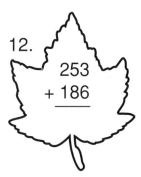
12.
253
+ 186

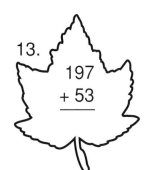
13.
197
+ 53

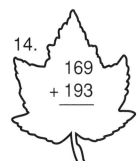
14.
169
+ 193

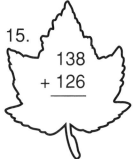
15.
138
+ 126

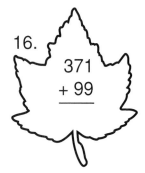
16.
371
+ 99

Color Code
yellow = 100–200   red = 201–300
brown = 301–400   orange = 401–500

Bonus Box: Make a chart to show how many leaves there are of each color.

Note To The Teacher: Duplicate one copy. Write numbers in the leaves and in the code. Then duplicate a copy
for each student.

Capitalize On Johnny Appleseed!

Read each sentence.
Circle the letters that need to be capitalized.
The number of capitals needed is written in
the apple by each sentence.

 1. johnny appleseed was born on september 26, 1774.

 2. his real name was john chapman.

 3. he traveled through ohio and indiana planting apple orchards.

 4. there are many stories about johnny's adventures.

 5. some people claim he was a medicine man to the indians.

 6. others say he wore a pot on his head instead of a hat.

 7. still others claim johnny never wore shoes, summer or winter.

 8. none of these stories about johnny have been proven true.

 9. we do know that he eventually owned about 1,200 acres of orchards.

 10. until his death in 1845, he kept traveling and planting apple trees.

Bonus Box: On the back of this paper, write three sentences about apples. Be sure to use capitals where needed.

Native American Contributions

The Native Americans lived in America long before Columbus arrived. They were here before the Pilgrims, the colonists, or the pioneers. The pictures below show some of the things that the Native Americans shared with early settlers in America. We still use many of the items today.

Cut each picture apart.
Glue it in the correct category.

Things to wear	Used for hunting	Used for transportation	Household items

Bonus Box: How many of the items above do you have in your home? Make a list on the back of this paper.

©1997 The Education Center, Inc. • *The Mailbox® Superbook* • *Grade 3* • TEC452 • Key p. 319

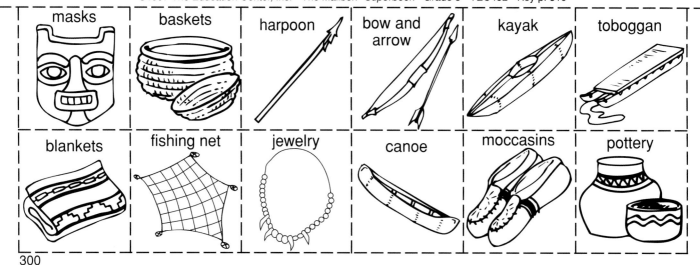

masks   baskets   harpoon   bow and arrow   kayak   toboggan
blankets   fishing net   jewelry   canoe   moccasins   pottery

Name_____

Columbus Day Word Find

Read each sentence.
Then find the bold words in the word-search puzzle.

```
A  R  C  O  L  U  M  B  U  S  C
S  F  A  D  G  J  O  S  V  Z  A
I  N  D  I  A  N  S  R  A  D  R
A  T  L  A  N  T  I  C  O  C  I
B  L  H  M  C  K  I  N  X  E  B
I  Q  U  E  U  R  O  P  E  G  B
N  W  T  R  M  P  E  Y  B  H  E
D  C  F  I  I  L  O  Q  U  Y  A
I  M  V  C  W  N  S  P  A  I  N
E  R  A  A  K  T  X  P  Z  S  J
S  A  N  S  A  L  V  A  D  O  R
```

Columbus wanted to cross the **Atlantic** Ocean by sailing west from Europe.

He was looking for a sea route to **Asia**.

Instead the route took him to the islands of the
    Caribbean Sea.

On October 12, 1492, his ships landed on an island
    that we now call **San Salvador**.

At that time, the people of **Europe** did not know
    about the **Americas**.

Columbus thought he was somewhere in the
    East **Indies**.

That is why Columbus called the people of the
    island *Indians*.

Five months later, he arrived back in **Spain** with news of his voyage.

It was not until 30 years later that people realized **Columbus** had never reached Asia.

Bonus Box: Columbus led three more expeditions to the New World. Find a fact about each of these voyages.

Halloween Handiwork

Complete each drawing.
Then color the pictures.

Bonus Box: On another sheet of paper, draw half of a symmetrical object. Ask a classmate to complete the picture.

©1997 The Education Center, Inc. • *The Mailbox® Superbook • Grade 3* • TEC452

Name_____

Why Are You Thankful?

Read each question.
Then write your answer in a complete sentence.

1. **Who** are you thankful for? _____

_____

2. **What** are you thankful for?_____

_____

3. **Where** are you thankful? _____

_____

4. **When** are you thankful? _____

_____

5. **Why** are you thankful? _____

_____

6. **How** do you show that you are thankful? _____

_____

Bonus Box: On another sheet of paper, draw a picture to show one of your answers.

Name_____ *Critical thinking*

Count On Winter!

Complete each sentence with information about winter.

One winter sport is_____ .

Two winter holidays are _____ .

Three winter months are _____ .

Four types of winter clothing are _____

_____ .

Five kinds of winter weather are _____

_____ .

Six things to do in the winter are _____

_____ .

Seven things you see in winter are _____

_____ .

Eight words to describe winter are _____

_____

_____ .

Nine things that keep you warm are _____

_____

_____ .

Ten things that are as cold as winter are _____

_____

_____ .

Bonus Box: On the back of this paper, tell what you like best about winter.

Dreidel Math

The dreidel game is played with a special top and game tokens.
Each player has ten game tokens.
To start the game, each player places one token in a center pile called a *kitty*.
Players take turns spinning the dreidel.
Each side of the dreidel directs the player to get tokens, lose tokens, or do nothing
  with the tokens.

Use the information in the boxes to answer the problems about a game of dreidel.
Show your work.

 **Nun**

The player does nothing.

 **Gimmel**

The player takes everything in the kitty. All other players give one token each to the new kitty.

 **Hey**

The player takes half the pot.
(If there is an uneven amount, the player takes half plus one.)

 **Shin**

The player adds one token to the kitty.

1. You have eight tokens.
   There are six tokens in the kitty.
   The dreidel lands on hey.
   How many tokens would you have at the end of the turn?

2. You have six tokens.
   There are five tokens in the kitty.
   The dreidel lands on shin.
   How many tokens would you have at the end of the turn?

3. You have nine tokens.
   There are seven tokens in the kitty.
   The dreidel lands on nun.
   How many tokens would you have at the end of the turn?

4. You have two tokens.
   There are four tokens in the kitty.
   The dreidel lands on gimmel.
   How many tokens would you have at the end of the turn?

5. You have ten tokens.
   There are three tokens in the kitty.
   The dreidel lands on shin.
   How many tokens would you have at the end of the turn?

6. You have seven tokens.
   There are eight tokens in the kitty.
   The dreidel lands on hey.
   How many tokens would you have at the end of the turn?

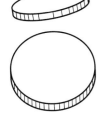

Scrambled Sleighs

Read the words on each sleigh.
Write the words in ABC order on the lines.

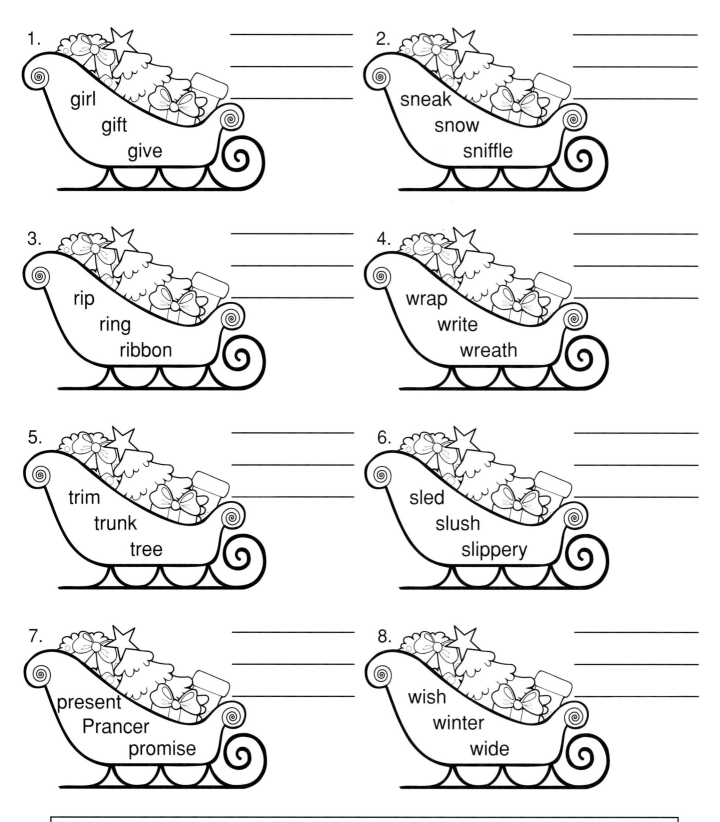

1. girl
   gift
   give

_____
_____
_____

2. sneak
   snow
   sniffle

_____
_____
_____

3. rip
   ring
   ribbon

_____
_____
_____

4. wrap
   write
   wreath

_____
_____
_____

5. trim
   trunk
   tree

_____
_____
_____

6. sled
   slush
   slippery

_____
_____
_____

7. present
   Prancer
   promise

_____
_____
_____

8. wish
   winter
   wide

_____
_____
_____

Bonus Box: Think of three words to describe Christmas. Write them in ABC order on the back of this page.

Name_____

Count Down The New Year!

Get ready to celebrate the New Year!
Write the times for the events on the lines.

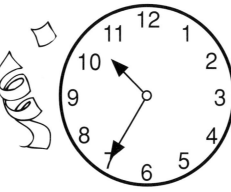

_____
The last guest arrives.

_____
Everyone puts on a
funny hat.

_____
We sit down to a late
supper.

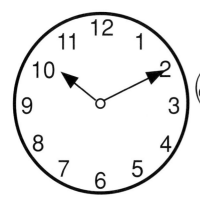

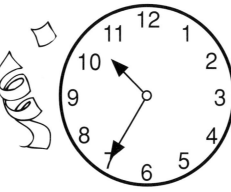

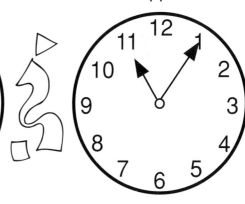

_____
We recall happy times
of the year.

_____
Is anyone getting
sleepy yet?

_____
There's less than an
hour to go!

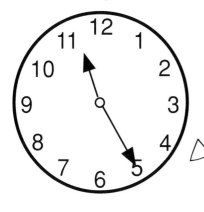

_____
Make your New Year's
resolution.

_____
Pass out the
noisemakers!

_____
Happy New Year!

Bonus Box: Did you make a New Year's resolution? Write about it on the back of this page.

Gung Hay Fat Choy!

What do these words mean? They mean "Happy New Year!" in Chinese.
Complete the crossword puzzle to find out more about this holiday.
Use the word bank to help you solve the puzzle.

Word Bank

dragon	money
lions	moon
firecrackers	month
red	lantern
drums	China

Across

1. The Chinese New Year begins with the first new _____ of the new year.
2. Dancers dressed as _____ can be seen in street parades.
3. In _____ , everyone celebrates his birthday during Chinese New Year.
4. Children are given _____ wrapped in red and gold paper.
5. _____ is an important holiday color.

Down

1. The New Year festivities last for almost a _____ .
2. When the first full moon appears, it is time for the _____ parade.
6. There is also a parade featuring a large _____ .
7. Noisemakers and _____ are used to scare away the old year.
8. As parades pass by, the air is filled with cheering, laughter, and the sound of beating _____ .

Bonus Box: Did you know that dragons are a symbol of good luck in China? On the back of this paper, draw a colorful dragon.

Valentine Values

If you had $5.00 to spend on valentine gifts, what could you buy?
Find the prices of the items on the chart.
Add the prices of the items below.
Then tell if you have enough money to buy each pair of gifts.

$4.25 $2.65 $ .50

$1.85 $ .75 $ .95

1.

Total cost _____
Could you buy it? _____

2.

Total cost _____
Could you buy it? _____

3.

Total cost _____
Could you buy it? _____

4.

Total cost _____
Could you buy it? _____

5.

Total cost _____
Could you buy it? _____

6.

Total cost _____
Could you buy it? _____

7.

Total cost _____
Could you buy it? _____

8.

Total cost _____
Could you buy it? _____

9.

Total cost _____
Could you buy it? _____

10.

Total cost _____
Could you buy it? _____

Bonus Box: If you had $10.00 to spend, which items would you buy?

African-American Champions

Find out about an important African-American.
Research to find information about one of the people listed below.

Thurgood Marshall
Jackie Joyner-Kersee
Marian Anderson
Martin Luther King, Jr.
Bill Cosby
Arthur Ashe
Maya Angelou

Benjamin Banneker
Mae Jemison
Rosa Parks
George Washington Carver
Alvin Ailey
Oprah Winfrey

My Report About _____

Date of birth: _____

Place of birth: _____

Occupation: _____

Accomplishments: _____

_____

_____

_____

Interesting fact(s): _____

_____

_____

_____

It's Presidents' Day

Color by the code:

red =

blue =

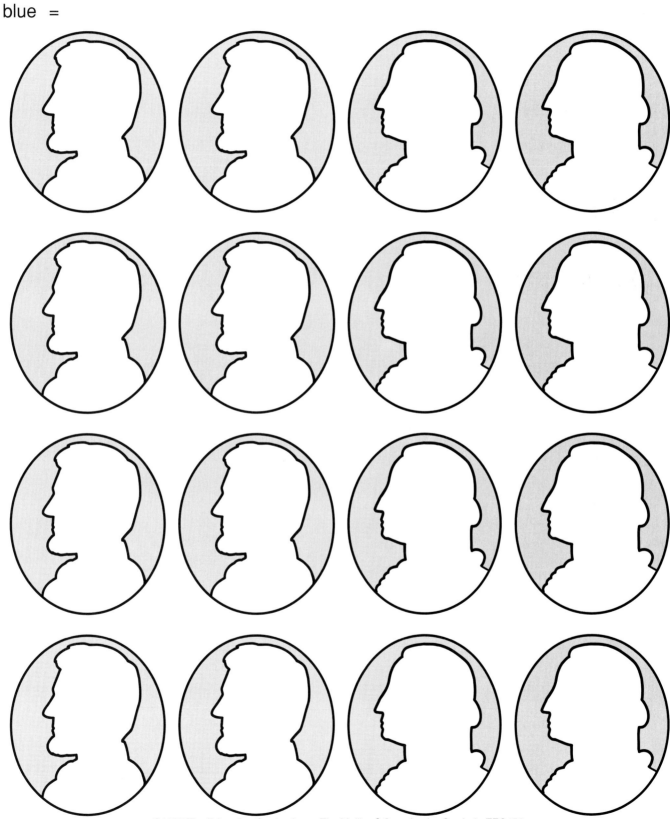

Note To The Teacher: Duplicate one copy. Program the code and the profiles to match (odd/even, fact/opinion, correct/incorrect). Then duplicate a class supply.

Shamrock Shenanigans

Use the word box to find an antonym for each word.
Write the antonym on the shamrock.
Then use one word from each shamrock to complete the sentences below.

tiny _____

end _____

never _____

few _____

dull _____

true _____

Word Box

bright   false
large   beginning
always   many

1. St. Patrick's Day is _____ celebrated on March 17.

2. It is a day when _____ people wear green.

3. One symbol of the holiday is a _____ green plant called a shamrock.

4. Another symbol of the holiday is a _____ man called a leprechaun.

5. Legend says that you can find a leprechaun's gold at the _____ of the rainbow.

6. Do you think that could be _____ ?

Bonus Box: On the back of this page, list ten things that are green.

Name_____ *Fractions*

"Eggs-tra" Special Fractions

Follow the directions for coloring the eggs.
Then write a fraction to answer each question.

1. Color two eggs pink and three eggs green. 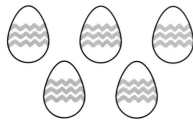 What fraction of the eggs are pink?_____	2. Color four eggs yellow and one egg red. 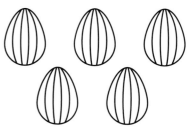 What fraction of the eggs are yellow?_____
3. Color two eggs blue and four eggs purple. 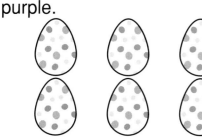 What fraction of the eggs are blue?_____	4. Color three eggs yellow and five eggs red. 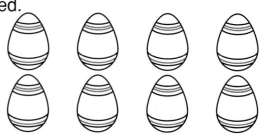 What fraction of the eggs are red? _____
5. Color six eggs orange and one egg pink. 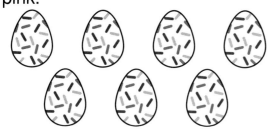 What fraction of the eggs are pink?_____	6. Color three eggs pink and two eggs yellow.  What fraction of the eggs are pink?_____
7. Color one egg blue and three eggs green. 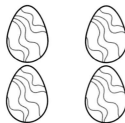 What fraction of the eggs are blue?_____	8. Color four eggs purple and four eggs green.  What fraction of the eggs are purple?_____

Bonus Box: On the back of this page, draw an egg for every person in your family. Color the adults yellow. Color the children purple. Write a fraction to show how many people in your family are children.

Celebrate Cinco De Mayo!

Cinco De Mayo is a Mexican celebration honoring a military victory in 1862. It takes place on the fifth of May. The celebration includes parades, fireworks, picnics, and pinatas.

Color the pinata.
Use the word box for help.

rojo—red
anaranjado—orange
amarillo—yellow
verde—green
azul—blue
morado—purple

©1997 The Education Center, Inc. • *The Mailbox® Superbook • Grade 3 •* TEC452

Bonus Box: What is your favorite color? Write it in Spanish on the back of this page.

My Marvelous Mom

Complete each sentence with information about your marvelous mom.

1. If my mom were a flower, she would be a _____

   because _____ .

2. If my mom were a song, she would be _____

   because _____ .

3. If my mom were a super hero, she would be _____

   because _____ .

4. If my mom were candy, she would be _____

   because _____ .

5. If my mom were a car, she would be a _____

   because _____ .

6. If my mom were a color, she would be _____

   because _____ .

7. If my mom were an animal, she would be a _____

   because _____ .

8. If my mom were a TV show, she would be _____

   because _____ .

Bonus Box: Think of ten words to describe your mother. Write them in the shape of a heart on another piece of paper. Give it to your mom on Mother's Day.

Synonyms For Super Dads

Read each sentence.
Use the word box to find a synonym for each word in bold.
Write the synonyms on the lines following each sentence.

Word Box				
intelligent	construct	stream	great	correct
repair	forest	glad	chef	grin

1. My dad is a **wonderful** guy! _____

2. Just thinking of him makes me **smile**. _____

3. He is always **happy** to spend time with me. _____

4. Sometimes we go fishing at the **creek**. _____

5. Other times we camp out in the **woods**. _____

6. My dad showed me how to **build** a birdhouse. _____

7. He also taught me how to **fix** a flat tire on my bike. _____

8. Dad is also a very good **cook**. _____

9. I think my dad is very **smart**. _____

10. When I ask him a question, he always knows the **right** answer. _____

Bonus Box: In what ways are you and your father alike? Write your answer on the back of this paper.

Name _____

What A Year!

Complete the sentences about your year in third grade.

My teacher's name was

Three of my friends were

My favorite subject was

The name of my school was

The funniest thing that happened this year was

HA HA HA HA HA

At recess I liked to

I liked learning about

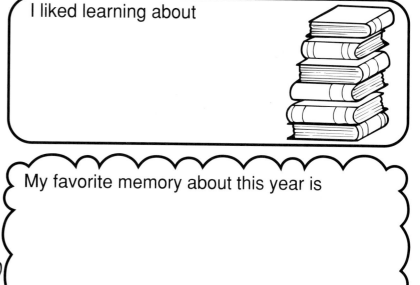

My favorite memory about this year is

Name _____ *Writing a friendly letter*

Welcome Aboard!

Write a letter to next year's third graders.
Tell them what to expect in the third grade.

©1997 The Education Center, Inc. • *The Mailbox® Superbook • Grade 3* • TEC452